Teaching Aquatics

John A. Torney, Jr.
Emeritus, University of Washington

Robert D. Clayton
Fort Collins, Colorado

Illustrations by
Barbara S. Jones
Moorhead State University
Moorhead, Minnesota

 **Burgess Publishing Company**
Minneapolis, Minnesota

Editorial: Wayne Schotanus, Anne Heller, J. D. Wicklatz
Copy Editor: Toni Johnson
Production: Morris Lundin, Pat Barnes
Cover Design: Priscilla Golz

Copyright © 1981 by John A. Torney, Jr. and Robert D. Clayton
Printed in the United States of America
Library of Congress Catalog Number 80-67566
ISBN 0-8087-3617-5

Burgess Publishing Company
7108 Ohms Lane
Minneapolis, Minnesota 55435

J I H G F E D C B A

Contents

Tables and Charts

Preface

For many years we have taught classes to prepare instructors in swimming and diving, with the help of materials gathered from the Red Cross, the YMCA, and other aquatic specialty groups and from master instructors. This information is scattered, and not all is accessible to the majority of the instructors. The purpose of this text, then, is to offer advice, gleaned from the materials and experiences of others, to the teacher of swimming and diving. We believe that the material contained herein will enable instructors to master their specialties more quickly.

The text is specifically designed for use in school or agency training programs for beginning aquatic instructors. We have tried to make our suggestions pertinent to the needs of any agency or group that sponsors swimming or diving instructional programs. The lifesaving chapter provides the reader with information on both the American YMCA and the American Red Cross (ARC) techniques.

We are convinced that expert aquatic instructors combine conceptual awareness of psychomotor and psychological learning strategies with the knowledge of correct skill performance. This combination promotes an effective learning experience, because expert instructors know why, what, and how. This text attempts to assist both beginning and experienced instructors in these areas. The first two chapters deal with the personal and conceptual foundations of successful instruction; the remaining chapters discuss and illustrate correct skill performance and explain effective teaching strategies for all recognized swimming skills, YMCA and ARC lifesaving skills, and the forward and backward dives. Furthermore, advice is given on teaching preschool children, youth, adults, and special populations. In all cases, the correct performance techniques are illustrated with line drawings and accompanied by lists of common performance errors.

Each chapter is organized to provide the reader with information in a logical sequence: introduction, discussion (and illustrations, where they are appropriate) of the skills and knowledge needed in a particular aquatic specialty, activities for swimming instructors, behavioral objectives that describe precisely what instructors should know, and current references. The chapter dealing with special populations, preschool children, and adults offers additional information on the organization and administration of programs for these groups.

Good teaching includes an analysis and evaluation. Performance analysis sheets for eleven strokes and three dives are provided; these may be used at water-side to develop the "photographic eye" that is common to competent instructors. Evaluation is discussed in Chapter 8, which provides sound advice for instructors either in a school or an agency situation.

While we do not believe this text is the complete authority on the subject, we are convinced that instructors will profit from reading and following the advice given, advice that we have in turn received from many colleagues and students over the years. Special mention should go to two professional colleagues who were of particular help in this revision: Mrs. Bee Hallett, Central Michigan University, and Dr. Lionel McIlwain, University of Toledo. In addition, Mrs. Barbara Aldrich typed (and retyped!) the manuscript. To these people, we give thanks.

As with our earlier book, our wives deserve credit for making possible the time and creative energy that goes into a writing project. Now that the task is over for the second time, we again acknowledge the patience, understanding, and even the gentle prodding of Marian Torney and Joyce Clayton.

December 1980   John A. Torney, Jr.
                                                                                  Robert D. Clayton

CHAPTER 1

Becoming a Competent Aquatic Worker

Certification and Competency
Aquatic Education
Using This Text

Everyone seeks to become competent in some area of work or play. By reading this book you show that you want to become a more competent swimming teacher. But how are competent teachers trained?

Usually, a young person joins a swimming team or a synchronized swimming group, takes a lifesaving course, and helps teach swimming classes or works as a lifeguard. If he or she is very enthusiastic about swimming, formal training certification may follow. After some years of preparation, a competent teacher may emerge. This text is designed to help you improve as a teacher.

This text is a summary of the experiences of the authors and other swimming teachers. It will give you information about most of the problems facing the beginning instructor. This information will be detailed enough to make your first years as an aquatic instructor less traumatic and embarrassing, but you should not regard this text as the complete source for all information you may need. Other publications, especially those of the American Red Cross (ARC) and the YMCA, should be consulted also. What works well for one may not work quite so well for others. The competent instructor is distinguished by an ability to combine the lessons of experience with new ideas and use them as a guide. We hope this book will help you to make a good start on the road to excellence.

CERTIFICATION AND COMPETENCY

Throughout this text we will use the terms "certified aquatic worker" or "certified aquatic instructor" with reference to people who have earned nationally recognized certification as teachers of swimming and diving, in programs such as the ARC's water safety instructor or the YMCA's aquatic specialist.

This text will be most valuable to beginners in formal aquatic worker training. Each national group has its own tests to screen applicants. A modified test (Table 1.1) has been developed for use in colleges and universities. The level of skill reached is expected to be the same, whether the instruction is given in a week-long aquatic school or in a school term. However, the longer term permits students to overcome initial shortcomings with additional practice.

Table 1.1 is a self-rating test. If you are seeking to enroll in a formal course for aquatic workers, rate yourself on each item. Your instructor may have you demonstrate any or all of the physical skill items and may add more. Meeting these standards is the first step toward becoming a certified aquatic worker.

Table 1.1. Self-Test for Prospective Certified Aquatic Workers

	Yes	No
1. Are you at least 17 years of age?		
2. Do you have a current lifesaving certificate?		
3. Do you have the ability to perform these psychomotor skills?		
a. Correct flutter kick (no bicycle action)		
b. Correct scissors kick (not inverted)		
c. Correct whip kick (wedge acceptable)		
d. Acceptable breathing in crawl stroke (face in water, rhythmic)		
e. Swim 500 yards nonstop (any combination of strokes, 11½ minutes)		
f. Carry a person of equal size with the cross-chest carry (25 yards)		
g. Enter water head first (1-meter board)		
4. Do you have these physical and attitudinal traits?		
a a. Energetic enough to demonstrate and teach aquatic skills for at least 45 minutes at one time		
b. Conscientious enough to read and think about written material		
c. Enthusiastic enough to master all aquatic skills (including diving)		

AQUATIC EDUCATION

If you meet the necessary physical and attitudinal requirements, you may wonder if you need this book. Consider the scope of knowledge a well-trained aquatic instructor is supposed to have mastered. A glance at the table of contents reveals that this text discusses the background information for teaching aquatic skills. It gives suggestions for performing and teaching almost all aquatic strokes and skills, including the basic dives, and presents material that will enable you to teach lifesaving skills. There are also suggestions on how to teach aquatic skills to preschool children, adults, and special populations. Finally, principles and procedures for the evaluation of swimming skills are discussed. A competent aquatic instructor is proficient in all these areas.

This text will provide basic knowledge in many areas of expertise. Further education is essential for one who wants to be a competent aquatic worker. Many of the specialized aquatic groups in the United States and Canada periodically hold short courses and workshops. The Council for National Cooperation in Aquatics (CNCA) was formed in 1945 to serve as a unifying force and forum for aquatics. Every two years, it holds conferences at which all are welcome. At these conferences, experts present both theoretical and practical information on a variety of topics.

Many CNCA members have specific certification and recognition programs, because they are convinced that we must constantly educate more and more citizens. We hope you will participate in some of these programs as you seek to become more expert in specific areas.

Table 1.2 shows the variety of aquatic teaching specialties available. In most U.S. universities, several different aquatic courses are taught; in some, it is possible to earn an aquatic minor. The Aquatic Council of the American Alliance of Health, Physical Education, Recreation and Dance (AAHPERD) provides a listing of schools that currently offer an emphasis in aquatics.

Table 1.2. Certification/Recognition Programs for Aquatic Workers

Specialty	Beginning Instructors	Master Instructors
Swimming	Universities throughout U.S. and Canada, ARC, YMCA, Boy Scouts, Canadian Red Cross Society (CRCS)	Aquatic Council of AAHPERD[1], ARC, YMCA, CRCS
Swimming for preschoolers	YMCA	
Lifeguarding	YMCA, ARC[2], United States Life Saving Assn., Royal Life Saving Society Canada	Aquatic Council of AAHPERD
Competitive swimming	Colleges throughout U.S. and Canada, YMCA, Canadian Amateur Swimming Assn.	Aquatic Council of AAHPERD, RC, YMCA[3]
Springboard diving	Colleges throughout U.S. and Canada, YMCA, Canadian Amateur Diving Assn.	Aquatic Council of AAHPERD, YMCA[3]
Swimming for special populations	ARC, YMCA[3]	Aquatic Council of AAHPERD, RC, YMCA[3]
Scuba	YMCA, National Assn. of Underwater Instructors (NAUI), Professional Assn. of Diving Instructors (PADI), National Assn. of Underwater Instructors, Canada (NAUIC), Assn. of Canadian Underwater Councils (ACUC)	YMCA[3], NAUI, PADI, NAUIC, ACUC
Small craft	ARC, YMCA	Aquatic Council of AAHPERD, CRCS
Surfing	YMCA[3]	
Synchronized swimming	YMCA, Canadian Amateur Synchro Swim Assn.	Aquatic Council of AAHPERD
Water polo	Colleges throughout U.S. and and Canada, YMCA, Canadian Amateur Water Polo Assn.	Aquatic Council of AAHPERD
Pool chemistry	Colleges throughout U.S. and Canada, local health departments, YMCA[3]	Aquatic Council of AAHPERD
Aquatic facilities manager	Colleges throughout U.S. and Canada, YMCA[3]	Aquatic Council of AAHPERD

Addresses of all groups will be found in References.

[1] The Aquatic Council of AAHPERD has annual aquatic institutes in most instructor specialties. The purpose is to develop master teachers, who will then conduct classes in their own locale.

[2] ARC Life Guarding course began in 1981. Neither the ARC Advanced Life Saving course nor the YMCA Senior Life-saving course are *lifeguarding* courses.

[3] American YMCA only

[4] Canadian YMCA only

USING THIS TEXT

Every chapter begins with a brief introduction that provides an outline of the material and, we hope, makes you eager to read on. Next, the chapter presents appropriate material, using various combinations of written text, illustrations, tables, and charts. At the ends of Chapters 2–8 we include a behavioral objectives section, which is to be read before beginning the study of that chapter. These objectives specify what is expected of students in our aquatic certification classes.

It is important that you first know the objectives and then study the material with the help of one or more of these techniques: redraw the diagrams; rephrase important points; add your own comments in the margin. In addition, some students will complete the written assignments at the end of the chapters. They will use the teaching suggestions with novice students and retain effective suggestions. Finally, these students will gain experience in all phases of the swimming program.

CHAPTER 2

Foundations of Successful Aquatic Instruction

Characteristics of a Competent Teacher
Knowledge of Aquatic Skills
A Sound Teaching Approach
Conditions Affecting Aquatic Instruction
Class Structure

Successful, competent aquatic instructors must have extensive knowledge of their subject matter and be able to demonstrate or describe numerous aquatic skills in terms that learners understand. Competent instructors have developed a sound teaching approach, which includes various strategies that will reduce fear and performance errors. They must consider the many factors that affect instruction, such as age and number of lessons. Finally, veteran aquatic workers have the ability to successfully teach a class because they have organized plans for safety, formations, testing, and other details of class structure.

CHARACTERISTICS OF A COMPETENT TEACHER

The list of essential qualities for superior swimming and diving teachers (Table 2.1) is formidable. Each of these points is important; training given by national groups to certified instructors requires at least minimum exposure to the first four. But the last characteristic—patience—is an absolute necessity. Some students just do not "catch on" to a needed skill even after many sessions of instruction. The teacher's temptation is to cease instruction of the skill, and this is sometimes done. However, truly competent instructors alter the explanation, devise a new drill, or organize practice in a different fashion to accomplish the task. Some instructors naturally have patience. Others must cultivate it. However patience is gained, it is essential.

KNOWLEDGE OF AQUATIC SKILLS

Most competent aquatic teachers are or have been above-average swimmers or divers. No research supports the idea that skilled performance in swimming is highly correlated to success in aquatic teaching. Nevertheless, the ability to accurately describe correct performance of all the aquatic skills detailed in Chapters 3, 4, 5, 6, and 7 must be viewed as essential. If you can already correctly perform all the skills shown in these chapters, great! But, it's likely that some may require practice. An excellent way to

Table 2.1. Essential Characteristics of Competent Swimming or Diving Teachers

Characteristic	Where Discussed in This Text
1. Knowledge of aquatics, which includes ability to:	
a. demonstrate or accurately describe correct performance of numerous aquatic skills	Chapters 3, 4, 5, 6
b. analyze and correct errors	Chapters 3, 4, 5, 6
2. Knowledge of a sound teaching approach, which includes ability to:	
a. use biomechanical principles in demonstration or explanations	Chapter 2
b. use teaching strategies appropriate to group	Chapters 2, 3, 4, 5, 6, 7
c. minimize fear in students	Chapters 2, 7
d. employ flotation devices as needed	Chapters 2, 7
3. Knowledge of factors that affect instruction, which includes consideration of:	
a. age of students	Chapters 2, 7
b. frequency, location, and quality of practice	Chapters 2, 7
c. learning plateaus	Chapters 2, 7
d. introduction of new skills	Chapters 2, 7
4. Knowledge of procedures and techniques, ability to:	
a. ensure safety of students	Chapters 2, 7
b. classify students	Chapters 2, 8
c. prepare appropriate objectives	Chapters 2, 8
d. construct sound lesson plans	Chapter 2
e. select effective drills and formations	Chapters 2, 3, 4, 5, 6
f. evaluate skills	Chapter 8
5. Patience	Chapters 2, 7

Adapted from American National Red Cross, *Swimming and Water Safety Courses: Instructor's Manual*, 1968, pp. 2–4.

develop skill in both performance and teaching is the reciprocal method of instruction (see p. 11), with another novice as your partner. Both of you will gain immensely from the practice sessions.

Demonstration of Correct Performance

The ability to analyze and correct mistakes has been cited as a characteristic of competent teachers. Some national certifying groups require that their instructors be able to demonstrate most of the strokes, dives, and skills shown in Chapters 3, 4, 5, and 6. Actual practice is thus required. There is a universal feeling (but no research to prove it) that instructors who can demonstrate are better teachers than those who cannot. However, the practical view is that correct demonstrations must be given.

Who should demonstrate—the instructor or a student? Most experienced instructors use student demonstrations, feeling that the learners are more apt to succeed if they know one of their classmates can do the skill. In addition, the instructor can maintain class control, make sure the demonstration is correct, and make appropriate comments to the demonstrator and the group. If no student can demonstrate correctly, then the instructor must. In certain instances, films or wall charts may be used, but live demonstrations generally are preferred.

Analysis of Performance

The term "photographic eye" denotes the ability to watch any part of a stroke or dive and instantly know what is right or what is wrong. A beginning instructor cannot easily separate the parts of a performance or relate exactly what should be done to improve the performance. This is an acquired trait developed only when the instructor can analyze or dissect a performance. Even though only teaching experience will develop the photographic eye to its sharpest degree, acquiring this ability should begin as early as possible.

Skill analysis sheets are specialized forms developed for the express purpose of analyzing the form of a swimmer or diver. Usually they contain a diagram of the skill, with a list of common errors. As the student demonstrates a skill, the instructor notes on the sheet exactly what is satisfactory and what is not, and then shows it to the student. Analyzing the form of fellow students is excellent training for all members of a class, and especially important for those who are becoming certified aquatic instructors. The use of the analysis sheet is much superior to the informal method of watching a swimmer and mentioning one or two faults. Performance analysis sheets are presented for every stroke and dive described in this text; they should help develop the photographic eye in aquatic instructors.

Correction of Performance

The ability to correct mistakes begins when they are recognized. A photographic eye, combined with a knowledge of what correct performance should be, is the starting point. The error should be explained in language appropriate to the maturity of the student. Next, the correct movement is demonstrated, followed by practice.

It is better to use praise ("good" or "that's right, but . . .") more often than criticism. Positive teaching (demonstrating what is being done right) is likewise recommended over negative teaching. The manner in which the correction is made is often more important than what is said. Above all, the teacher must not merely say to the learner, "That is wrong." Tell the student exactly what is wrong and indicate specifically how the performance can be improved.

A SOUND TEACHING APPROACH

"Teaching approach" is a vague, ill-defined term encompassing a number of issues based upon research into teaching methods. Our view is that a sound teaching approach implies that the instructor is knowledgeable about the basic aquatic teaching strategies, practice conditions that lead to efficient learning, appropriate use of biomechanical principles, and, perhaps the key to all successful aquatic instruction, reduction of fear in the learner.

The "Why" of Swimming

For years, excellent teachers have been stressing "why" a skill should be performed in a certain way, rather than just "how" to do it. Evidence suggests that students learn more effectively when both "how" and "why" are emphasized.

In swimming, "why" is answered by basic biomechanical principles. The problem facing the aquatic instructor is to recognize that the explanation and demonstration of the various principles must be adjusted for different age groups. Table 2.2 indicates the two basic categories of biomechanical prin-

Table 2.2. Biomechanical Principles of Movement in the Water

Biomechanical Principles and Explanations	Examples of Teaching Techniques

I. Floating

    A. Floating—interaction of gravity, buoyancy, and density of an object in the water
    B. Gravity—the downward pull on an object
        1. Center of gravity—imaginary point on land around which the weight of an object is centered
        2. Line of gravity—imaginary vertical line that passes through the center of gravity.
    C. Buoyancy—upward force on an object immersed in liquid
        1. Buoyancy (upward force)—equal to the weight of the liquid it displaces (Archimedes' Law)

Explanation	Examples and Rationale
The force that holds a swimmer up is equal to the weight of the amount of water displaced by the swimmer's body.	Have persons of different sizes do tuck float. Larger persons generally float well *unless* they are muscular.
	Float vertically, face down. Slowly raise head. Head removed from water decreases amount of liquid it displaces, and thus body tends to sink. Body also sinks until weight of the water displaced is equal to body weight.

        2. Center of buoyancy—imaginary point that represents the center of gravity of a body in the water

Explanation	Examples and Rationale
As center of gravity changes, the center of buoyancy changes. The center of buoyancy is normally found in the chest region (when the lungs are filled with air).	Prone float, slowly raise head. The body will rotate (feet going down, head coming up), because the weight of head moves upward causing body to sink.
	Back float by pushing off from side. As momentum slows, the feet will sink until center of buoyancy reached.
	Float on back, arms outstretched. Slowly move arms overhead (keeping them underwater). Feet will rise as the center of buoyancy moves from lungs toward hips.
	Prone float, slowly bring knees up to chest. Body rotates (feet down, head up), because shortened leg length raises center of buoyancy toward chest.

    D. Density—the ratio of the weight of the body to the weight of an equal amount of water

Explanation	Examples and Rationale
A body will float only if its density is less than the density of the water.	Have persons of different body types (muscular, thin, fat, short, tall) float. Differences in floatability due to differences in density and lung capacity.
Density depends upon lung capacity and body composition. Inflating lungs increases body volume without adding much weight.	Have persons float with lungs partially filled, and then float with lungs completely filled. With lungs completely filled. With lungs filled, people float better.

Table 2.2–*continued*

Biomechanical Principles and Explanations	Examples of Teaching Techniques
Explanation	**Examples and Rationale**
Bone and muscle weigh more than fat.	Have males and females float. Females have extra layer of subcutaneous fat, and thus tend to float better.

II. Motion

A. Inertia—an object remains at rest (or in motion) unless acted upon by an outside force (Newton's First Law)

Explanation	**Examples and Rationale**
Friction of water is an outside force which slows body.	Prone position, push off from wall. Friction causes body to gradually slow down.
	Survival float in middle of pool (person will stay in the same relative position).
	Survival float next to pool inlet (person will be "pushed away" from inlet by current of water).
	Compare force necessary to swim 10 feet pushing off wall rather than standing start.

B. Resistance—factors that slow body movement through water

Explanation	**Examples and Rationale**
Speed through water, negative movements of limbs, density of swimmer, eddy resistance, unstreamlined body all tend to increase resistance, and thus reduce motion.	Using less force, a lighter swimmer can move same speed as heavier person (assuming equal skill, arm length, arm strength).

C. Action and reaction—for every action there is an equal and opposite reaction (Newton's Third Law)

Explanation	**Examples and Rationale**
To go forward, you must push backward.	Prone float, arms in advance of body. Press arms vigorously toward bottom; note rise of shoulders followed by sinking.

D. Leverage—for every aquatic movement there is an optimum angle for leg and arm position

Explanation	**Examples and Rationale**
To increase the force of propulsion, the distance between the fulcrum and the load must be shortened.	Partner stands behind swimmer who is standing in chest deep water. Compare backward force generated in crawl stroke with windmill arm action (e.g., straight arm in both recovery and propulsion phase) versus bent arm recovery and propulsion.

Adapted from American Red Cross, *Swimming and Water Safety*, 1968, pp. 43-51; Arnold and Freeman, 1972, pp. 27-32; Canadian Red Cross Society, *National Instructor Guide and Reference*, pp. 29–42; Midtlyng, 1974, pp. 7-12; personal communication from Dr. Nancy Oyster, Colorado State University.

ciples with explanations and examples of sub-principles that reinforce the main concept. If possible, explanations suitable to the age level should be followed by movements designed to reinforce the concept.

Basic Teaching Strategies

Four of the many basic principles of motor learning have particular application to the teaching of aquatic skills. First, simple movements can best be learned by wholes, but complex movements can usually best be learned by emphasizing the largest part possible. Second, the learning rate is hastened if the student has favorable past physical and mental experiences in the skill. Third, the learning rate is impeded if the person is fearful, cold and shivering, or tired. Finally, the whole movement is more than the sum of its parts. These principles govern the selection of the particular teaching strategy that should be used.

Many experts feel that the best way to teach people to swim is by the "whole" method (show them the skill, then let them practice). Others will tell you that practice of the parts (kick, pull, breathing, and coordination) is necessary before an efficient stroke is attained. Still others maintain that the progressive-part teaching strategy (practice the kick, practice the arm stroke, practice the kick and arms together, and so on) is the way swimming should be taught. All these strategies are effective at one time or another, but none of them alone is guaranteed to produce efficient swimmers.

The Whole-Part-Whole Method. The rationale behind this method is that most aquatic skills are simple ones; either repetitive and continuous (e.g., the crawl stroke, where the arms, legs, and breathing are repeated), or composed of few movements (e.g., the pike surface dive involves bending at the waist, lifting the straight legs vigorously toward the ceiling, sinking vertically as the weight of the legs overcomes buoyancy).

Research has shown that many swimming skills can be taught more quickly, and just as correctly, by the whole-part-whole method than by the traditional progressive-part method. Johnson (1972) and Smith (1972) both have excellent commentaries on this method. These articles should be studied by all certified aquatic workers.

The whole-part-whole method involves the following steps:

1. After making sure fear is not a deterring factor, demonstrate the entire skill.
2. Have each learner, alone or in a group, perform the skill as best he or she can.
3. Select the most important error (e.g., failure to bend at a ninety degree angle in the pike surface dive is more serious than failure to keep legs straight and together), and give advice on overcoming the error.
4. Continue to offer advice to overcome errors, even though the entire skill is practiced.
5. If an error persists after three to five trials, have the student practice only on that part.
6. Continue to work on the whole, and the needed parts, until the skill is performed correctly.

Two obvious advantages to this method are that a large number of learners can correctly perform very quickly, and students are highly motivated because they are practicing only the parts they cannot perform correctly. Notice that the whole-part-whole method involves continuous observation and correction by the instructor; it does not include repetitious and unsupervised practice.

This teaching strategy is most successfully used by experienced instructors, who have background and experience in analyzing strokes, who have devised several techniques for perfecting parts of a particular skill, and who have a more highly developed photographic eye. Beginning instructors should try the whole-part-whole method, though it is more difficult for them.

The Progressive-Part Method. The pure "part" method is seldom, if ever, used in teaching swimming. Instead, the traditional Red Cross and YMCA aquatic training programs advocate the progressive-part method. These training programs have been very successful, as shown by the thousands of competent instructors produced. Most instructors trained by the Red Cross or YMCA still advocate the progressive-part method, because they know it works.

Teaching progressions, detailed later in this text, are an essential feature of this teaching strategy. A progression may be defined as the sequential steps in teaching a certain skill. For example, when teaching the crawl stroke with the progressive-part method, the instructor will first have students practice the flutter kick, then the arm stroke, then the combination. Breathing is then practiced and added to the skills that have already been learned. There are no universally accepted progressions for any stroke; some teachers probably reverse the steps and still succeed. Beginning instructors are handicapped in formulating their own progressions because they usually have forgotten how they learned the stroke or dive. Teaching progressions are of importance to the student because they lead from the simple to the complex skills; they are of even greater importance to the instructor because they enable teaching with the confidence that comes from knowing what the next step will be. The instructor's confidence is evident to the student, and this in turn makes the progression more effective.

Throughout the next four chapters of the present text, the reader will find suggested progressions for every stroke, skill, and dive discussed. The beginning instructor would be well advised to use these progressions until experience leads to the formulation of new ones. Development of new progressions is desirable, providing the following guidelines are considered:

1. The progression should begin with an explanation, and preferably a demonstration, of one part of the skill. (In diving, it is sometimes impossible to demonstrate an individual part of a dive. The learner is then instructed to concentrate attention on one part only.) This explanation should be complete and in language the student can understand.
2. Correct physical practice of the first part is done enough times to ensure reasonably consistent performance.
3. The next part is explained and demonstrated.
4. This second part is practiced until it can be done.
5. Steps 1 and 2 are repeated for each additional part until the whole stroke, dive, or skill is learned.

The Reciprocal Method. Mosston (1966) described seven distinct teaching styles. One of them—the reciprocal method, also called partner teaching—has been advocated by swimming authorities for some years. This method is effective in teaching swimming, if the students are mature enough to give and receive directions. This method makes use of two persons—the learner and the teacher. (Call the teacher a "coach"; in our society, the coach is highly respected!) Each person in turn practices the skill under the watchful eye of his or her partner. The instructor must tailor the skills to each learner and coach, decide the skills to be done and what features to emphasize in each segment of the practice. He or she must converse with the coach, who, in turn, advises the learner. There is no doubt that the reciprocal method would provide the teacher with aides. Just how young the learner and partner may be to achieve the desired results needs to be determined. The concept is sound; the details are yet to be settled.

Which Method to Use? The trend is clearly toward using the whole-part-whole method, because students are more motivated, attention can be focused on parts that need improvement, and because correct performance can result more quickly. But, the method cannot be used indiscriminately. A group of beginners scattered all over the swimming area could present severe safety problems for the instructor attempting to work with each person individually. Proper organization, including qualified teacher aides, would be needed. After taking the proper safety precautions, we recommend beginning with the whole skill. If the age, background, or fears of the learners prevent adequate performance of the whole skill, proceed to the parts, using whatever progressions or techniques that are appropriate. Return to teaching the whole skill as quickly as possible, emphasizing the parts as needed.

The progressive-part method is still essential in some instances. For example, we have found the sidestroke progression given on page 65 to be very useful, whatever the age of the group. Likewise, the single trudgen is difficult to master unless the sidestroke–overarm sidestroke lead-up progression (see p. 77) is used. The progressive-part method seems to be more suited for younger learners (ages three to seven), who have not had much water experience, whose motor coordination is still developing, and whose attention span is short.

The reciprocal method seems to have most promise when the instructor is experienced, and can quickly spot errors to be corrected by the partner. Beginning instructors might spend excessive time in clearly explaining to the partner how to correct an error with the result that the actual swimming time is reduced greatly.

Fear Reduction

Overcoming fear is an essential task, because fear is a tremendous barrier to learning. Table 2.3 summarizes some guidelines for various age groups. Remember that a combination of these techniques is apt to be needed.

Table 2.3. Guidelines for Overcoming Fear

Age Level	Comments
All age groups	Stress "why" (in appropriate language) as well as "how" Achieve early success in swimming (any method) a short distance Have warm water if possible Use peer demonstration Encourage, but don't force, students to attempt skill Build confidence day by day, not in one all-out effort Realize success breeds confidence, and vice versa Use a variety of teaching techniques, gimmicks Give praise when warranted Use criticism sparingly
Especially useful for preschool groups	Practice underwater skills Employ game activities Use flotation devices Teach in shallow water Experiment with buoyancy and change of body position
Especially useful for elementary-age groups	Practice underwater skills Employ game activities Use partner (reciprocal) method
Especially useful for teenagers	Use partner (reciprocal method) Encourage trials when peers are not watching (if can be safely done)
Especially useful for adults	Use verbal explanations that can be understood Achieve early success in survival floating (drownproofing), vertical floating, and/or elementary backstroke Ensure successful experience in deep water

Flotation Devices

Flotation devices are any artificial aids (kickboards, buoyant belts, inner tubes) that help a swimmer stay afloat. Until the mid-1950s, few instructors regularly used such devices, feeling that they had two insurmountable disadvantages: (1) the swimmer could develop a false sense of confidence and become discouraged in trying to move unaided; and (2) the beginner who loses the device suddenly could be in great danger unless he or she could already propel himself or herself. Even though kickboards were found in every pool, they were to be used as arm support only by those who already had water skills. They were not to be used to help a beginner "float."

Increased use of flotation devices began with the rapid spread of the "tiny-tot" swim programs. These youngsters were too short to reach the bottom of a three-foot pool, and their social and physical immaturity prevented the success of the usual instructional techniques. Instructors saw buoyant belts, kickboards, and inner tubes as the primary means of letting young persons (ages six months to six years) move safely in the water without having to be carried. The results of using flotation devices were so good in terms of swimmer and parental acceptance that scarcely a preschool program in the U.S. today does not use such devices.

Many excellent instructors do not make extensive use of the flotation aids. In general, the YMCA and the private pool programs make more use of flotation aids than does the Red Cross programs. In theory, flotation devices would be beneficial for a swimmer of any age, but in practice they are much more commonly used in teaching the very young.

Why do the majority of instructors use such devices? Table 2.4 summarizes both the pros and cons of this issue.

In summary, even though research does not conclusively prove the definite advantage of using flotation devices, they are commonly used. There is no evidence that students are harmed in any way from their use. Chart 2.1 depicts and discusses the common devices used today.

Table 2.4. Flotation Devices–Should They Be Used?

Advantages	Disadvantages
1. Students are safer in the water, especially in those classes where parents are working with their small children.	1. Safe commercial flotation devices are expensive.
2. The students (and their parents!) have less fear, and thus adjust to the water more quickly.	2. The devices are sometimes "borrowed" from the swimming area and never returned.
3. Students learn skills more quickly.	3. Quite often, lifeguards will not permit them to be used in recreational swim sessions.
4. Student's attention can be focused on one aspect of a skill (e.g., kick, arm stroke) without worrying about staying afloat.	4. They encourage parents and beginners to use unsafe devices (e.g., vinyl floating ducks, small boards) in out-of-class swimming in backyard pools and beaches.
5. More water space of the pool can be used safely.	
6. Longer instructional periods can be scheduled, because swimmer fatigue is lessened.	

Our view: Limited research evidence, and much practical experience indicate that safe flotation devices should be used in swim programs. Their use in unsupervised situations is not recommended, and thus they should be securely stowed away when not used in a class.

Chart 2.1. Suitable Flotation Devices and Their Uses

Styrofoam Devices

A. Devices can be made out of broken kickboards. Cut into 6″–7″ widths, cut out two holes, insert a safe belt (see below) through two holes. Two devices can be used if more support needed.

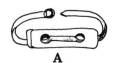

Be sure belt is strong (nylon webbing preferred) and that fastening device is safe. Check often!

B. A device can also be made by *securely* fastening a safe belt to one pull buoy (used to immobilize legs for kicking practice).

C. Most instructors prefer devices strapped to waist, rather than around upper back. Preschool children, however, function better in a vertical position.

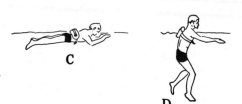

More difficult to use strapped to stomach than to back.

D. Most useful for young (6 months-6 years) students.

Small Inflatable Tubes

E. If small inner tubes are used, strap down valve stem. Air in tubes can be reduced, thus providing less support if desirable. Remember—anything that can be inflated can also be deflated!

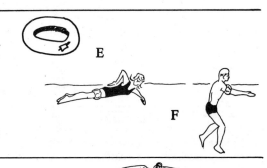

F. Most useful on legs (as arm stroke is practiced) or upper arms (treading arm action).

Will impede proper movements unless on upper arm or leg.

Inflatable Belts

G. Commercially made. Inflate by blowing up.

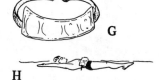

H. Easier to wear on stomach than styrofoam devices.

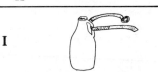

Plastic Bottles

I. One-gallon plastic milk jugs or bleach bottles are very suitable. Using a safe belt, fasten to upper back of person.

Kickboards

J. Styrofoam or plastic models are best; wood is too heavy and dangerous. Some models come with hand-holds.

Chart 2.1 *—continued*

K. Grasp so that body position closely approximates desired swim position.

L. Harder to use while on back.

Broken easily if thrown or slapped on water. Use broken ones for styrofoam devices (see A above).

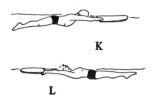

CONDITIONS AFFECTING AQUATIC INSTRUCTION

Knowledge of skills and possession of a sound teaching approach represent but two essential characteristics of a competent aquatic instructor. Consideration of such practical items as age, practice locations, speed of learning, and others are often the difference between effective and ineffective instruction, and will be discussed in this section.

Age Level of the Students

Special sections in Chapter 7 contain specific advice concerning swim programs for preschoolers and for senior citizens. Usually, these two age groups do not learn as rapidly as the students of in-between age. The ARC text, *Swimming and Water Safety* (1968, Chapter 3), summarizes succinctly important considerations concerning the different age groups. Table 2.5 is based on this source, but contains additional comments.

Frequency and Length of Practice Periods

Regardless of the method of teaching you are using, you must consider the length of time to practice each part or stroke. "Massed" practice is when a certain skill is practiced for a length of time, (e.g., twenty minutes), while "distributed" practice is when the twenty minutes of practice is distributed over several days. Research suggests that for people learning a skill, distributed practice over a several-day period seems to be the best. On the other hand, experienced performers (such as advanced swimmers) perhaps benefit most if they have massed practice on a stroke. The age of the learners is related to the length of time a swimmer should practice one stroke. It may be necessary for a young beginner group to take four five-minute sessions to practice floating. An older group could accomplish this in two ten-minute sessions.

The Location of Practice

Where should students practice? The usual procedure is for them to get into the water and practice—and this seems to make sense. However, land drill (standing or lying on the pool deck or beach) has been recommended since 1798. It is also possible to practice mentally. However, swimming research (Clayton, 1963, pp. 188-89) has not shown that either land drill or mental practice were significantly beneficial to beginning male swimmers when either was used in conjunction with water practice. It is conceivable that either method (or both) would aid in the learning of aquatic activities, but instructors will continue to believe that the best place to learn to swim is in the water, until they are shown that this is untrue. In learning to dive, however, it is common to use diving sand pits, trampolines, and visual aids.

Table 2.5. Guidelines for Teaching Different Age Levels

Age Level	Comments
Preschool children	Use imitation, not explanation, as the source of learning. Water temperature should be higher than for others; activity prevents shivering! Keep lessons short; make drills gamelike and fun. Competition sometimes encourages a child who is afraid to try a new skill; it discourages those who are fearful. Use swimmer aides; have parents help, if they will. Don't expect significant aquatic skills to develop in all the students; forewarn each parent of this possibility.
Elementary school children	Demonstration by peers, and much student activity, yield greatest results. Make instruction fun. Use swimmer aides for those who are not making sufficient progress. Watch for show-offs who attempt a skill they cannot do.
Teenagers	Beware of embarrassing a student. Allow more free time for practice (not free play). Demonstration by fellow students is more effective than demonstration by the instructor.
Adults	The primary task is to build confidence. Stress survival floating and swimming on back. Even though they listen politely, avoid talking too much. Distributed practice is usually more successful than massed practice. Expect great variations in skill level after the third or fourth session.

Adapted from American National Red Cross, *Swimming and Water Safety,* 1968, Chapter 3. Used by permission.

The Quality of Practice

One of the most popular myths of all times is "Practice makes perfect." A moment's reflection will reveal that this simply cannot be true. If so, why can't experienced bowlers consistently roll games of 250 to 300? Why can't all veteran golfers consistently shoot close to par? The most obvious aquatic example is the diver who cannot learn a certain dive. He or she tries the dive over and over, but seldom with success. It should be obvious that practice alone will not make a perfect performance. This concept of practice should be rephrased to read, "Correct and sufficient practice leads toward perfection." The key words in this phrase are "correct" and "sufficient." The primary job of the teacher, then, is to make certain that students are practicing correctly. A secondary job is to enable them to practice this correct form a sufficient length of time. Because skills can be practiced either correctly or incorrectly, sufficient practice on incorrect skills will result in incorrect performance.

Learning Plateau

As learning progresses, a plateau may be reached when the rate of leaning slows or stops. This is especially true of beginners, who make very rapid progress for a few sessions, but suddenly seem to cease learning. They become discouraged, and quite often (especially adults) stop coming for lessons. The experienced instructor expects this learning plateau and avoids discouragement by such devices as:

1. Introducing a new stroke or skill even though the person has not mastered the previous stroke
2. Spending more time in review than on new skills
3. Using distributed practice periods rather than massed
4. Using varied explanations of the same stroke or skill

Introduction of New Skills

Teaching involves judicious addition of new skills to those previously learned. When to add new skills is puzzling to beginning teachers. Not everyone in the class will master a skill at the same time, perhaps because of the plateaus that occur in learning. To complicate matters, the average class contains a marked deviation in skill level. Some instructors add new skills rather often, their theory being that the students will become bored if this is not done. The other view is that the students will become discouraged if skills are added too rapidly, before the previous ones have been thoroughly learned. There is no universally accepted rule as to when to review, and when to teach a new skill. Many instructors progress to new skills when 65 to 70 percent of the class members can perform the old skill satisfactorily. The old skill is reviewed in subsequent sessions until virtually everyone can master it and then it is not practiced again on a class basis.

CLASS STRUCTURE

If you can demonstrate skills, have a good understanding of a sound teaching approach, and have considered the practical conditions that affect instruction, are you ready for the first class? Not quite. There are still a few details of class structure that must be considered.

Safety and Emergency Procedures

Essential provisions for safety are often overlooked. Perhaps common sense will aid you, but reflective thinking about the material in Table 2.6 might prevent a tragic accident.

Skills Your Students Already Possess

One of the first things a beginning aquatic instructor will learn is that the mere possession of a certificate (an intermediate swimmer card, for example) does not mean that the person is capable of performing all the skills required to earn that card. Therefore, you must have some way of evaluating your class to see what skills each student possesses. Consider the following ways of assessing skill level before, or at least during, the first class period.

1. Give the final skill test that you plan to use. Obviously, any student who can satisfactorily perform the skills should not be in that class. After the test, you will know exactly how skilled each student is.
2. Select the three or four most difficult skills from the final test. If these can be done by a student, it is probable that he or she is in the wrong group.
3. Have each student swim a width (or less) of these strokes:
    a. backstroke (if the student cannot do so, he or she is probably a beginner)
    b. crawl stroke (if the student cannot do this or the backstroke, he or she is probably a beginner)
    c. breaststroke (if the kick is not correct, the student is probably an intermediate; if the stroke is correct in all details, the student is almost always in the advanced swimmer stage)

Table 2.6. Safety and Emergency Procedures

Safety

Rescue equipment (poles, heaving lines, spine board, first aid kit, rescue tube, etc.) must be available, visible, and usable.

Assign lifeguards to each class (essential at lake or ocean, desirable in pool).

Maintain appropriate teacher-pupil ratio (approximately one teacher to 15 beginners, one teacher to 22 intermediate and advanced swimmers).

Swim from deep to shallow water, not vice versa.

Practice facing shallow end.

Conform to legal requirements concerning safety (e.g., post depths, first aid equipment).

Provide safe swimming environment.

Post and enforce rules.

Dismiss class on pool deck or beach, not while students are in water.

Lock doors of swimming area when class dismissed.

Post emergency numbers by phones; establish emergency reporting system.

Require first aid training of all aquatic workers.

Always know where each student is.

Emergency Procedures

Rescue victim, administer only necessary first aid.

Call rescue squad.

Clear pool or beach.

Source: Dick McFeters, American National Red Cross safety services representative.

4. The breaststroke is the one best single stroke to rate students. An overall rating for form could be used, awarding points on this basis:
   0 points—no conception of the stroke—beginner
   1 point—poor form in both arms and legs—advanced beginner
   2 points—incorrect kick, but arms reasonably good—intermediate
   3 points—form and power acceptable, but no glide—advanced
   4 points—good form—advanced
5. Have each student swim the basic strokes and demonstrate any other aquatic skills that you desire (e.g., surface dive, floating). Rate each student on a scale of 1 (poor) to 4 (excellent). Determine the maximum number of points that can be scored and place each student in the appropriate category. Chart 2.2 illustrates one such device.

How Much Time and Help Will You Have?

The overall length of all the class periods is easily ascertained, but how much of that time will be spent in instruction? Teaching assistants will permit the class to be segregated by ability levels. Will such help be available? The answer to these questions will greatly affect the organization of your program.

What Do You Plan to Accomplish?

What are the objectives or standards of the course? When teaching a Red Cross or YMCA course, for example, the objectives and standards for each class are clearly stated, and you are expected to follow them. Your job is to represent the sponsoring group as faithfully as possible and to make your course exactly like one offered in any other sector of the country.

Chart 2.2. Scale for Rating Students

Directions: Demonstrate the skill, then ask each student to perform it. Rate 0 (cannot perform); 1 (poor); 2 (average); 3 (good); 4 (excellent).

Name	Crawl				Back			Side				Survival Float			
	Arms	Kick	Breath	Coordination	Arms	Kick	Coordination	Arms	Kick	Breath	Coordination	Arms	Kick	Coordination	Etc. *
Pete Salmon	3	4	3	3	2	2	1	4	4	4	4	1	1	1	
Will Dolphin	4	2	1	2	4	4	4	3	1	3	2	3	2	3	

*Strokes and skills appropriate to the level of instruction can be used, or the same rating scale can be used for all levels. The fewer points scored by a student, the less proficient.

Teaching in a school situation presents certain other problems. The instructor must decide the purpose of the course and the skills to be taught. The usual practice is to follow the Red Cross program and award certificates. Parents and students expect this and the cooperation of the local Red Cross chapter makes this feasible. However, if you follow a progressive physical education program, then you must provide for different levels of aquatic instruction in the same class. This is a difficult problem to solve. Using the skilled students as teacher aides is a common practice, but you also have an obligation to help these students acquire new aquatic skills. Such a program must be highly organized, and carefully considered objectives and standards must be developed at the outset.

Must Lesson Plans Be Made?

Competent teachers, we have said, must be able to formulate complete lesson plans. Experienced teachers might smile at this dictum, because very few ever appear on the pool deck with a carefully formulated, written lesson plan. However, the competent teacher *does* have lesson plans formulated in his or her mind. These plans are composed primarily of the commonly used teaching progressions and skill sheets that describe performance goals for students to attain by the end of the course. The American Red Cross has prepared some lesson plans to guide teachers (*Swimming and Water Safety Courses: Instructor's Manual,* 1968, Sections 5-9). Experienced instructors tend to develop their own plans, however. Only the poor instructor truly has no lesson plan to follow.

Table 2.7 summarizes, describes, and suggests approximate time allotments for each element. The ages of students, their skill levels, and the complexity of the new material will cause plans to vary from situation to situation, but the elements presented should be the basis for virtually all class sessions.

Value of Drills and Formations

A drill is a specific movement or series of related movements by which the student practices a single aspect of a stroke or dive. For example, one drill for improving the crawl stroke would be flutter kicking with a board. Students may practice drills individually or as a class. When several students are involved in the same drill, practice is more effective and use of water space is more economical if those students practice in some kind of formation or pattern. These formations are devised to emphasize special aspects of each stroke to be practiced. There are numerous formations, but they are all variations of the basic patterns shown in Chart 2.3.

Table 2.7. Lesson Plan Elements, Descriptions, and Time Allotments

Element	Description of Element	Percentage of Class Time
Introduction	What will be done today	Less than 5%
New material*	Explanation, demonstration, directed practice of new material	25%–40% depending upon complexity of skill, ease of learning, etc.
Old material*	Review skills taught previously	50%–60%
Individual practice	Supervised practice of previously taught skills	5%–20%

*Quite often, the new material is a continuation of the old. For example, the back glide and regaining the feet have been taught before, and now the arm stroke for the elementary backstroke will be taught. Thus, the explanation and demonstration include the old material, or perhaps the old material is practiced before the new material is presented.

Chart 2.3. Basic Formations for Swimming Practice

Description	Pattern
1. *Wave formation.* The group is formed into one or more lines (counting off if necessary). One line at a time is sent to the opposite side of the pool. This is especially good for kicking, pulling, and breathing drills.	
2. *Stagger formation.* The group is formed into lines, as in the wave formation, but the individual members leave from the side one at a time. This is useful when individual appraisal must be made.	
3. *Circle formation.* The group is in either a small or a large circle and all are performing the same skill at the same time. This is useful when swimming lengths or for individual appraisal.	
4. *Single-file formation.* The individual follows the person in front. This is useful for individual appraisal.	
5. *Corner formation.* The group is formed into a semi-circle in one corner of the pool. This is especially useful for stroking practice or when the instructor needs to demonstrate to a group.	

Chapter 8 presents a detailed discussion of evaluation devices in aquatics. If you teach for one of the national groups, its skill sheets are fairly explicit and the standards should be known to you. In a school situation, you must consider this before you organize your class.

CLASS ASSIGNMENTS

1. After securing permission from the instructor, observe a swimming class (preferably a beginning class). Comment upon these facets:
   a. Were skills demonstrated? If so, by whom—the teacher, student aide, student?
   b. Was there evidence that the instructor possessed a photographic eye?
   c. Did the explanations of the skills cover "how to do it," "why to do it," or both?
   d. What method—whole-part-whole, progressive-part, or reciprocal—was used by the instructor?
   e. Was there evidence of fear in the swimmers? If it was overcome, how?
   f. Was there any evidence that the teacher had thought about the special needs of the age group being instructed?
   g. Were new skills introduced at an appropriate time?
   h. Was there evidence of course objectives? lesson plans? evaluation?
   i. Were the drills and formations effective?
   j. Were the students safely working most of the time?

2. With another person, demonstrate to each other the various biomechanical principles outlined in Table 2.2. Devise new examples from those given in the text.

3. Based upon the class you observed or another class with which you are familiar, construct a lesson plan for the next class. Use Table 2.7 as your guide. Include diagrams of formations/drills you would use.

4. Assume you are going to begin to teach the class you observed or a beginning class of ten year olds. Devise a sheet that will indicate when they are ready for your intermediate class.

BEHAVIORAL OBJECTIVES

Quite often, the aquatic leader's course is taught in a situation where it is possible for students to spend more time than in the concentrated weekend or week-long aquatic school. Also, many colleges and universities have aquatic courses as part of their regular curricula. In these situations, it is expected that students will study this text more thoroughly—and quite often the instructor will test more thoroughly!

Below will be found specific objectives for Chapter 2. If desired by the instructor, these could be used as the basis of the examination on this chapter.

After study of this chapter, students should be able to respond correctly (based on the material in this chapter) to questions that require them to list important points, to diagram formations. They should be able to perform any or all of the tasks listed below.

1. List and explain the five characteristics of a competent aquatic instructor.
2. Indicate how these three elements—demonstration, analysis, and correction of performance—are interrelated.
3. Explain how these biomechanical principles apply to aquatics: (a) buoyancy, (b) density, (c) centers of gravity and buoyancy, (d) static equilibrium, (e) inertia, (f) resistance, (g) action and reaction, and (h) leverage.
4. Describe the advantages and disadvantages of these teaching strategies: (a) whole-part-whole, (b) progressive-part, (c) reciprocal.
5. Fear reduction techniques are important to a successful teacher. List four such techniques you would use with beginners three to ten years old, thirteen to nineteen, and over twenty-one.
6. What are the pros and cons about using flotation devices for beginners?

7. Define these terms or concepts, as used in this text: (a) massed, distributed practice, (b) correct and sufficient practice, (c) learning plateau, (d) introduction of new skills.
8. Be able to list the safety equipment available in a designated aquatic facility, and give the phone number(s) of the local rescue groups.

REFERENCES

American National Red Cross. *Swimming and Water Safety.* Washington, D.C.: American National Red Cross, 1968, Chapters 2, 3, and 4.

——. *Swimming and Water Safety Courses: Instructor's Manual.* Washington, D.C.: American National Red Cross, 1968, pp. 2–29.

Arnold, Lloyd, and Freeman, Robert W. *Progressive Swimming and Springboard Diving Program.* New York: National YMCA Program Materials, 1972, pp. 11–27.

Canadian Red Cross Society. *National Instructor Guide and Reference.* Toronto: Canadian Red Cross Society, 1977, pp. 13–138.

Clayton, Robert D. "The Efficacy of the Land-Drill, Implicit Rehearsal, and Water-Practice Methods in Teaching the Breast Stroke and Crawl Stroke to College Men." Microcarded dissertation, University of Oregon, 1963.

Fisher, Joseph C. *Reduce or Control Fear of the Water.* 1980. Contact the author, 81 Crestwood Drive, Mt. Pocono, Pennsylvania 18344.

Johnson, Marion L. "A Case for Using Large Motor Tasks." *JOHPER,* March 1972, pp. 29–31.

Midtlyng, Joanna. *Swimming.* Philadelphia: W. B. Saunders Company, 1974.

Mosston, Muska. *Teaching Physical Education.* Columbus, Ohio: Charles E. Merrill Publishing Company, 1966.

Smith, Murray. "Teaching Methods in Swimming and Water Instruction." *Waters of the World: Conservation and Use.* Manassas, Va.: Council for National Cooperation in Aquatics, 1972, pp. 58–66.

Vanderbeck, Edna R. "It Isn't Right but I Don't Know What's Wrong with It." *JOPER,* May 1979, pp. 54–56.

CHAPTER 3

Performing and Teaching Essential Aquatic Skills

Floating
Rhythmic Breathing and Bobbing
Kicking
Treading Water
Swimming on the Stomach
Swimming on the Back
Standing Dive
Personal Flotation Devices
Cramps
Artificial Resuscitation
Assists and Escapes

The goal of all aquatic teachers is to make each student safe in the water. A safe swimmer must be able to stay afloat for at least five minutes, to enter the water either head or feet first, and to cope when trouble arises. If a swimmer can meet these requirements, the teacher can be fairly confident that almost any aquatic activity can be enjoyed with a reasonable degree of safety.

To be safe in the water, certain skills must be learned. The American National Red Cross, the YMCA, and similar groups have established definite skills for their beginning courses. This chapter will describe those major skills and one other we feel is essential. A school program of beginning swimming should include these skills. Each student must demonstrate proficiency in these skills before graduating from the beginner stage.

The skills defined in Table 3.1 represent standards for a beginner course in swimming. Though expectations vary for different age groups, we recommend that these skills be taught all swimming classes. For beginners, the standards would serve as a final examination; for all other classes, the items would serve as a screening device.

FLOATING

Floating is defined as a means of staying at or near the surface of the water with minimum effort for an indefinite period. Because a greater proportion of their weight is made up of muscle and bone, which are nonfloating substances, most males are poorer floaters than females. In fact, only about 2 percent of white males and 30 percent of black males are considered absolute nonfloaters (Lanoue, 1963, p. 105). The majority of males consider themselves nonfloaters, however, because they cannot keep their feet at the surface while lying on their backs. Our definition of floating makes no mention of

Table 3.1. Essential Aquatic Skills and Standards

Skill	Expectations for Beginners		
	Ages 5–10	Ages 11–16	Age 17+
1. Floating			
a. Vertical (face up, motionless or nearly so)	30 seconds	1 minute	1 minute
b. Survival floating	2 minutes	5 minutes	7 minutes
2. Rhythmic breathing and bobbing	1 minute (6 feet of water)	1 minute (7 feet of water)	1 minute (8 feet of water)
3. Kicking (flutter, scissors, breaststroke)	30 feet each	45 feet each	60 feet each
4. Treading water (using hands and feet)	30 seconds	1 minute	1 minute
5. Backstroke (finning, elementary backstroke, or crawl)	30 feet	60 feet	60–75 feet
6. Front crawl stroke	30 feet	45 feet	60–75 feet
7. Water entry and swim (any stroke)	Standing or running entry, swim 30 feet	Standing or running entry, swim 30 feet	Standing or running entry, swim 30 feet
8. Use of life jacket	Demonstrate	Demonstrate	Demonstrate
9. Release of cramps	Demonstrate	Demonstrate	Demonstrate
10. Mouth-to-mouth resuscitation	Explain	Explain	Explain
11. Assists and escapes	Demonstrate	Demonstrate	Demonstrate

where the legs must be; common sense dictates that the position of the head is more important than that of the feet. If the head stays at or near the surface with no more than an intermittent arm press or kick for at least ten seconds, the body is floating.

The floats described in this section are all essential skills for the beginner. The ability to float ensures that, in case of fatigue or an aquatic accident, the swimmer can remain at or near the surface while gathering the strength and wit essential to survival. Beginning swimmers also gain confidence, an important element in learning, when they can float successfully and easily.

While we advocate the whole or whole-part-whole methods of teaching (see Chapter 2), we think it better to teach floating skills by the progressive-part method. At the beginning of a course, you will not know much about the skill and fear levels of the students. The progressions described in the charts are safe and effective for all levels.

The Tuck Float

Which floating skills to teach is an unsettled question among instructors. Traditionally, the tuck, the prone, and the supine floats are all taught as means to an end. The tuck float is generally taught first, so the instructor can quickly ascertain which students float well naturally. Furthermore, the tuck position is taken when regaining the feet after the prone glide and when removing clothing in the water. Chart 3.1 shows the tuck float—the floating position and the method of regaining the feet.

Chart 3.1. Performance Techniques for the Tuck Float

Techniques	Illustration	Performance Errors
A. Begin with shoulders in water and large amount of air in lungs, place face in water, look downward.		A. Failing to submerge face. Failing to look downward.
B. Tuck chin close to chest, wrap arms around tucked legs. Float in this position for 3–6 seconds.		B. Failing to pull knees up to chest (instead, shoulders forced down). Failing to hold floating position long enough.
C. To regain feet, raise head as the feet are lowered.		C. Raising head before feet are lowered.

We do not recommend any special method of teaching the tuck float, but it is important that the instructor is able to observe the entire class. Learning to float with a partner standing by in case of trouble is a desirable method of instilling confidence in beginners. Stress the proper method of regaining the feet.

The Prone Float

The prone or face-down float is usually taught after the tuck float. This necessary skill is the basic position for the front crawl stroke, the breaststroke, and the trudgen strokes. Chart 3.2 depicts this float.

Chart 3.2. Performance Techniques for the Face-down (Prone) Float

Techniques	Illustration	Performance Errors
A. Begin with tuck float.		A. Failing to submerge face. Failing to look downward. Failing to pull knees up to chest.
B. Extend arms and legs in opposite directions. Float in this position for 3–6 seconds.		B. Failing to keep face submerged. Failing to keep ears between extended arms. Failing to float long enough.
C. To regain feet, resume tuck float first, then stand.		C. Failing to bend hips and knees before attempting to stand.

The teaching progression for the prone float is ordinarily based upon learning the tuck float first and then extending the arms and legs as described in Chart 3.2. However, some instructors find that the progression shown in Chart 3.3 is useful, especially with students who cannot perform the tuck float easily.

Chart 3.3. Teaching Progression for the Face-down Float (Shallow Water)

Step 1	Step 2	Step 3
Partner faces student and grasps hands. Student faces shallow water.	Student takes breath, places face well into the water.	Student lifts feet off bottom; partner retains grip.
Step 4	**Step 5**	**Step 6**
Partner faces student and grasps hands. Student faces shallow water.	When student is at ease in Step 3, partner releases grip. Student assumes standing position, without help, if possible.	Partner observes, but does not touch, student floating in prone position.

The Supine Float

The supine or face-up float must be taught before any kind of backstroke can be attempted. Chart 3.4 presents the techniques, illustrations, and major and common performance errors of this float.

Chart 3.4. Performance Techniques for the Face-up (Supine) Float

Techniques	Illustration	Performance Errors
A. Begin with arms at sides, legs bent enough so that shoulders are in water. Place back of head in water, lean backward and push gently with feet to place body in horizontal back-down position.	A	A. Failing to submerge shoulders. Keeping entire head out of water. Throwing body backward with vigor.

Chart 3.4—*continued*

Techniques	Illustration	Performance Errors
B. Float on back with ears in water, face up, arms at sides, feet well off bottom. Arms may be extended at sides.		B. Raising head or hands above the surface. Failing to look upward at sky or ceiling.
C. Slowly move arms out from sides and beyond head, causing feet to rise, but not to reach, the surface. Float in this position.		C. Moving arms too quickly. Expelling air in lungs. Overarching the body. Letting hips bend and sink.
D. To regain feet, return arms to sides and lift face out of water as knees are bent. Swing feet under knees toward hips. Arms may be pressed downward and backward if desired. *Note:* This is a difficult and fearful step for some beginners.		D. Raising arms above water surface. Attempting to stand while body is straight. Moving vigorously.
E. When feet are under hips, raise head and come to standing position.		E. Attempting to stand before feet are under hips. Raising head before feet are under hips.

Chart 3.5 depicts the teaching progression for the supine float. As with the prone float, this progression is designed to utilize a partner until the student gains confidence.

Chart 3.5. Teaching Progression for the Face-up (Supine) Float

Step 1	Step 2	Step 3

Partner stands behind student; both face deep water. Partner supports back of student's head as it is placed in water. Student looks at sky or ceiling.	Student *gently* pushes off bottom, arms at side. Partner retains support. Partner helps student regain feet.	Student slowly moves arms sideward and forward toward ears; arms stay in water at all times; partner retains support.

Chart 3.5—*continued*

Step 4	Step 5	Step 6

When floating position is reached, partner withdraws support but remains available for help. Flotation device on stomach may be used.	Student moves arms back to side and regains feet by putting feet under buttocks and face toward stomach. Partner helps by lifting student's upper back.	Partner observes but does not touch student floating in supine position and regaining feet.

The Vertical Floats

Two methods of vertical floating—face down and face up—are shown in Chart 3.6. Women and most children can usually perform either with ease, but men who are not good floaters find the face-down method better. The face-down or "deadman's" float is not what most people consider to be a desirable skill. However, it is the basis for the technique known as drownproofing.

Chart 3.6. Performance Techniques for the Vertical Floats

Techniques	Illustration	Performance Errors
Face Down A. Following a deep breath, extend arms forward (as in prone) float); tuck chin. Float in this position 5–10 seconds. Arms and legs may be spread if desired.	A	A. Failing to submerge face. Holding float position too briefly. Exhaling breath.
Face Up B. Extend legs with feet below hips, extend arms sideward, take and hold a deep breath, press chest upward, place back of head in water, and look upward. C. Hold breath for 3–5 seconds, exhale half of air in lungs and quickly inhale a like amount. On succeeding trials, lengthen to 10–15 seconds the time the breath is held.	B and C	B. Failing to arch back, press hips forward and place back of head in water. Failing to place feet under hips. Failing to assume floating position slowly and gently. C. Breathing out slowly. Breathing out more than one-half of air in lungs. Failing to breathe in immediately after breathing out.

The vertical floats may be taught in shoulder-deep water, using a partner to provide support if needed. However, we recommend that these be taught in deep water if possible, using the progression shown in Chart 3.7.

Chart 3.7. Teaching Progression for the Vertical Floats (Deep Water)

Face Down

Step 1	Step 2	Step 3
	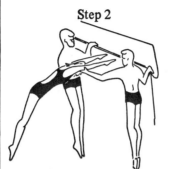	
Partners on either side of student. Student puts hands on trough, feet underneath. Arms are wide, with chest next to wall.	Student takes breath, puts face in water. Partners support (not lift) student by placing near hands under shoulder. Student removes hands from trough and floats.	Partners observe the floater; help only if needed.

Face Up

Step 1	Step 2	Step 3
		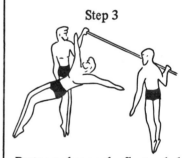
Partners on either side of student. Student has back to wall, arms outstretched grasping deck, feet underneath (not out).	Student takes breath, looks at sky or ceiling, removes hands from wall; partners support student with near hands under shoulder. Student holds breath, then exhales and inhales quickly.	Partners observe the floater; help only if needed.

The Glides

A glide is merely a float with motion. Because the forward movement aids the student in floating, the glides are considerably easier for some students. For this reason, certain instructors teach the glides before the floats. Charts 3.8 and 3.9 describe and illustrate the teaching progressions for the prone or face-down glide and the supine or face-up glide.

Chart 3.8. Teaching Progression for the Face-down Glide

Step 1	Step 2	Step 3
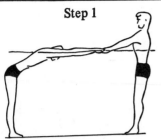		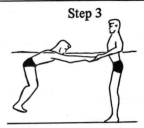
Student faces shallow water. Partner grasps hands of student, who leans forward, takes breath, and puts face in water.	Partner walks backward. Student "stretches" out.	Student regains feet by bringing knees underneath, raising head and pressing down with arms. Partner provides support.

Step 4	Steps 5 and 6
	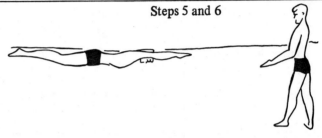
Student *gently* pushes off wall (or off bottom by leaning forward and pushing), and glides to partner, 6–10 feet away.	Partner backs up 3–5 feet each time student adds length to glide. Partner aids student in regaining feet. Student performs glide; partner is ready to assist if needed.

Chart 3.9. Teaching Progression for the Face-up Glide

Step 1	Step 2	Step 3

Student grasps wall as shown, back of head in water. Partner supports head. (If no wall, bend knees so shoulders are in water.)	Student gently presses with feet, stretches out with arms at sides. Partner walks backward, supporting head. Student must look at sky or ceiling.	Student regains feet as in supine float. Partner assists.

Chart 3.9—*continued*

Step 4	Steps 5 and 6
	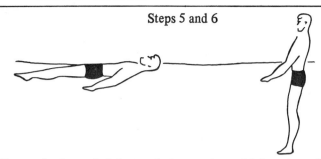
Student pushes off wall and glides to partner, 6–10 feet away. Partner helps student regain feet if necessary.	Partner backs up 3–5 feet each time student adds length to glide. Student performs glide; partner ready to assist if needed.

Survival Floating (Drownproofing)

Drownproofing, developed by Fred Lanoue, is a technique of staying afloat and moving in the water. It has become world famous because "it guarantees that (unless you are: 1) held or pinned underwater; 2) dazed or unconscious in the water; 3) so badly cramped or injured you are useless in the water; or, 4) faced with an impossible problem in thickness of foam, rate of heat loss, etc.) you will survive any water accident regardless of age, sex, or condition." (Lanoue, 1963, p. 13).

Aquatic specialists have been concerned about drownproofing in recent years for two reasons. First, the term itself implies virtual immunity to drowning if the technique is used correctly. Since even the best of swimmers can drown, the term "survival floating" has been substituted by some authorities. Second, death due to heat loss (hypothermia) is a very real hazard in many water accidents that occur outside of heated pools. The head is most subject to heat loss of the parts of the body. Because drownproofing calls for repeated immersion of the face, the technique may accelerate the onset of hypothermia even as it permits the person to stay afloat. (See discussion on personal flotation devices, pages 51–52.)

There is no doubt that in warm water and for short periods of time, drownproofing is superior to other forms of unaided floating. For this reason, it must be mastered by all swimmers. At the same time, students should realize that some heat loss will always occur, and that if floating and treading water can keep the head dry, so much the better.

The survival floating technique demonstrated in Chart 3.10 is suitable for almost all women and young children and for men who are naturally good floaters.

Most men do not float as well as women. The techniques described and illustrated in Chart 3.11 are designed for them.

Finally, Lanoue adapted his technique for the people who need it most, the nonfloaters. The basic difference is that there is no resting phase for nonfloaters. They must continually be moving forward, sinking, or coming back to the surface. Chart 3.12 illustrates the survival floating technique for nonfloaters.

The teaching progression for drownproofing is basically the same as for floating. Lanoue (1963, pp. 74-77) advocated teaching drownproofing in deep water, but we prefer to begin in shoulder-deep water. Chart 3.13 discusses and illustrates our technique.

Chart 3.10. Performance Techniques for Survival Floating (Women and Young Children)

Techniques	Illustration	Performance Errors
A. *Rest.* Vertical floating position, arms and legs dangling, face in water. Hold an ordinary amount of air in the lungs.		A. Raising face out of water.
B. *Get ready.* Slowly raise the arms so that they are at the surface. *Position* the legs for a scissors kick.	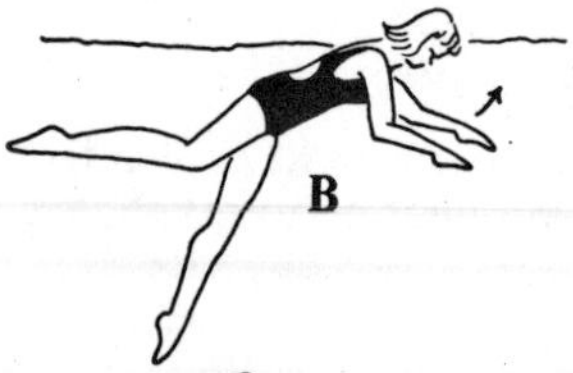	B. Raising arms too fast. Failing to move legs into position for delivery of a scissors kick.
C. *Exhale and rise.* Press the hands down toward bottom; at same time, exhale through nose.	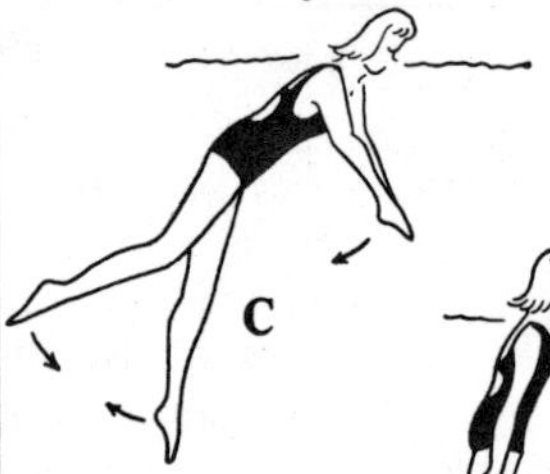	C. Failing to exhale. Pushing hands and arms backward rather than downward.
D. *Stay at surface.* Inhale as soon as chin is at surface. Continue to press arms and legs downward.		D. Trying to rise too far out of water.
E. *Rest.* Place face in the water. Remain motionless as body settles underwater and then regains floating position.	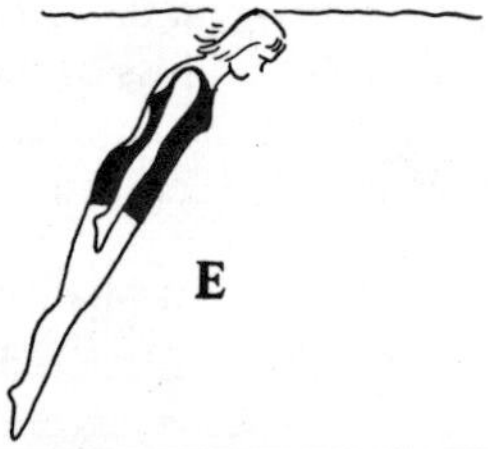	E. Failing to lower the face into water. Moving before the body regains floating position.

Adapted from Lanoue, *Drownproofing* (Prentice-Hall, 1963), pp. 15–18. Used by permission.

Chart 3.11. Performance Techniques for Survival Floating (Buoyant Men)

Techniques	Illustration	Performance Errors
A. *Rest.* With lungs full of air, assume position with head forward and face in water, arms and legs dangling, floating with back of head at surface.	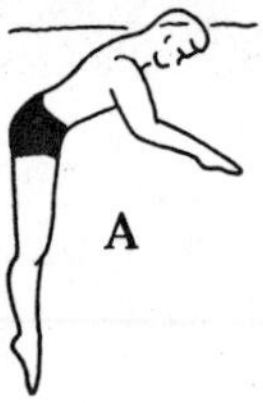	A. Raising or holding the face out of water.

Chart 3.11–*continued*

Techniques	Illustration	Performance Errors
B. *Get ready to breathe.* Raise the forearms leisurely to surface in front of head. Place forearms parallel to each other. Prepare to scissors kick.	B	**B.** Raising the forearms too vigorously. Failing to place arms and/or legs into correct position.
C. *Exhale.* Without moving the arms or legs from their position, raise the head so the chin just nears the water's surface. As head is raised, exhale through the nose. Finish exhaling just as the chin reaches the surface.	C	**C.** Failing to exhale. Moving the hands and/or legs.
D. *Inhale.* The instant the chin clears the surface, begin the inhalation through the mouth. Kick with the feet and sweep out with palms of hands until the arms are extended sideward. Inhablation should be finished just as the arms are extended sideward and the kick is finished.	D	**D.** Treading water (to take 2-3 breaths). Pressing arms toward bottom. Inhaling through the nose. Kicking and moving arms too vigorously, thus causing body to rise too high in the water.
E. *Stay at surface.* As inhalation is finished, body will sink. As head settles below the surface, force arms downward (legs may be kicked). Place face in water.	E	**E.** Failing to lower the face into the water.

Adapted from Lanoue, *Drownproofing* (Prentice-Hall, 1963), pp. 24–29. Used by permission.

Chart 3.12. Performance Techniques for Survival Floating (Nonfloaters)

Techniques	Illustration	Performance Errors
A. *Get to the top.* As soon as the head settles underwater, lower the face into the water, bend the elbows and hold arms close to chest. Ready the feet for a scissors kick. Deliver the kick to propel the body toward the surface.	A	**A.** Failing to lower the face into the water. Failing to deliver the kick.

Chart 3.12—*continued*

Techniques	Illustration	Performance Errors
B. As soon as the kick is completed, sweep the arms slowly but forcefully backward until they reach the sides. Sweep the arms slightly downward to push the body to the surface while traveling 3–5 feet forward.	B	B. Failing to travel (concentrating on up and down movement instead).
C. *Get ready to inhale.* Allow legs to settle as forward momentum is lost. Place legs into scissors kick position as arms are gently recovered toward surface.	C	C. Failing to let legs settle before moving them into position for delivery of scissors kick. Moving arms to surface too quickly and vigorously.
D. *Exhale.* Deliver scissors kick as arms are pressed downward and air is exhaled. Expel air just as chin reaches water surface.	D	D. Exhaling before the chin reaches the surface.
E. *Inhale and sink.* Press with palms as arms move outward. Allow body to settle after breath is taken and face is placed in water.	E	E. Raising the mouth too far above the surface of the water. Failing to lower the face into the water.

Adapted from Lanoüe, *Drownproofing* (Prentice-Hall, 1963) pp. 29–32. Used by permission.

RHYTHMIC BREATHING AND BOBBING

The term "rhythmic breathing" is self-explanatory, but it is frequently associated with "bobbing." Bobbing is a method of alternately rising above and sinking below the surface. Because it is virtually impossible to bob more than four or five times without breathing, these two skills are frequently combined in one drill.

Rhythmic breathing is extremely important, because proper and efficient form in several strokes requires that the face be in the water most of the time.

Chart 3.14 illustrates the techniques for bobbing in shallow water and in deep water. Rhythmic breathing is obviously a part of this skill.

Bobbing and rhythmic breathing are taught together, for obvious reasons. Before beginning, it is wise to remind swimmers that water will not go up the nose if a "trickle" of air is allowed to escape while the body is submerging. Nose clips are acceptable, but we recommend that a swimmer first try to

Chart 3.13. Teaching Progression for Survival Floating

Step 1	Step 2	Step 3

Students stand in shoulder-deep water, facing shallow end. Practice coordination of arm press-exhalation-head lift-inhalation-head drop.	Students travel across pool in shoulder-deep water. (Identify those who are poor floaters; they will need more help than others.) Flotation devices on the back will be helpful to some.	Students enter deep water, with partner on each side. Student faces wall and practices. Add kick where needed. Partners keep student close to wall. (In lake, use advanced swimmers as guards.)

Step 4	Step 5	Notes
		Practice Step 1 during the first two or three sessions. Set goals (30 consecutive, successful breaths, for example). Add Step 2. When virtually everyone can do Step 2, go to deep water for remainder of steps.
Students go across deep end of pool, staying next to edge. Then go length of pool, again next to edge.	Students perform survival floating in one place for a period of time.	

Chart 3.14. Performance Techniques for Bobbing

Techniques	Illustration	Performance Errors
Shallow Water A. Take a breath; sink below surface by bending knees and raising arms overhead. B. Extend legs to push off bottom. C. As face emerges above the surface, lower the arms, exhale and inhale. D. Repeat Steps A, B, and C rhythmically and in sequence.	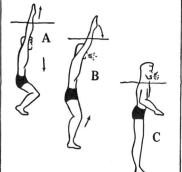	A. Failing to submerge completely. B. Leaning too far forward or too far backward from vertical. C. Exhaling before emerging above surface. D. Pausing for longer than 2 or 3 seconds between submersions.

Chart 3.14—*continued*

Techniques	Illustration	Performance Errors
Deep Water E. After taking a breath, descend to bottom by extending arms overhead (very buoyant persons may have to expel some air). Variations include: 　1. Using a sculling action with the hands overhead (a continual upward-pushing motion with the palms). 　2. Using a reverse pull (lowering the arms to the thighs and then pulling sideward and upward with palms facing upward). F. Push off bottom and pull arms down to thighs. (If a lake bottom is soft mud, it probably is better to omit push-off). G. To move forward, incline body slightly forward when pushing off bottom. H. Emerge at surface. Exhale and inhale. Thrust arms overhead. I. Repeat Steps E, F, G, and H rhythmically and in sequence.	E.1　　E.2 F　　　G H	E. Bending at hips or knees. Extending the feet backward or forward from vertical. 　1. Failing to push upward with palms. 　2. Thrusting the arms upward instead of exerting a pull upward. F. Failing to pull arms through to thighs. Failing to execute a vigorous pull. Failing to execute a vigorous push-off. G. Inclining body forward too much. H. Exhaling before reaching surface. Failing to rise high out of water on emerging. I. Failing to perform actions in sequence.

keep water out of the nose by this method or even by holding the nose. Face masks and goggles are sometimes used.

To practice bobbing, students stand in chest-deep water facing the instructor, and then bob up and down in place. When most have mastered this, a single file of students can cross the pool (or a given distance), again in chest deep water.

Bobbing in deep water is more difficult to master, hence our recommendation of distributed practice sessions. The students should try, one at a time, to go as far into deep water as they can. They should go close to the side of the pool or dock (Chart 3.15A). If instruction is taking place in open water, a line of advanced swimmers may be placed along the intended route (3.15B). These "lifeguards" tread water, and only move if needed. Whether in a lake or in a pool, traveling from the shallow to the deep water is easier for most beginners. They should have some experience in starting in the deep water, however.

Chart 3.15. Teaching Bobbing in Deep Water

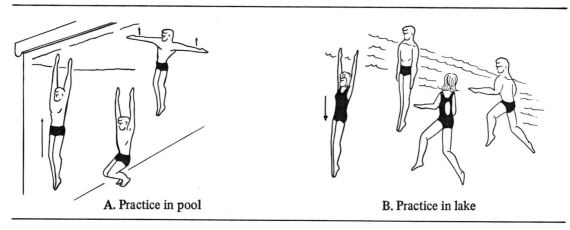

A. Practice in pool   B. Practice in lake

Rhythmic breathing should also be practiced while standing in waist-deep water. Chart 3.16A shows a swimmer with one ear in the water and the face to the side. After inhaling, the face is rolled into the water and the breath exhaled (3.16B). The head is then rolled back to the original position (3.16 A). To practice breathing for the breaststroke and butterfly stroke, bring the face forward until the chin is out of the water (3.16C) and then lower it while the arm movement continues (3.16D).

Chart 3.16. Breathing Drills

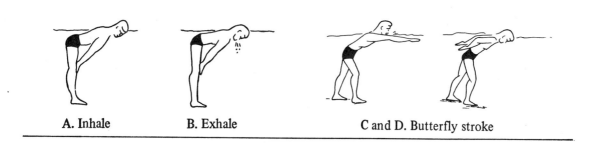

A. Inhale   B. Exhale   C and D. Butterfly stroke

KICKING

Kicking may be defined as propelling the body through the water by means of leg movements. Many beginners seldom use their legs, but the importance of kicking as the primary source of power for many strokes is soon realized. Many instructors spend more time in the beginner course on kicking than they do on any other single phase. Because the flutter kick is less efficient, these instructors devote most of their efforts to the scissors and breaststroke kicks.

The Flutter Kick

The flutter kick on the stomach begins by pointing the toes. If the toes are not pointed, the kick will be too weak to be effective. As a matter of fact, it is possible to move backward if the toes are hooked enough!

Chart 3.17. Performance Techniques for the Flutter Kick

Techniques	Illustration	Performance Errors
Stomach (Prone) Position A. Extend legs, point toes. Move feet alternately up and down 12–15 inches. Have slight bend at knees, bring heels to surface, limit the amount of splash. Emphasize "down" beat and kicking from hips.	A	A. Bending too much at knees (causing bicycle-riding movement). Causing too much splash. Bending too little at knees. Using a kick that is too narrow and tense. Failing to point toes.
Back (Supine) Position B. Extend legs, point toes. Move feet alternately up and down 12–15 inches. Have slight bend at knees, limit the amount of splash. Emphasize "up" beat and kicking from hips.	B	B. Bending too much at knees (causing knees to be above surface). Having feet too low in the water. Using a kick that is too narrow. Failing to point toes.

The Breaststroke Kicks

The preferred whip kick and the older wedge kick are two kinds of breaststroke kicks. Both begin and end in the same position, but the spread of the knees, the propulsive thrust, and the power of the kicks vary. The wedge kick is seldom taught anymore, but remains useful for people with knee problems.

Chart 3.18. Performance Techniques for the Breaststroke Kicks

Techniques	Illustration	Performance Errors
Whip A. Knees hip width apart as they are lowered downward, heels stay together and at surface as they are brought as close to buttocks as possible.	A	A. Knees too close together. Bringing knees forward and under stomach.

Chart 3.18—*continued*

Techniques	Illustration	Performance Errors
B. Lower leg rotates outward as toes pointed outward. Feet are outside of knees. Thighs do not move. Movements in A and B are gentle.		**B.** Separating knees as thighs move outward. Pointing the toes backward. Recovering the legs too forcefully.
C. Body moves ahead as feet and lower leg complete rotary motion, ending with legs straight and toes pointed backward.		**C.** Applying too little effort to the completion of rotary movement. Legs not completely closed.
D. Glide for 3-6 seconds with legs extended and toes pointed backward.		**D.** Beginning next kick without pause for glide.
Wedge **E.** Extend legs and point toes backward.		**E.** Bending the knees. Failing to point toes.
F. Move knees sideward, bring heels toward buttocks (heels are almost touching toes), point outward.		**F.** Pointing the toes of one foot inward (causing scissors kick). Lowering knees toward bottom instead of outward.
G. Move heels to outside, partially straighten legs, point toes outward. Actions in steps E, F, and G should be gentle, drifting actions.		**G.** Continuing to point toes backward. Recovering the legs too quickly and too vigorously.
H. Press legs backward and squeeze together. Point toes backward at end of the press.		**H.** Applying too little effort during the press. Underemphasizing the press and overemphasizing the squeeze. Pointing toes backward during press.
I. Glide for 3-6 seconds with legs extended and toes pointed.		**I.** Failing to glide.
Inverted Whip Kick **J.** Drop heels to bottom, keeping knees just below surface. Keep knees together, toes pointed outward.		**J.** Lifting knees upward out of water. Failing to keep thighs at surface. Failing to point toes outward.

Chart 3.18—*continued*

Techniques	Illustration	Performance Errors
K. Begin rotary motion as feet circle outward and toward surface (toes remain pointed outward).	K	K. Straightening leg diagonally outward rather than rotary motion.
L. Body moves ahead as feet and lower legs complete rotary movement, ending with legs straight and toes pointed backward.	L	L. Failing to bring feet back up to surface. Applying too little effort to the completion of the rotary movement. Legs not completely closed.
M. Glide for 3-6 seconds with legs extended close together with toes pointed.	M	M. Beginning next kick without pause for glide.
Inverted Kick (Wedge) N. Spread knees 15-18 inches. Lower heels downward, keeping knees just below surface.	N	N. Bringing knees above surface.
O. Extend lower legs by moving feet outward. Point toes outward.	O	O. Extending legs by lowering thighs. Pointing toes upward.
P. Straighten legs as they are pressed backward and squeezed together. Point toes back by end of press.	P	P. Expending too little effort on press or squeeze. Pointing toes backward.
Q. Glide for 3-6 seconds.	Q	Q. Recovering legs for next kick without pause for glide.

The Scissors Kicks

The scissors kicks, used in the sidestroke and in lifesaving, are shown in Chart 3.19.

Teaching the Kicks

The whole or whole-part-whole teaching method we advocate in most situations mean that you should observe a whole stroke before spending time on the kick alone. However, it is our experience that

Chart 3.19. Performance Techniques for the Scissors Kicks

Techniques	Illustration	Performance Errors
Regular		
A. Rest the upper leg directly upon the lower, with both legs extended and toes pointed.	A	A. Bending at the knees and ankles (body position is not streamlined).
B. Bend the legs at the knees and bring the heels up to just behind the buttocks.	B	B. Bringing the knees too far in front (near stomach). Failing to bend knees.
C. Move the legs into a striding position, the upper leg forward. Make leg actions parallel to surface. Point toes of upper leg outward in front of body, toes of lower leg to rear of body. Movements in A, B, and C should be gentle.	C	C. Extending lower leg forward. Lowering the under leg toward bottom. Making actions too quick and vigorous.
D. Straighten legs as they are squeezed rearward and together. Point toes during squeeze. Stop the squeeze when legs are together.	D	D. Using a breaststroke kick. Failing to straighten legs before the squeeze. Expending too little effort. Squeezing legs past each other (as in flutter kick).
E. Assume a stretched, streamlined position. Glide for 3–6 seconds.	E	E. Failing to glide.
Inverted		
F. Rest the upper leg directly upon the lower, with both legs extended and toes pointed.	F	F. Bending at the knees and ankles (body position is not streamlined).
G. Bend the legs at the knees and bring the heels up to just behind the buttocks.	G	G. Bringing the knees too far in front (near stomach). Failing to bend knees.
H. Move the legs into a striding position, with the *lower* leg *forward* and the *upper* leg *backward*. Make leg actions parallel to surface. Movements in F, G, and H should be gentle.	H	H. Extending upper leg forward. Lowering the under leg toward bottom. Making actions too quick and vigorous.

Chart 3.19—*continued*

Techniques	Illustration	Performance Errors
I. Straighten legs as they are squeezed rearward and together. Point toes during squeeze. Stop the squeeze when legs are together.	I	I. Using a breaststroke kick. Failing to straighten legs before the squeeze. Expending too little effort. Squeezing legs past each other (as in flutter kick).
J. Assume a stretched, streamlined position. Glide for 3–6 seconds.	J	J. Failing to glide.

the majority of beginners will not kick efficiently in any stroke and will profit greatly if they practice the kicks alone.

Usually the progressive-part method of teaching any kick begins by having the student hang on to the trough and wall (Chart 3.20A) or brace in shallow water (3.20B). Practicing the scissors kick requires a different method of grasping the wall (3.20C). The instructor moves back and forth, observing everyone's kick. Occasionally, the instructor should enter the water, grasp the ankles of a student, and control the leg movement. Make corrections to the entire group after they have kicked awhile and need a rest, but individual corrections can be made when the other students are still kicking.

As quickly as possible, proceed to a free-floating prone or back glide, with or without a kickboard. Some instructors, who feel that the form of the kick is more important than the distance covered, do not advocate the use of kickboards for beginners. The matter is debatable. If a kickboard is used, Chart 3.20D shows how to hold it without altering the proper position of the body in the water.

Chart 3.20. Positions for Kicking Practice

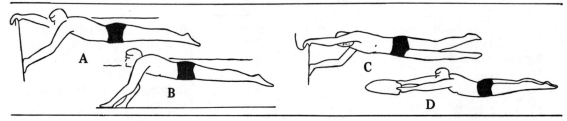

TREADING WATER

Treading is a way of remaining at the surface of and keeping the head above water. Its importance is readily apparent the first time a swimmer needs to orient himself or herself or take three or four breaths while clearing air passages of extra water.

Chart 3.21 describes and depicts the skills involved in treading water.

Treading water is taught in the same fashion as vertical floating or survival floating. The student will master the arm movements and then practice in shoulder-deep water, first by standing erect and then with the knees bent. In deep water, hanging on the wall while practicing *all* the kicks (to see which one is preferred) will prove beneficial. Finally, the student attempts to tread while facing the wall and the partner. Use of flotation belts sometimes is desirable.

Chart 3.21. Performance Techniques for Treading Water

Techniques	Illustration	Performance Errors

Arm Movements
 	
A. With palms facing downward and with elbows bent so that hands are 12 inches in front of chest, tilt thumb down, move hand sideward (as in spreading butter on piece of bread).
 	
B. After hands have moved about 24 inches outward, reverse the tilt. Return hands to original position.
 	
Leg Movements
 	
C. Use any of these kicks:
  1. Wide, slow flutter
 	
  2. Scissors
 	
  3. Breaststroke
 	
  4. Eggbeater (breaststroke, one leg at a time)
 	
Coordination
 	
D. Move arms and legs simultaneously.
Keep head erect.
Retain one-half of air in lungs or more.
Make movements as slow as possible without losing effectiveness.
		A. Failing to tilt hands. Facing palms more upward than downward.
		
		B. Failing to reverse tilt of hands.
		
		C. 1. Making the kick too fast or too narrow.
		  2. Kicking too hard or too fast and causing expenditure of too much effort.
		  3. Kicking too hard, causing body to surge out of water and sink down.
		  4. Same as C.3 above.
		
		D. Allowing the body position to deviate from vertical. Failing to hold air in the lungs.

SWIMMING ON THE STOMACH

Swimming on the stomach is best described as a simultaneous kicking of the legs with some form of arm pull. Everyone wants to learn the front crawl, which is often considered the "only" way to swim!

A more practical value of the front crawl is that it helps the swimmer to see where he or she is going and to avoid being surprised by waves when trying to breathe.

Whether to teach the human stroke (one arm pull to one flutter kick) or the dog paddle (one arm pull to three flutter kicks) depends, for the most part, on the age of the learner. Many youngsters find the crawl-stroke breathing difficult to combine with the over-water recovery of the arms. These students will learn the dog paddle readily. Ordinarily, teenagers and adults dislike being taught the dog paddle, but will respond to instruction in crawl stroke or elementary backstroke. We are, therefore, unwilling to recommend either the human stroke or dog paddle as a stroke to be taught to everyone.

The Front Crawl Stroke

Chart 3.22 describes and illustrates the front crawl stroke and points out common performance errors. The crawl stroke can be performed with two, four, six, or eight kicks, but the six-beat crawl is by far the most common for beginners.

Almost everyone has attempted with limited success to swim the crawl stroke (incorrectly called "free style," which really means "any style"). Instruction should begin with a demonstration of the

Chart 3.22. Performance Techniques for the Front Crawl Stroke

Techniques	Illustration	Performance Errors
Leg Movements A. Extend legs, point toes. Move feet alternately up and down 12-15 inches. Have slight bend at knees, bring heels to surface, limit the amount of splash. Emphasize "down" beat and kicking from hips.		A. Bending too much at knees (causing bicycle-riding movement). Causing too much splash. Bending too little at the knees. Using a kick that is too narrow and tense. Failing to point toes.
Arm Action B. Arms are always opposite each other. Extend one arm, fingers entering water first directly in front of shoulder (as other arm pulls.		B. Permitting elbow to enter water prior to hand entry. Entering hand in front of opposite shoulder.
C. "Settle" hand and forearm 8–12 inches below water.		C. Entering hand in front of face and pushing hand forward before pulling backward.
D. Bend arm, pull, and then push it back until nearing hips.		D. Failing to bend arm to obtain best leverage. Failing to pull completely through.
E. List elbow out of water, bring forearm forward, extend arm to original position.		E. Keeping arm straight. Thrusting arm forward instead of swinging from the shoulder. Failing to relax arm during recovery.

Chart 3.22—*continued*

Techniques	Illustration	Performance Errors
Coordination F. Combine, usually, six kicks to one arm cycle (one stroke with each arm). G. Keep kicking and pulling action continuous.	F and G	F. Failing to deliver the same number of kicks to each arm pull (inserting a scissors kick with one arm pull). G. Executing the kicking and pulling actions independently of each other.
Breathing H. Position the face to "look ahead" underwater (water line at hairline).	H (see C)	H. Carrying head above water or too low in the water.
I. Exhale during pull and push of one arm. Roll head to that side; keep lower ear in water.	I (see D and E)	I. Exhaling during arm recovery. Lifting head rather than rolling it for breathing.
J. Inhale during recovery of same arm; return head to "look ahead" position.	J (see E and C)	J. Trying to inhale after arm on breathing side is entering the water.

complete stroke with emphasis on the kick and arm motion. Students should then imitate the demonstrator. Usually, if students swim until they need a breath (approximately twelve feet) they will quickly perform a fairly effective crawl stroke. Students should continue to swim short distances until errors in the kick or arm movement are eliminated. Then, demonstrate the complete stroke again with an emphasis on breathing. The students then swim more short distances until enough air is inhaled to enable them to swim farther.

A progressive-part method for teaching the crawl stroke is shown in Chart 3.23. Many instructors begin their progression with a demonstration of the whole stroke and then a demonstration of the part to be practiced. It must be remembered that all students will not progress at the same rate. Although the teaching progression shown will be appropriate for all in the class, teaching must relate to the skill differences between individuals. Some skills in the progression will be acquired quickly, and others (e.g., breathing) may require extensive practice.

Flotation devices are helpful to young students, but generally not to adults. The embarrassment of the device usually outweighs its benefits for this group.

SWIMMING ON THE BACK

The greatest advantages of swimming on the back are ease of learning and simplicity of performance. It is entirely possible for a group of beginners (age seven or more) to learn to swim fifty feet on their backs (flutter kick, finning combination) in the first class session.

There are two possible strokes on the back that can be mastered by beginners. The easiest one (but one universally accepted as the best one for beginners to learn first) has no formal name, but is a com-

Chart 3.23. Teaching Progression for the Front Crawl Stroke

Step 1	Step 2	Step 3
Students do prone glide first, then start flutter kick. Go as far as one breath allows a beginner.	In waist-deep water, students assume straddle position, bend at hips, brace self with forward leg. Practice arm stroke.	Students push off, glide 2–3 seconds, *add* kick for next 2–3 seconds, *add* arms. Stop when breath is needed. Do not permit pulling and kicking to begin at same time.

Step 4	Step 5	Notes
Students stand in waist-deep water, practice arm stroke plus breathing.	Students glide, add kick, add arms for two cycles, add breathing.	Massed practice for Steps 1–3 is profitable, but breathing practice (Step 4) should be done in distributed fashion. If Step 3 is not done well, it is virtually impossible to achieve success in Step 5.

bination of flutter kicking and hand finning. Finning is a movement whereby the forearms are moved from the side to a position about eighteen inches from the body and then pushed back until they touch the sides again. A continuous flutter kick, combined with finning, will effectively move the body through the water. Because the face is out of the water all the time, breathing presents no particular problem. See Chart 3.24 for this stroke.

A second way of swimming on the back is by use of the elementary backstroke (Chart 3.24). In the performance of this stroke, the swimmer combines an inverted whip kick (preferred) or wedge kick with a simultaneous underwater recovery and pull-and-push with both arms.

Correct form requires that the stroke be performed with an inverted whip kick or a wedge kick. However, at times when form is not a factor, a swimmer with a strong scissors kick may choose to use this kick if it is more effective than the inverted whip kick or the wedge kick.

Chart 3.24. Performance Techniques for Swimming on the Back

Techniques	Illustration	Performance Errors
Finning A. Recover arms from position alongside thighs to position with hands about 18 inches outward from body. Point fingers outward, face palms backward.	A	A. Facing palms downward. Bringing hands to less than 18 inches from sides. Failing to point fingers outward.
B. Push palms forcefully backward toward feet and thighs.	B	B. Pushing hands downward rather than backward and toward thighs.
C. Repeat the pull-push in continuous action. Add an inverted flutter kick for faster progress.	C	C. Failing to push backward continuously.
Elementary Backstroke D. Assume glide position on back with eyes looking straight upward, ears underwater, arms at side, legs together, hips at surface, and body in straight, streamlined position.	D	D. Sagging at hips. Raising head upward and/or forward. Raising hands above surface.
E. Bend elbows as fingers move up (tickling) the side. Bend knees and drop heels downward (inverted whip kick).	E	E. Keeping arms straight. Bringing arms above surface. Bringing hands over chest. Recovering arms and legs too abruptly and vigorously.
F. When fingers reach armpit, draw elbows in to ribs and point fingers forward and outward (to bisect the angle between neck and shoulders). Begin whip kick leg recovery, or continue inverted whip kick leg recovery.	F	F. Bringing hands out of the water.
G. Extend arms diagonally outward and forward.	G	G. Extending arms within the angle between shoulders and lower body.

Chart 3.24—*continued*

Techniques	Illustration	Performance Errors
H. Begin arm pull backward to thighs. When arms are opposite hips, roll palms downward in order to increase efficiency of pull (see backstroke arm action, Chart 4.8). Begin propulsion phase of kick. Complete arm and leg propulsion phases at same time, if possible. Exhale and inhale immediately.	H	H. Failing to roll palms when opposite hips. Failing to start arm and leg action at same time. Executing a leg kick or arm stroke either too gently or too forcefully.
I. Glide for 2–4 seconds.	I (see D)	I. Inclining head too far forward or backward. Failing to glide.

The instructor will find that the elementary backstroke is so quickly mastered by supine floaters that it might as well be taught first. If a student has difficulty with this stroke, however, the flutter-finning stroke is recommended.

Once again, consider the whole method first. After making sure that students can regain their feet after a supine float, let them imitate the stroke demonstrated. Ordinarily, the arms will do most of the work, and the kick will be very weak. Have students concentrate on covering a given distance in the fewest possible strokes.

Should the whole method prove too difficult, Chart 3.25 shows the traditional teaching progression.

Chart 3.25. Teaching Progression for the Elementary Backstroke

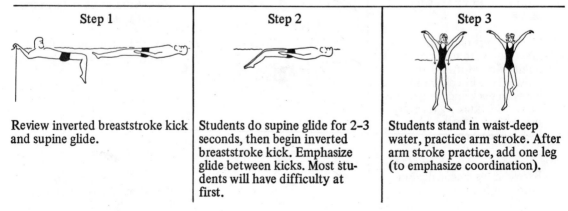

Step 1	Step 2	Step 3
Review inverted breaststroke kick and supine glide.	Students do supine glide for 2–3 seconds, then begin inverted breaststroke kick. Emphasize glide between kicks. Most students will have difficulty at first.	Students stand in waist-deep water, practice arm stroke. After arm stroke practice, add one leg (to emphasize coordination).

Chart 3.25—*continued*

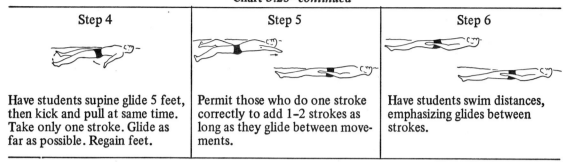

Step 4	Step 5	Step 6
Have students supine glide 5 feet, then kick and pull at same time. Take only one stroke. Glide as far as possible. Regain feet.	Permit those who do one stroke correctly to add 1–2 strokes as long as they glide between movements.	Have students swim distances, emphasizing glides between strokes.

STANDING DIVE

Diving is any means of entering the water headfirst. For young swimmers, the ability to dive means status, but any swimmer might need to enter the water quickly and cover a distance rapidly at some time. The student must be reminded that if the feet are placed higher than the head during the dive, there is little danger of landing on the stomach.

Chart 3.26 depicts successful performance techniques for the standing dive.

Chart 3.26. Performance Techniques for the Standing Dive

Techniques	Illustration	Performance Errors
A. Stand, toes curled over edge of deck.		A. Failing to curl toes over edge of deck or raft.
B. Bend at knees and place extended arms over ears. Focus eyes on spot under the surface and about 5 feet outward from edge of deck.		B. Bending knees at more than 60 degree angle. Extending arms in front of chest. Focusing eyes on distant spot on surface.
C. Lose balance; keep arms over ears.		C. Failing to fall forward off balance. Taking spot on surface, instead of on bottom, as point of aim.
D. Push vigorously with legs, causing feet to rise upward; arms remain straight and over ears.		D. Falling off balance without extending legs. Raising head from between the arms. Bending at hips and knees after take-off.

Chart 3.26–*continued*

Techniques	Illustration	Performance Errors
E. Enter water with hands about 3 feet from deck or dock, arms, body and legs straight, toes pointed. F. After feet enter water, rise to surface by pointing diagonally upward with fingers and raising head slightly.		E. Bending knees and raising head as body enters water. F. Arching back and inclining hands upward too much. Pulling arms backward to thighs.

Chart 3.27. Teaching Progression for the Standing Dive

Step 1	Step 2	Step 3
Students sit, aim for a spot 3 feet ahead. Fall forward. Hands enter water as legs are pushed vigorously.	Students kneel, aim for spot 5 feet ahead. Fall forward. Hands enter water as one leg (braced against solid object) pushes vigorously.	Students stand on one leg, keep other leg straight as it is raised behind body. Bend forward at the hips as the leg is raised behind the body. Enter water about 5 feet in front.

Step 4	Step 5	Step 6
		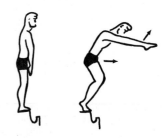
Students crouch, bend both knees. Fall forward and push back with legs by straightening knees as balance is lost.	Students do beginner standing dive, but beginning with arms extended overhead (Chart 3.26).	Students begin with arms at side. As balance is lost, arms are raised overhead and dive is completed as before (Chart 3.26).

Very few people dive successfully on the first attempt. Therefore, most teachers advocate a definite teaching progression, described in Chart 3.27, which begins with a sitting dive and moves to first a kneeling dive, then a one-legged standing dive.

PERSONAL FLOTATION DEVICES

A personal flotation device (PFD) which keeps the head and face out of the water is a necessity for two reasons—basic survival, and reduction of heat loss in cold water. It is a widespread myth that any Coast Guard–approved PFD is a life preserver; Chart 3.28 shows that only Types I and II ensure than an unconscious person will float with the face out of water, and thus preserve life. All the PFDs shown are Coast Guard approved, however.

Chart 3.28. Personal Flotation Devices

Type	Purpose	Illustration
I. Life preserver	Turn an *unconscious* person from a face downward position to a vertical or slightly backward position; has more than 20 lbs. buoyancy. Recommended for offshore cruising.	
II. Buoyancy vest	Same as Type I except that buoyancy is at least 15.5 lbs. Recommended for inshore cruising.	
III. Special purpose device	Keep a *conscious* person in a vertical or slightly backward position; has at least 15.5 lbs. buoyancy. Recommended for water skiing, lake activities.	
IV. Buoyant cushion, ring buoy	Designed to be thrown, not worn; has at least 16.5 lbs. buoyancy.	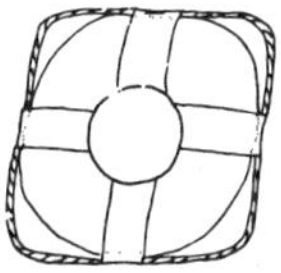 

Adapted from U.S. Coast Guard, *Personal Flotation Devices: Requirements for Recreational Boats,* pamphlet, no date.

Hypothermia

As mentioned earlier, hypothermia (death due to heat loss) is the greatest threat to survival in cold water. Hayward, Eckerson, and Collis (1975) presented data showing that swimmers wearing standard life jackets could survive longer in cold water than those who treaded water or practiced drownproofing. Life jackets have two advantages over treading water or drownproofing: (1) they keep the head out of the water with minimum energy expenditure, and (2) they insulate the body. Drownproofing, because of periodic head immersion, caused the greatest heat loss in cold water and led to the conclusion that it should not be attempted in water colder than 20°C (68°F). Finally, even though the huddle technique shows slightly greater estimated survival time, the problems of adjusting life jackets so that victims can huddle closely are such that, for most victims in most water accidents, the HELP position was the most desirable. Table 3.2 gives illustrations and results depicting this information.

Table 3.2. Flotation Techniques in Cold Water

	Huddle	HELP*	Standard	Treading	Survival Floating
Brief description of technique	Wearing life jackets, 3 persons face each other, huddling as close as possible. See Chart 3.29H.	Wearing life jacket, person grasps it tightly, draws legs up. See Chart 3.29G.	Wearing life jacket, person "stands" in water.	Standard technique See Chart 3.21.	Standard technique See Charts 3.10, 3.11, 3.12.
Water Temperature	Estimated Survival Time in Water				
5°C (41°F)	3.0 hours	2.8 hours	2.0 hours	1.5 hours	1.1 hours
10°C (50°F)	4.0 hours	3.8 hours	2.6 hours	2.0 hours	1.4 hours
15°C (59°F)	6.2 hours	6.0 hours	4.1 hours	3.1 hours	2.3 hours

*HELP = Heat Escape Lessening Posture.

Selections from the pamphlet *Man in Cold Water,* based mainly on the scientific research of John S. Hayward, Martin L. Collis, and John D. Eckerson, are reprinted in Appendix A. It succinctly explains information that should be known by all who would venture on or near cold water. Free copies of the pamphlet are available; see References for address. A film is also available.

Beginners should be acquainted with the various types of personal flotation devices, be aware of the dangers of hypothermia, and practiced in effective use of life jackets. Chart 3.29 describes techniques of life jacket use.

Chart 3.29. Life Jacket Safety Techniques

Techniques	Illustration	Performance Errors
Water Entry While Wearing a Life Jacket A. Keep arms crossed over the chest, hands grasping top of jacket.	A	A. Failing to grasp jacket firmly (thus causing jacket to hit the chin).
Donning a Life Jacket While in Water B. Tread water (feet alone). Insert head into opening. C. Fasten strap after pulling it behind back. or D. Tread water (feet alone). Spread jacket on water (outside down), insert arm in proper hole. E. Roll back into jacket, thrusting other arm into proper arm hole. F. Fasten topmost tie, then others in descending order. Refasten ties (top to bottom), making them tight as possible.	B C D E F	B. Lifting jacket out of water (rather than just lifting opening for head). C. Failing to fasten strap. D. Lifting jacket out of water to insert arm. E. Failing to roll into jacket. F. Not fastening ties tight enough.
HELP Procedure G. Clutch front of life jacket tightly to chest, keep arms very close to sides. Raise knees to where upper thighs contact bottom of jacket. Rest chin on top of jacket (assuming that chin stays out of water).	G	G. Floating somewhat on back, allowing back of head to be in water. Not keeping thighs pressed tightly against bottom of jacket.

Chart 3.29—*continued*

Techniques	Illustration	Performance Errors
Huddle Procedure H. Two or three persons face each other, shift life jackets to side and back, hug adjacent persons so that chests are as close together as possible. Legs intertwined.	H	H. Failure to shift jacket off chest, thus not gaining warmth of adjacent person. Not intertwining legs.

CRAMPS

Cramps are described by the layman as "knotting of a muscle." This can be crucial, because the swimmer cannot use the affected muscle if the cramp is severe. Virtually all cramps occur in limbs or fingers; stomach cramps are apparently very rare and thus need not be of great concern to swimmers (Lanoue, 1963, pp. 97-98).

Because cramps occur when a muscle is contracted (or knotted), the logical treatment is to cause the muscle to stretch. Kneading or massaging is also sometimes effective. Most authorities recommend that swimmers float and massage the affected muscle very forcefully even after a cramp has disappeared, because cramps are seldom completely eliminated in a short time. For cramps in the calf or instep, gentle and steady pulling of the toes toward the knee while massaging the affected part seems effective. Chart 3.30 illustrates these various massaging positions.

When the students are attentive (which usually means not chilled or exhausted) the instructor can explain what a cramp is and demonstrate how a limb is stretched and/or massaged. Students should practice floating in various positions and the kneading and stretching movements that relieve cramps.

Chart 3.30. Treatment for Cramps

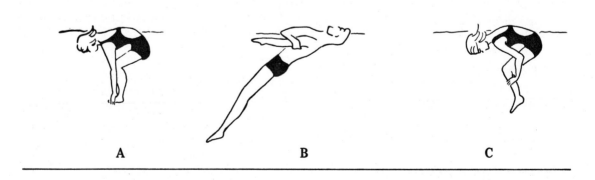

A   B   C

ARTIFICIAL RESPIRATION

Drowning is death by suffocation and always a danger in an aquatic environment. Artificial respiration is defined as a means of keeping victims of near-drowning alive until they are able to resume breathing on their own. The YMCA, ARC, and the American Medical Association all recommend the mouth-to-mouth method as the most effective for the semitrained layman to use. It is easily learned; in fact, there is an instance where a six-year-old boy successfully revived his younger brother by this method.

Chart 3.31 describes and illustrates mouth-to-mouth resuscitation. This is the method officially recognized by the American National Red Cross, and thus should be considered the standard technique.

Teaching about Artificial Respiration

When the students are dry, warm, and attentive, the instructor should explain, illustrate with models, and show at least one movie that demonstrates this technique. The American Red Cross does not recommend actual person-to-person practice. It is a simple technique and hygienic considerations outweigh any possible advantage of actual practice. Some instructors use a special training manikin, which is cleaned after each use with a 70 percent isopropyl alcohol solution. We recommend that a movie suitable to the age of the group and not conflicting with accepted techniques be shown first. The technique should then be explained, the training manikin used, and the movie shown again. Beginning instructors may think it a waste of time to show the movie twice, but audiovisual experts say that the first showing has limited value. Mouth-to-mouth resuscitation is so important that is should be taught well and reviewed in *every* class.

ASSISTS AND ESCAPES

All swimmers, not just those taking lifesaving, must know how to safely assist others in the water. Most of the techniques shown in Chapter 6 (Lifesaving) are obviously beyond the capabilities of beginning swimmers. However, Charts 6.1 and 6.2 depict how to assist by reaching and throwing the ring buoy; both can be done by beginners. Instructors should have students practice extending arms, towels, poles, kickboards, sweatshirts—anything that is available in a pool or beach area.

Escapes are sometimes needed by beginners; other beginners, in their fright, may grab the nearest person when they swallow too much water or lose their footing. The most important things for beginners to remember are: (1) don't panic, take a few seconds to assess the situation; (2) pry off the hand, arms, or legs with calm and deliberate pressure; (3) don't go underwater if possible; and (4) if going underwater, grab a "bite of air." Whether to deliberately practice escapes with young beginners is debatable; anticipating being grabbed may be too frightening. However, beginners are in real danger if grabbed, and thus should at least be told what to do.

CLASS ASSIGNMENTS

1. Teach a beginner as many of the skills outlined in the chapter as possible. Keep a daily account of the progress; focus attention each session on material in one of the segments in Chapter 2 (e.g., teaching strategies, introduction of new material, flotation devices).

2. Talk to an experienced swimming instructor. How many of the skills mentioned in this chapter does he or she teach to beginners? Name the two or three skills regarded as the most important?

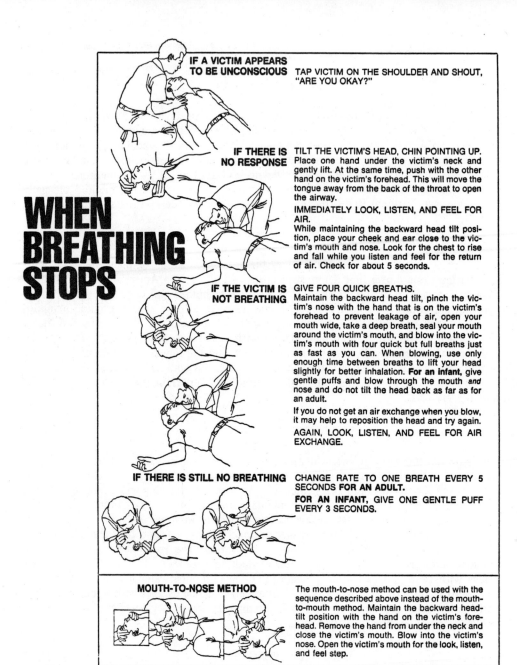

WHEN BREATHING STOPS

IF A VICTIM APPEARS TO BE UNCONSCIOUS TAP VICTIM ON THE SHOULDER AND SHOUT, "ARE YOU OKAY?"

IF THERE IS NO RESPONSE TILT THE VICTIM'S HEAD, CHIN POINTING UP. Place one hand under the victim's neck and gently lift. At the same time, push with the other hand on the victim's forehead. This will move the tongue away from the back of the throat to open the airway.

IMMEDIATELY LOOK, LISTEN, AND FEEL FOR AIR.

While maintaining the backward head tilt position, place your cheek and ear close to the victim's mouth and nose. Look for the chest to rise and fall while you listen and feel for the return of air. Check for about 5 seconds.

IF THE VICTIM IS NOT BREATHING GIVE FOUR QUICK BREATHS. Maintain the backward head tilt, pinch the victim's nose with the hand that is on the victim's forehead to prevent leakage of air, open your mouth wide, take a deep breath, seal your mouth around the victim's mouth, and blow into the victim's mouth with four quick but full breaths just as fast as you can. When blowing, use only enough time between breaths to lift your head slightly for better inhalation. **For an infant,** give gentle puffs and blow through the mouth *and* nose and do not tilt the head back as far as for an adult.

If you do not get an air exchange when you blow, it may help to reposition the head and try again.

AGAIN, LOOK, LISTEN, AND FEEL FOR AIR EXCHANGE.

IF THERE IS STILL NO BREATHING CHANGE RATE TO ONE BREATH EVERY 5 SECONDS **FOR AN ADULT.**

FOR AN INFANT, GIVE ONE GENTLE PUFF EVERY 3 SECONDS.

MOUTH-TO-NOSE METHOD The mouth-to-nose method can be used with the sequence described above instead of the mouth-to-mouth method. Maintain the backward head-tilt position with the hand on the victim's forehead. Remove the hand from under the neck and close the victim's mouth. Blow into the victim's nose. Open the victim's mouth for the look, listen, and feel step.

For more information about these and other life-saving techniques, contact your Red Cross chapter for training.

AMERICAN RED CROSS   **ARTIFICIAL RESPIRATION**

Poster 1002
Rev. April 1978

Chart 3.31. Performance Techniques for Mouth-to-Mouth Resuscitation
Poster from American Red Cross. Used by permission.

3. Talk to an experienced instructor. What are the chief problems in teaching beginners of various age groups?

4. Using the analysis sheets in Appendix B evaluate a partner on his or her performance in the elementary backstroke and the crawl stroke. Discuss the results, demonstrate the correct techniques, and attempt to eliminate all errors.

BEHAVIORAL OBJECTIVES

Almost all instructors will teach beginners at some time. Therefore, we expect our students to be able to respond correctly (based on material in this chapter) to questions calling for brief written answers or diagrams, and to meet the standards indicated for the essential aquatic skills.

1. Describe the specified number of the major and common performance errors usually found in the following skills: (a) survival floating by nonfloaters—2, (b) crawl stroke—4, (c) elementary backstroke—4, (d) standing dive—2, (e) scissors kick—2, (f) whip kick—2.

2. Be able to explain and diagram these skills: (a) survival floating as *you* do it, (b) treading water, (c) artificial respiration, (d) bobbing (deep water), (e) HELP posture with personal flotation device.

3. Based on the concepts given in Chapter 2, describe appropriate teaching strategies for teaching skills to specific groups using these techniques: (a) supine float—five year olds—whole method; (b) crawl stroke—teenagers—whole, then progressive-part method; (c) standing dive—young adults —progressive-part method; (d) elementary backstroke—ten year olds—whole, then progressive-part method; (e) treading—teenagers—whole, then reciprocal method.

4. Meet the minimum standard for certified aquatic workers for each of the essential aquatic skills given below.

Skill	Standard
Vertical float	Motionless (or nearly so) for 60 seconds
Bobbing	8 feet of water for 60 seconds
Survival floating	4 minutes arms alone 4 minutes legs alone 12 minutes combined
Treading water	1 minute arms alone 1 minute legs alone
Kicks: Flutter	30 feet
Whip	30 feet
Wedge	30 feet
Scissors	30 feet
Inverted whip	30 feet
Inverted flutter	30 feet
Crawl stroke	30 feet
Elementary backstroke	30 feet
Standing dive	Legs straight, toes pointed, body in straight line, little splash

Form for all skills to be as described in this text.

REFERENCES

American National Red Cross. "Basic Water Safety Course." *Lifesaving: Rescue and Water Safety Instructor's Manual.* Washington, D.C.: American National Red Cross, 1974, pp. 27–29.

——. *Swimming and Water Safety Courses: Instructor's Manual.* Washington, D.C.: American National Red Cross, 1968, pp. 30–54.

——. *Swimming and Water Safety.* Washington, D.C.: American National Red Cross, 1968, pp. 9–35, 55–57, 62–66, 97–105, 110–120.

Arnold, Lloyd C., and Freeman, Robert W. *Progressive Swimming and Springboard Diving Program.* New York: National YMCA Program Materials, 1972, pp. 39–50, 52.

Bernhartsen, John C. "Cold Water Primer." *JOPER,* May 1979, pp. 52–53.

Canadian Red Cross Society. *National Instructor Guide and Reference.* Toronto: Canadian Red Cross Society, 1977, pp. 39–55, 60–63, 77–86, 90–93, 174.

Gorman, Patricia J. "Developing an Understanding of Action-Reaction in Flutter Kicks." *NAGWS Guide* (Aquatics, July 1979–July 1981). Reston, Va.: AAHPERD, 1979, pp. 47–55.

Hallett, Bee, and Clayton, Robert, eds. *Course Syllabus: Teacher of Swimming.* Reston, Va.: AAHPERD, 1980.

Hayward, John S., Eckerson, John D., and Collis, Martin L. "Effect of Behavioral Variables on Cooling Rate of Man in Cold Water." *Journal of Applied Physiology,* June 1975, pp. 1073–77.

Lanoue, Fred R. *Drownproofing.* Englewood Cliffs, N.J.: Prentice-Hall, Inc., 1963.

Man in Cold Water. Pamphlet, no date. Dr. J. S. Hayward, Department of Biology, University of Victoria, P.O. Box 1700, Victoria, British Columbia, Canada V8W 2Y2.

Vanderbeck, Edna R. "Use of the 'Standing Float' in Learning to Tread Water." *NAGWS Guide* (Aquatics July 1979–July 1981). Reston, Va.: AAHPERD, 1979, pp. 36–38.

FILMS

American National Red Cross. *Freestyle* and *Elementary Backstroke.* Super 8 mm cartridges. See local ARC office.

——. *Skilled Swimming.* 16 mm, color, sound. See local ARC office.

Counsilman, James. *Swimming.* 16 mm, color, sound. *Learning to Swim.* 8 mm cartridges. Wolverine Sports, Ann Arbor, Michigan 48104.

Man in Cold Water. 16 mm, color, sound. Media and Technical Services, University of Victoria, Victoria, British Columbia, Canada V8W 2Y2.

WALL CHARTS

Illustrated American Swimming Techniques. CPR. Youngbluth Co., P.O. Box 186, Homestead, Florida 33030.

FILM STRIPS

Freestyle. Elementary Backstroke. Super 8 mm cartridges. Mariner III, Box 38246, Hollywood, California 90038.

Hypothermia and Cold Water Survival. Recreational Boating Institute, Inc., c/o University of Tulsa, 600 South College, Tulsa, Oklahoma 74104.

CHAPTER 4

Performing and Teaching Other Aquatic Skills

Sidestroke and Overarm Sidestroke
Breaststroke
Butterfly Stroke
Back Crawl Stroke
The Trudgen Strokes
Inverted Breaststroke
Turning at Pool Ends
Surface Diving
Underwater Swimming
Clothing Inflation

The essential aquatic skills discussed in Chapter 3 represent what should be known by everyone. Beginning a new class with a short screening test based on those essential skills will accomplish two important goals: (1) the instructor will know quickly what essential skills must be taught and (2) the students will be reminded of the essential skills to be mastered. After this initial test and instruction, the skills presented in this chapter should be taught.

The skills and techniques described in this chapter correspond roughly to those required in intermediate and advanced swimming classes. Because many of our readers now teach or will teach swimming courses in schools, we have indicated logical content and standards for two different levels of instruction (Table 4.1). For Red Cross or YMCA courses, the content is already established by the organization and must be followed exactly.

Students seeking aquatic instructor certification have already achieved high levels of skill and are sometimes tempted to pay only cursory attention to this chapter. However, our experience tells us that it is rare for even one student in an instructor's class to correctly demonstrate each of the skills and techniques in this chapter without additional practice. For example, are you absolutely sure that you can swim the breaststroke correctly? Many of the students in an instructor's class cannot. What about demonstrating correct form in the butterfly stroke? the single and double trudgen strokes? the trudgen crawl?

You might ask, "Why must I be able to demonstrate all the skills in this chapter?" The practical answer is that aquatic certification standards require or strongly suggest it. This is based on the belief that ability to demonstrate enables a person to become a better teacher. Most valuable to prospective

Table 4.1. Skills and Standards for Intermediate and Advanced Swimming Courses

Skills	Standards of Performance	Intermediate	Advanced
1. Flutter kick on stomach	No major errors	40–50 yds.	—
2. Crawl stroke arm action	No major errors	20–25 yds.	—
3. Front crawl stroke	No major errors	40–50 yds.	100 yds.
4. Elementary backstroke	No major errors	40–50 yds.	100 yds.
5. Scissors kick	No major errors	40–50 yds.	—
6. Sidestroke arm action	No major errors	20–25 yds.	—
7. Sidestroke (preferred side)	No major errors	40–50 yds.	100 yds.
8. Overarm sidestroke (preferred side)	No major errors	—	100 yds.
9. Breaststroke kick (wedge, whip)	No major errors	40–50 yds. (one type)	40–50 yds. (both types)
10. Breaststroke arm action	No major errors	20–25 yds.	—
11. Breaststroke	No major errors	40–50 yds.	100 yds.
12. Dolphin kick	No major errors	20–25 yds.	—
13. Butterfly arm action	No major errors	10–15 yds.	—
14. Butterfly stroke	No major errors	—	50 yds.
15. Flutter kick on back	No major errors	20–25 yds.	—
16. Back crawl stroke	No major errors	—	100 yds.
17. Single trudgen stroke	No major errors	—	100 yds.
18. Double trudgen stroke	No major errors	—	100 yds.
19. Trudgen crawl stroke	No major errors	—	100 yds.
20. Inverted breaststroke	No major errors	—	100 yds.
21. Turning at pool ends (stomach, back, side)	No major errors	Demonstrate all	—
22. Surface dives (tuck, pike, feet first)	No major errors	Demonstrate any one	Demonstrate all
23. Underwater swim	No push off	10 ft.	30 ft.
24. Dive from board	No major errors	Standing (front)	Running (front) Standing (back)
25. Clothes inflation (wearing shirt, pants, shoes)	Float (any position) for 2 min. after inflation	Inflate pants while wearing other clothes	Inflate shirt and pants
26. Continuous swim (any combination of strokes)	No time limit	200 yds.	500 yds.
27. 200-yd. continuous swim (50 yds. each of breaststroke, sidestroke, elementary back, and crawl or trudgen)	No major errors	—	6:40 or less

teachers in this chapter are the teaching progressions for eleven strokes, and discussions and diagrams of open turns, surface dives, underwater swimming, and clothing inflation. Even if you have had extensive teaching experience, we think that this chapter can help you. Specific behavioral objectives for certified aquatic instructors will be found at the end of the chapter.

Before concentrating on new strokes, a review of the front crawl and the backstrokes would be beneficial.

SIDESTROKE AND OVERARM SIDESTROKE

The sidestroke is primarily a resting stroke, featuring a powerful scissors kick, followed by a long glide. The glide is an essential characteristic of the stroke. This stroke is comparatively easy to teach and is especially useful in instructing adults because the breathing problems inherent in the crawl and breast-strokes are absent. In our experience, children and younger adults are not especially keen on learning the sidestroke because it is not a racing stroke. Even though the overarm sidestroke was used in international swimming meets until 1904, basically it is not suited for speed.

The scissors kick, arm action, coordination, and breathing used in the sidestroke are shown and discussed in Chart 4.1. The use of the inverted scissors kick and the lack of a glide, are very common errors.

Chart 4.1. Performance Techniques for the Sidestroke

Techniques	Illustration	Performance Errors
Scissors Kick A. Rest the upper leg directly upon the lower, with both legs extended and toes pointed. B. Bend the legs at the knees and bring the heels up to just behind the buttocks. C. Move the legs into a striding position, the upper leg forward. Make leg actions parallel to surface. Point toes of upper leg outward in front of body, toes of lower leg to rear of body. Movements in A, B, C should be gentle. D. Straighten legs as they are squeezed rearward and together. Point toes during squeeze. Stop the squeeze when legs are together.		A. Bending at the knees and ankles (body position is not streamlined. B. Bringing the knees too far in front (near stomach) Failing to bend knees. C. Extending lower leg forward. Lowering the under leg toward bottom. Making actions too quick and vigorous. D. Using a breaststroke kick. Failing to straighten legs before the squeeze. Expending too little effort. Squeezing legs past each other (as in flutter kick).

Chart 4.1—*continued*

Techniques	Illustration	Performance Errors
Arm Action E. Assume glide position with trailing arm extended over hip, leading arm extended forward, body on side, head turned to bring chin toward upper shoulder so mouth is out of water.	E	E. Allowing trailing arm to drift in front of or behind body line. Bending either arm at elbow. Failing to be perfectly on the side.
F. Pull leading arm outward, downward, and inward toward chin. Bend elbow of trailing arm and bring hand toward chin.	F	F. Pressing the leading arm toward pool bottom rather than pulling parallel to water surface. Ending the pull of leading arm too soon.
G. Place the hand of the trailing arm over the hand of the leading arm as they meet in front of chin.	G	G. Failing to have hands meet in front of chin.
H. Lower the elbow of leading arm, point fingers forward, extend arm forward with palm facing downward. Push trailing arm completely back to thigh.	H	H. Pulling trailing arm to thigh before extending leading arm. Pulling both arms toward feet at the same time.
Coordination and Breathing I. Begin the stroke by pulling with leading arm.	I	I. Beginning leg recovery before leading arm begins to pull.
J. After leading arm has begun pull, begin recovery movement with other three limbs.	J	J. Beginning the movement of all four limbs at the same time. Pulling leading arm and kicking at same time.
K. Finish pull of leading arm, extend leading arm forward, pull with trailing arm, and deliver kick. Exhale.	K	K. Kicking before leading arm is in position to be extended forward.
L. Streamline the body. Inhale. Glide for 2–3 seconds.	L	L. Failing to glide. Turning the entire body onto the back to raise the face to breathe.

The overarm sidestroke is basically the same as the sidestroke, except that the arm recovery occurs above water for the sake of speed. See Chart 4.2.

It is much easier to teach these strokes to a beginner than to one who has learned them incorrectly. The person who has learned incorrectly usually has an inverted scissors kick and cannot "get the power" from the correct kick. The easiest way to overcome this problem is to simply have the student roll over. He or she will then be doing the same kick, but it will be the correct one.

Chart 4.2. Performance Techniques for the Overarm Sidestroke

Techniques	Illustration	Performance Errors
Scissors Kick A. Rest the upper leg directly upon the lower, with both legs extended and toes pointed.		A. Bending at the knees and ankles (body position not streamlined).
B. Bend the legs at the knees and bring the heels up to just behind the buttocks.		B. Bringing the knees too far in front (near stomach). Failing to bend knees.
C. Move the legs into a striding position, the upper leg forward. Make leg actions parallel to surface. Point toes of upper leg outward in front of body, toes of lower leg to rear of body. Movements in A, B, C should be gentle.		C. Extending lower leg forward. Lowering the under leg toward bottom. Making actions too quick and vigorous.
D. Straighten legs as they are squeezed rearward and together. Point toes during squeeze. Stop the squeeze when legs are together.		D. Using a breaststroke kick. Failing to straighten legs before the squeeze. Expending too little effort. Squeezing legs past each other (as in flutter kick).
Arm Action E. Assume glide position with trailing arm extended over hip, leading arm extended forward, body on side, head turned to bring chin toward upper shoulder so mouth is out of water.		E. Allowing trailing arm to drift in front of or behind body line. Bending either arm at elbow. Failing to be perfectly on the side.

Chart 4.2—*continued*

Techniques	Illustration	Performance Errors
F. Pull leading arm outward, downward, and inward toward chin. Bend elbow of trailing arm and recover it over the surface to a point in front of face. Keep elbow high during recovery and entry.	F	F. Recovering trailing arm underwater. Pounding trailing arm into water. Overreaching with trailing arm (causing body to roll onto stomach).
G. Place the hand of the trailing arm over the hand of the leading arm as they meet in front of chin.	G	G. Failing to have hands meet in front of chin.
H. Lower the elbow of leading arm, point fingers forward, extend arm forward with palm facing downward. Push trailing arm completely back to thigh.	H	H. Pulling trailing arm to thigh before extending leading arm. Pulling both arms toward feet at the same time.
Coordination and Breathing I. Begin the stroke by pulling with leading arm.	I	I. Beginning leg recovery before leading arm begins to pull.
J. After leading arm has begun pull, begin recovery movement with other three limbs.	J	J. Beginning the movement of all four limbs at the same time. Pulling leading arm and kicking at same time.
K. Finish pull of leading arm, extend leading arm forward, pull with trailing arm, and deliver kick. Exhale.	K	K. Kicking before leading arm is in position to be extended forward.
L. Streamline the body. Inhale. Glide for 2-3 seconds.	L	L. Failing to glide. Turning the entire body onto the back to raise the face to breathe.

When instructing students, it will help to remind them that the sidestroke consists of three distinct movements. First, pull with the leading arm. Then, the legs and other arm are brought up, out, and pushed back. Last and most important, glide. Beginners will make quicker progress if the instructor constantly emphasizes that the strokes start with the leading arm, not with the kick.

The arm action of the sidestroke has been likened to picking an apple out of a tree, transferring it from the picking hand to the other and putting it in a sack at the hip as the picking hand goes back for another apple. This analogy has proved very useful in implanting the concept of the leading arm pulling first to keep the body moving before the remaining arm and the legs are recovered (see Chart 4.1F). It also helps for swimmers to imagine that water is pulled down to the chest area with the leading arm, and then the same water is pushed down to the feet with the other arm.

As before, we recommend the whole or whole-part-whole methods of instruction. Demonstration in slow motion and at regular speed with comments on the kick, arms, coordination, and glide will enable some students to perform an acceptable stroke quickly. For those who have trouble (almost always with the arm-leg coordination), Chart 4.3 suggests a usable progression. Frequent demonstrations of the whole stroke as the parts are perfected will be beneficial.

Chart 4.3. Teaching Progression for the Sidestroke

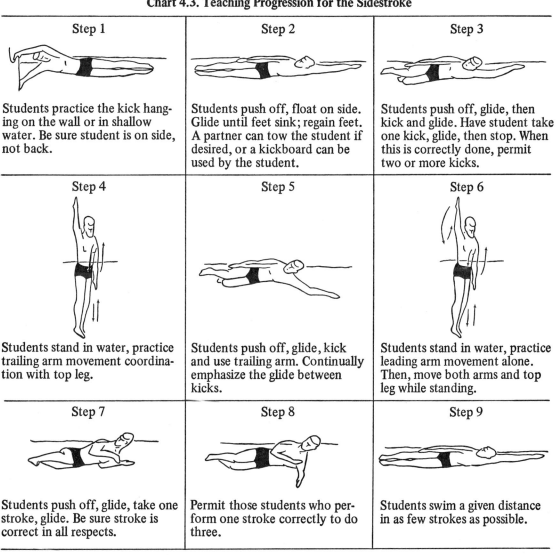

Step 1	Step 2	Step 3
Students practice the kick hanging on the wall or in shallow water. Be sure student is on side, not back.	Students push off, float on side. Glide until feet sink; regain feet. A partner can tow the student if desired, or a kickboard can be used by the student.	Students push off, glide, then kick and glide. Have student take one kick, glide, then stop. When this is correctly done, permit two or more kicks.
Step 4	Step 5	Step 6
Students stand in water, practice trailing arm movement coordination with top leg.	Students push off, glide, kick and use trailing arm. Continually emphasize the glide between kicks.	Students stand in water, practice leading arm movement alone. Then, move both arms and top leg while standing.
Step 7	Step 8	Step 9
Students push off, glide, take one stroke, glide. Be sure stroke is correct in all respects.	Permit those students who perform one stroke correctly to do three.	Students swim a given distance in as few strokes as possible.

The overarm sidestroke is not taught until the sidestroke is performed adequately. It is the same stroke except for the overarm recovery, so here too the whole method works extremely well.

BREASTSTROKE

In the United States, most instructors teach the crawl stroke, the backstroke, and the sidestroke before they teach the breaststroke. Europeans usually teach the breaststroke first. Perhaps this accounts for the fact that Europeans usually perform the stroke much better than Americans. Because it is not a very fast stroke, most American swimmers in our experience are not motivated enough to learn it correctly. It requires a powerful kick, and if this is lacking, the arm pull of the stroke has to be wrong (i.e., all the way back to the hips) to achieve satisfactory momentum.

The whip kick and the wedge kick used in the breaststroke were introduced in Chapter 3. The kicks, arm stroke, coordination, and breathing are described in Chart 4.4.

Chart 4.4 Performance Techniques for the Breaststroke

Techniques	Illustration	Performance Errors
Whip A. Knees hip width apart as they are lowered downward, heels stay together and at surface, as they are brought as close to buttocks as possible.		A. Knees too close together. Bringing knees forward and under stomach.
B. Lower leg rotates outward as toes pointed outward. Feet are outside of knees. Thighs do not move. Movements in A and B should be gentle.		B. Knees separate as thighs move outward. Toes pointed backward. Recovery legs too forcefully.
C. Body moves ahead as feet and lower leg complete rotary motion, ending with legs straight and toes pointed backward.		C. Applying too little effort to the completion of rotary movement. Legs not completely closed together.
Wedge D. Extend legs and point toes backward.		D. Bending the knees. Failing to point toes.
E. Move knees sideward, bring heels toward buttocks (heels are almost touching toes), point outward).		E. Pointing the toes of one foot inward (causing scissors kick). Lowering knees toward bottom instead of outward.

Chart 4.4—*continued*

Techniques	Illustration	Performance Errors
F. Move heels to outside, partially straighten legs, point toes outward. Actions in steps D, E, and F should be gentle, drifting actions. G. Press legs backward and squeeze together. Point toes backward at end of the press.		F. Continuing to point toes backward. Recovering the legs too quickly and too vigorously. G. Applying too little effort during the press. Underemphasizing the press and overemphasizing the squeeze. Pointing toes backward during press.
Arm Action H. Glide with face down and ears between extended arms. I. Bend elbows and press arms backward and downward; keep elbows close to surface. J. As elbows reach the shoulder line, move them inward to a point in front of chest and under chin. K. After hands reach position under chin, extend them forward to gliding position.		H. Holding head above surface. Failing to glide. I. Pulling arms outward (as in rowing a boat). Pulling arms under center of body. J. Pressing the hands back to the hips or thighs. K. Failing to stretch arms to full extension. Failing to lower head to position between arms.
Coordination and Breathing L. After glide, press arms backward. Maintain extension of legs. Inhale as arms begin pull. M. As hands move inward toward chest, begin leg recovery. Lower face into water.		L. Recovering legs while arms are pulling. Raising head too late. Performing the leg kick and arm pull at the same time. M. Holding head up, with face not in water.

Chart 4.4—*continued*

Techniques	Illustration	Performance Errors
N. Kick with legs as arms recover to gliding position.	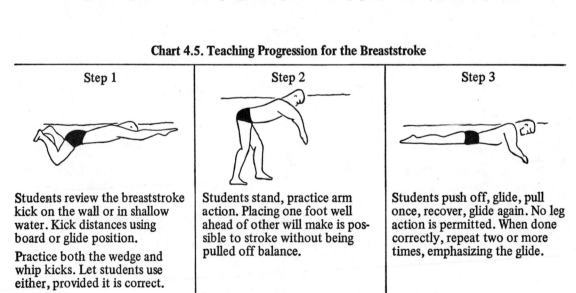	N. Extending the arms after kick has been delivered.
O. Glide with entire body in straight line. Exhale at end of glide.		O. Beginning arm pull immediately after extending the arms.

The breaststroke we describe can be continued by the swimmer for long distances without undue effort, if the kick is reasonably effective. The swimmer is resting while gliding and gets good distance from each stroke. This could be called "form" stroking to distinguish it from the competitive breaststroke. When swum by a competitor in good physical condition, the glide is eliminated in order to travel a comparatively short distance in the shortest possible time.

Most students in an intermediate or advanced swimming class will be able to swim a good breaststroke in thirty minutes if the whole method is used. Demonstrations in slow-motion and at regular speed, accompanied by instructor comments, are essential. First, students should concentrate on the timing of the pull, kick, and glide. Accentuating the glide will help learners. When the timing is acceptable, students should continue to swim the whole stroke while concentrating on either the kick or arms. Finally, when these two elements have been mastered, focus on the breathing. It is sometimes desirable to let students practice with their heads out of the water, so they can hear instructions and make corrections while practicing. If needed, a progressive-part teaching progression (Chart 4.5) may be used.

Chart 4.5. Teaching Progression for the Breaststroke

Step 1	Step 2	Step 3
Students review the breaststroke kick on the wall or in shallow water. Kick distances using board or glide position. Practice both the wedge and whip kicks. Let students use either, provided it is correct.	Students stand, practice arm action. Placing one foot well ahead of other will make is possible to stroke without being pulled off balance.	Students push off, glide, pull once, recover, glide again. No leg action is permitted. When done correctly, repeat two or more times, emphasizing the glide.

Chart 4.5—*continued*

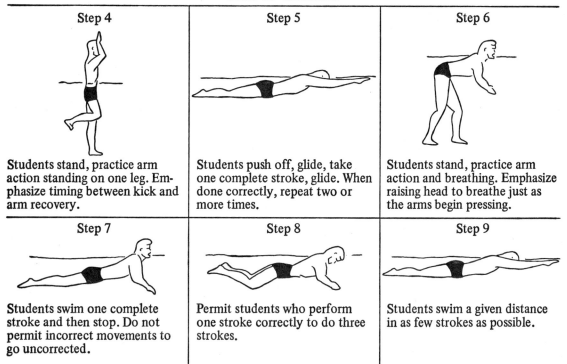

Step 4	Step 5	Step 6
Students stand, practice arm action standing on one leg. Emphasize timing between kick and arm recovery.	Students push off, glide, take one complete stroke, glide. When done correctly, repeat two or more times.	Students stand, practice arm action and breathing. Emphasize raising head to breathe just as the arms begin pressing.

Step 7	Step 8	Step 9
Students swim one complete stroke and then stop. Do not permit incorrect movements to go uncorrected.	Permit students who perform one stroke correctly to do three strokes.	Students swim a given distance in as few strokes as possible.

BUTTERFLY STROKE

The butterfly stroke is the only stroke invented by an American. David Armbruster, a former swimming coach at the University of Iowa, first demonstrated the stroke in 1935. It was not accepted as an official stroke until nearly twenty years later. The butterfly is the second fastest swimming stroke, ranking just behind the crawl. Because this stroke requires much strength in the arms, most beginners and intermediates find it extremely difficult to do. For the same reason, it has limited value for lifesaving.

The butterfly employs the dolphin kick, best described as a double-leg flutter kick. Arm action can be described as a double-crawl stroke movement. Chart 4.6 diagrams and explains the kick, arm action, coordination, and breathing of this stroke.

The instructor will find that unless students are permitted to swim comparatively short distances of the butterfly stroke, they become so arm-weary that correct practice is impossible. Swimming without breathing is essential before the leg and arm coordination can be mastered; thus swimming more than fifteen yards is not advised. The "one-stroke kicking" drill may be used effectively: the swimmer kicks lengths while in a gliding position without a board. When a breath is needed, only one arm stroke is taken, and then the kicking continues. This drill has two advantages: (1) the legs are given the practice they need, and (2) the swimmer does not have to be continually thinking about his legs, arms and breathing all at once. At first, the distance kicked should be short (ten yards) but as soon as a strong dolphin kick is developed, the distance should be lengthened.

Chart 4.6. Performance Techniques for the Butterfly Stroke

Techniques	Illustration	Performance Errors
Kick A. Assume face-down position with legs together, toes pointed. Bend slightly at knees. B. Press feet vigorously downward and backward, keeping thighs at about same level in water. C. Force legs upward. Keep legs extended until near end of rise. D. Bend knees slightly in preparation for downward and backward press.	A B C D	A. Bending too much at the knees (causing feet to come out of water). B. Pressing feet backward and with no downward emphasis. C. Moving hips downward rather than forcing legs upward. Having too much up-and-down movement of hips. D. Bending too much at the knees.
Arm Action E. Extend arms, with slight bend at elbows. Submerge arms 10–12 inches in water. F. Bend at elbows. Pull and push hands backward toward feet until arms are extended along sides. G. Begin arm recovery by lifting elbows upward. Swing arms forward over the water. Lower chin toward chest. H. Enter hands in water in front of shoulders. Glide briefly, chin on chest.	E F G H	E. Pressing down too far or too hard (causing head to rise too high and feet to sink. F. Failing to bend arms to obtain best leverage for push. Gliding with arms at sides. Leading with elbows, not pushing with hands. G. Pushing arms forward instead of swinging from shoulders. Dragging arms in water. H. Placing elbows in water before hands enter.
Coordination and Breathing I. Raise chin out of water and inhale during arm press. Kick (downward) during the late part of backward press of arms.	I	I. Raising head too high in order to breathe. Raising head as kick is delivered.

Chart 4.6—_continued_

Techniques	Illustration	Performance Errors
J. Second kick (downward) as arms enter water. Lower face into water. Exhale slowly or hold breath until just prior to inhalation. Undulate the spine and legs to obtain a porpoiselike action.	J	**J.** Failing to return the face into the water. Being stiff in the spine and legs.

The majority of instructors use the progressive-part method shown in Chart 4.7 when teaching the butterfly stroke. Steps 2, 8, and 9 in this chart depict how the whole method would be used, following a demonstration of the stroke.

Chart 4.7. Teaching Progression for the Butterfly Stroke

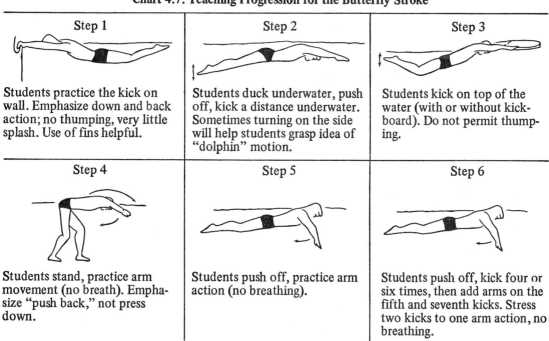

Step 1	Step 2	Step 3
Students practice the kick on wall. Emphasize down and back action; no thumping, very little splash. Use of fins helpful.	Students duck underwater, push off, kick a distance underwater. Sometimes turning on the side will help students grasp idea of "dolphin" motion.	Students kick on top of the water (with or without kickboard). Do not permit thumping.

Step 4	Step 5	Step 6
Students stand, practice arm movement (no breath). Emphasize "push back," not press down.	Students push off, practice arm action (no breathing).	Students push off, kick four or six times, then add arms on the fifth and seventh kicks. Stress two kicks to one arm action, no breathing.

Chart 4.7—*continued*

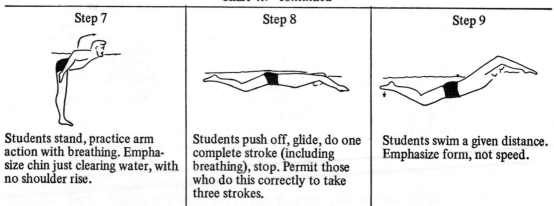

Step 7	Step 8	Step 9
Students stand, practice arm action with breathing. Emphasize chin just clearing water, with no shoulder rise.	Students push off, glide, do one complete stroke (including breathing), stop. Permit those who do this correctly to take three strokes.	Students swim a given distance. Emphasize form, not speed.

BACK CRAWL STROKE

The back crawl stroke is comparatively easy for most swimmers, young and old, to learn. It is a good stroke for beginners because breathing poses no problems; however, this is counterbalanced for most adults in our classes, because they prefer to see where they are swimming. Because swimming is most often taught in pools, instruction in the open turn should also accompany this stroke.

The flutter kick on the back (first described in Chapter 3) is used for this stroke.

The arm stroke, coordination, and breathing for the back crawl are discussed and diagrammed in Chart 4.8.

Chart 4.8. Performance Techniques for the Back Crawl Stroke

Techniques	Illustration	Performance Errors

Kick
 	
A. Extend legs, point toes.
  Move feet alternately up and down 12–15 inches.
  Have slight bend at knees.
  Limit the amount of splash.
  Emphasize "up" beat and kicking from hips.
	A	A. Bending too much at knees. (causing knees to be above surface).
		  Having feet too low in the water.
		  Using a kick that is too narrow.
		  Failing to point toes.

Arm Action B. Extend leading arm forward and extend trailing arm along side.	B	B. Crossing the leading arm behind the head.

Chart 4.8–*continued*

Techniques	Illustration	Performance Errors
C. Bend leading arm at elbow 90° angle, elbow toward pool bottom. Hand about 6 in. below surface. Pull hand and arm to a point opposite the shoulder. Begin recovery of trailing arm (little finger leading).	C	C. Failing to drop elbow toward bottom. Failing to place elbow (and thus hand) deep enough in water. Failing to bend at elbow (causing either sideward or downward pull). Delaying recovery of trailing arm. Pointing the elbow toward the feet (thus causing hand to slip through water).
D. Rotate leading arm, hand and forearm pushing toward hips while elbow remains in place. Continue recovery of trailing arm by upward and overhead.	D	D. Failing to rotate hand and forearm. Failing to lift entire recovery arm above surface. Throwing recovery arm to side rather than upward.
E. As hand and forearm near hips, continue to push until palm faces downward toward pool bottom. Enter the recovering arm into water (little finger first) above the shoulder. *Note:* Limited side-to-side roll aids arm pull and recovery.	E	E. Failing to complete arm push until palm is downward. Failing to keep arms opposite one another (letting one remain at side until other catches up). Entering elbow of recovery arm before hand. Pounding whole recovery arm into water (thus creating hole in water). Rolling to a sidestroke position.
Coordination and Breathing F. (Usually) deliver six flutter kicks to the pull-push-recovery cycle of both arms (three up-kicks to one arm pull).	F	F. Kicking less than two times to each complete arm pull. Permitting arms and legs to work independently of each other. Letting hips sag (causing "sitting down" in water).
G. Keep back of head in water, with eyes looking upward. Breathe when convenient and need is felt.	G	G. Raising head and looking toward feet. Inclining head too far back (causing water to surge over face).

Once the swimmer can float and kick on the back, the back crawl stroke can be taught. A demonstration, followed by swimming the whole stroke, usually produces acceptable backstrokes in a single class period. The progressive-part method, sometimes needed, is shown in Chart 4.9.

Chart 4.9. Teaching Progression for the Back Crawl Stroke

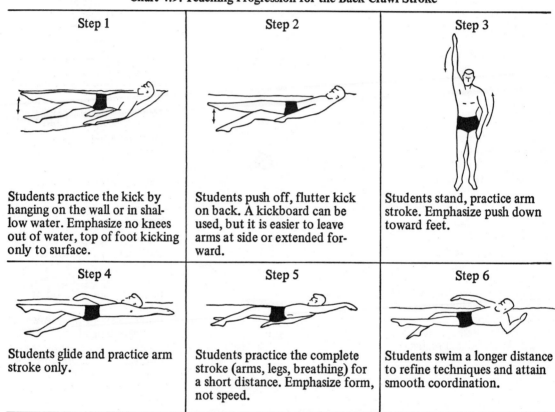

Step 1	Step 2	Step 3
Students practice the kick by hanging on the wall or in shallow water. Emphasize no knees out of water, top of foot kicking only to surface.	Students push off, flutter kick on back. A kickboard can be used, but it is easier to leave arms at side or extended forward.	Students stand, practice arm stroke. Emphasize push down toward feet.
Step 4	**Step 5**	**Step 6**
Students glide and practice arm stroke only.	Students practice the complete stroke (arms, legs, breathing) for a short distance. Emphasize form, not speed.	Students swim a longer distance to refine techniques and attain smooth coordination.

THE TRUDGEN STROKES

The trudgen is the only stroke named after a person—John Trudgen, an Englishman. Although they are not taught very often in beginning or intermediate classes, trudgen strokes are quite common, because many people unknowingly have taught themselves the stroke. The trudgen strokes feature an extreme body roll and glide (akin to the gliding position of the sidestroke) with the arm action of the crawl stroke. Those who have taught themselves to swim find it easier to breathe by rolling the entire body than to roll the head. This body roll is accompanied by a scissor or breaststroke kick. It has three advantages: (1) it is an overhand stroke, which both adults and children like to be able to do, (2) it permits more time for breathing, and (3) it is less tiring, permits more rest and relaxation, and yet is faster than the elementary backstroke, sidestroke, or breaststroke. All in all, it is often advisable to perfect adults' trudgen strokes rather than have them spend excessive time trying to master the crawl stroke.

In the single trudgen stroke only one kick is delivered in conjunction with a complete arm cycle. The double trudgen features two kicks to each arm cycle, delivered as each arm recovers. A narrower scissors kick is preferred, but a swimmer with a good breaststroke kick can sometimes move more easily with that leg action. Chart 4.10 depicts the single trudgen stroke, and Chart 4.11 the double trudgen stroke.

Chart 4.10. Performance Techniques for the Single Trudgen Stroke

Techniques	Illustration	Performance Errors
Kick A. Deliver a scissors kick as learned for sidestroke but make the stride separation of the legs narrower.		A. Making stride too narrow. Making stride too wide. Failing to kick vigorously.
Arm Action B. Assume a gliding position on the side as learned for sidestroke.		B. Failing to assume the correct gliding position.
C. Execute simultaneously a crawl stroke pull with leading arm and a crawl stroke recovery with trailing arm.		C. Thrusting the trailing arm forward instead of swinging the arm forward over water from shoulder.
D. Recover leading arm as trailing arm pulls. Resume gliding position on side.		D. Failing to recover trailing arm over water.
Coordination and Breathing E. Assume a gliding position on one side.		E. Gliding on stomach. Gliding on back.
F. Roll onto stomach as leading arm pulls and trailing arm recovers.		F. Failing to roll far enough onto stomach for trailing arm to be lifted clear of the water. Kicking during recovery of trailing arm.
G. Recover leading arm forward and bring legs into position for scissors kick as body is rolled from stomach to side and as trailing arm begins pull. Deliver kick and complete pull of trailing arm. Exhale.		G. Pulling trailing arm through to thigh before recovering the legs for kick. Lifting trailing arm for recovery immediately after pull to thigh.
H. Glide on side and inhale.	H (see E)	H. Failing to glide on side.

Chart 4.11. Performance Techniques for the Double Trudgen Stroke

Techniques	Illustration	Performance Errors
Kick A. Deliver a scissors kick as *each* arm is recovered.	 A	A. Executing a kick that is too narrow. Failing to kick with equal vigor on each side.
Arm Action B. Execute the crawl stroke recovery and pull of the arms.	 B	B. Making the pull and/or recovery of one arm shorter than that of the other arm.
Coordination and Breathing C. Assume a position with one arm extended forward and other arm trailing at thigh. Execute a scissors kick as leading arm is pulled backward to thigh and trailing arm is recovered forward. *Note:* Some instructors permit a breath to be taken as each arm is thrust forward. Glide on one side. Length of glide may be long for resting or may be brief.	 C	C. Permitting the kick to precede or to follow the arm pull.
D. Roll onto stomach and to opposite side. During the roll, recover the arm that now is at the thigh, pull with the opposite arm and execute a second scissors kick. *Note:* Some instructors permit a breath to be taken as each arm is thrust forward. Glide on one side (may be long or brief).	 D	D. Permitting the kick executed when rolling to one side to be weaker than the kick executed when rolling to the other side. Failing to glide even briefly on at least one side.
E. Substitute a breaststroke kick for each scissors kick (limited or no body roll is induced). This variation is especially beneficial to a swimmer with a strong breaststroke kick.	 E	E. Failing to pull the arms through completely. Failing to clear arms over surface on recovery.

Chart 4.12. Teaching Progression for the Single and Double Trudgen Strokes

Step 1	Step 2	Step 3
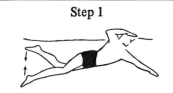	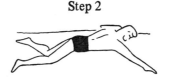	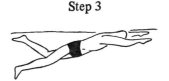
Students review the overarm sidestroke, but consciously rolling more on the stomach with each stroke. Emphasize glide and body roll.	Students switch to single trudgen by recovering both arms above water. Be sure both arms are pushed all the way back, and that glide is present.	To prepare for double trudgen, students practice scissors kick on alternating sides. Exaggerate body roll if necessary, but don't permit inverted scissors.

Step 4	Step 5
	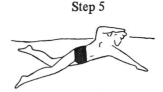
Students swim single trudgen but exaggerated roll to stomach. (Glide between arm pulls if going to use breaststroke kick.)	Students add second kick as second arm is recovered. Students can say to themselves, "Kick and glide, kick and glide" as each arm is recovered. Recovering arms underwater (human stroke) helpful in learning timing.

Most instructors are not too eager to teach the trudgen strokes, because they themselves do not swim the strokes well. If it is remembered that the basis for these strokes is the overarm sidestroke, the progression shown in Chart 4.12, which is essentially the whole method, will be easy to use.

The Trudgen Crawl Stroke

It is not uncommon to see self-taught swimmers use the trudgen crawl stroke. They have seen other swimmers use a crawl stroke so they try it, but because they roll their bodies to breathe, the natural tendency is to use the trudgen crawl rather than the crawl stroke. The trudgen crawl is a combination of three flutter kicks, one scissors (or breaststroke) kick, and two arm strokes. A pronounced glide follows the kick. The breathing is the same as described earlier. See Chart 4.13 for these skills.

As mentioned earlier, if students have taught themselves the trudgen, it is almost always the trudgen crawl. The whole method of instruction is suitable for use with such students. When teaching the stroke to people who are having problems, the progression shown in Chart 4.14 is suitable.

INVERTED BREASTSTROKE

The inverted breaststroke is primarily a resting stroke and is performed most easily by swimmers who possess a good wedge or whip kick. A single glide usually follows the kick, but a variation (shown

Chart 4.13. Performance Techniques for the Trudgen Crawl Stroke

Techniques	Illustration	Performance Errors
Kick A. Deliver three flutter kicks as one arm is pulling. B. Deliver a single scissors kick as other arm is pulling.	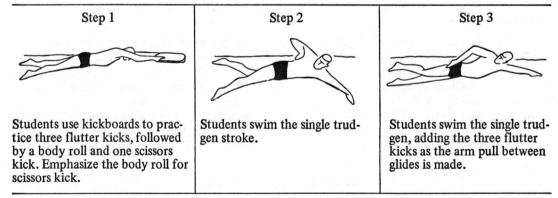	A. Bending too much at knees. Failing to point toes. B. Performing a wide flutter kick instead of a scissors kick.
Arm Action C. Execute the arm action as learned for the single trudgen stroke.		C. Failing to recover each of the arms above the surface.
Coordination and Breathing D. Assume a sidestroke glide position. Execute three flutter kicks as the leading arm pulls backward and trailing arm recovers forward. Execute the scissors kick and arm action of single trudgen stroke. Exhale and inhale. Glide on the side.		D. Executing too many flutter kicks (causing interference with recovery of the legs for delivery of scissors kick). Finishing the scissors kick as trailing arm goes forward. Gliding on stomach, not side.

Chart 4.14. Teaching Progression for the Trudgen Crawl Stroke

Step 1	Step 2	Step 3
Students use kickboards to practice three flutter kicks, followed by a body roll and one scissors kick. Emphasize the body roll for scissors kick.	Students swim the single trudgen stroke.	Students swim the single trudgen, adding the three flutter kicks as the arm pull between glides is made.

in Chart 4.15) is much superior in terms of efficient movement through the water. This variation, also called the double-gliding backstroke, emphasizes an arm pull followed by a glide, and then an arm recovery followed by a glide.

Chart 4.15. Performance Techniques for the Inverted Breaststroke

Techniques	Illustration	Performance Errors
Kick **A.** The inverted whip kick is preferred, but the inverted wedge is acceptable. **Inverted Whip Kick** 1. Drop heels to bottom, keeping knees just below surface. Keep knees together, toes pointed outward. 2. Begin rotary motion as feet circle outward and toward surface (toes remain pointed outward). 3. Body moves ahead as feet and lower legs complete rotary movement, ending with legs straight and toes pointed backward. **Inverted Kick (Wedge)** 4. Spread knees 15–18 inches. Lower heels downward, keeping knees just below surface. 5. Extend lower legs by moving feet outward. Point toes outward. 6. Straighten legs as they are pressed backward and squeezed together. Point toes back by end of press.	A.1 A.2 A.3 A.4 A.5 A.6	A. 1. Lifting knees upward out of water. Failing to keep thighs at surface. Failing to point toes outward. 2. Straightening leg so that it goes diagonally outward rather than a rotary motion. 3. Failing to bring feet back up to surface. Applying too little effort to the completion of the rotary movement. Legs not completely closed together. 4. Bringing knees above surface. 5. Extending legs by lowering thighs. Pointing toes upward. 6. Expending too little effort on press or squeeze. Pointing toes backward.

Chart 4.15—*continued*

Techniques	Illustration	Performance Errors
Arm Action B. Assume gliding position with arms extended in direction of progress.	B	B. Failing to extend arms.
C. Pull arms down to shoulder level, rotate palms downward while pushing hands to thighs.	C	C. Failing to apply sufficient force with pull and push of arms to provide momentum.
D. Recover arms by bending at elbows, hands close to body, elbows slowly leading hands toward the shoulders.	D	D. Recovering arms so force-fully that momentum is retarded. Recovering hands over the chest rather than outside of shoulders.
E. When hands reach shoulders, drop elbows toward bottom, push hands to extended position.	E	E. Causing water to be splashed over the face by not dropping elbows or by moving arms too fast.
F. Glide until legs start to drop.	F	F. Failing to hold glide long enough.
Coordination and Breathing G. Pull (and push) with arms. Legs remain in streamlined gliding position. Exhale and inhale at the end of the pull.	G	G. Bending legs immediately after completion of the kick.
H. As the hands approach shoulder level, recover the legs.	H	H. Recovering the legs before beginning the recovery of the arms.
I. Kick as the arms are extending forward into gliding position.	I	I. Kicking before the hands begin their move into the gliding position.
J. Glide, and hold breath.	J	J. Failing to hold glide until feet start to drop.
Variation K. Pull (and push) with arms, legs remaining in gliding position. Exhale and inhale.	K	K. Bending legs immediately after completion of the kick.

Chart 4.15—*continued*

Techniques	Illustration	Performance Errors
L. Glide until feet start to drop.	L	L. Failing to hold glide long enough.
M. Recover arms and deliver leg kick as shown in Illustration I.	M	M. Kicking before the hands begin their move into the gliding position.
N. Glide and hold breath.	N	N. Failing to hold glide until feet start to drop.

Both the whip and the wedge kicks have been described earlier in Chapter 3. When done on the back, the technique is essentially the same as when done on the stomach. Chart 4.15 presents the kick, arm action, coordination, and breathing of the inverted breaststroke.

Because this stroke normally will not be taught until the swimmers are skilled in the other basic strokes, it is usually easy to teach by the whole method. But, a progression is sometimes needed. A suggested progression is shown in Chart 4.16.

When doing this stroke for an ARC or YMCA test, the correct arm action (one glide) must be used. For practical purposes, most students prefer the two-glide variation because of the greater distance traveled per stroke.

TURNING AT POOL ENDS

Swimming lengths in a pool requires that some efficient way of turning must be known. Open turns are taught to all swimmers; closed turns are taught to those who have a possible racing career ahead of

Chart 4.16. Teaching Progression for the Inverted Breaststroke

Step 1	Step 2	Step 3
Students practice the kick. Emphasize keeping the knees under the water.	Students stand, practice arm stroke with kicking action of one leg. Students can repeat out loud "Pull, kick and recover, glide."	Students swim the stroke. Practice the variation (with two glides). Student can say, "Pull, glide, kick and recover, glide."

them. The essential difference between these turns is that the swimmer takes a breath during an open turn, and does not do so during a closed turn.

The Crawl, Side, Back, and Breaststroke Open Turns

Charts 4.17 and 4.18 depict the skills needed for the crawl stroke, sidestroke, and backstroke open turns. The competitive breaststroke turn is essentially that shown here in Chart 4.19, but the underwater action is much more demanding. If the skill of the group warrants, it is better to teach the competitive turns right away.

The push-off and the glide should be taught before the more difficult elements of the turn. First, practice these skills until they have been mastered. The swimmer should then stand about eight feet from the wall in the shallow water, push off, and glide into the wall. The turn itself is then practiced, omitting the push-off. All swimmers have a favorite hand, and it is wise to let them practice more with this hand at first than the other. They must feel confident using that hand before they are ready to try the other. When they can do the turn fairly well, then they must be forced to practice with both hands. Swimming short distances and using whichever hand comes up is an effective way of accomplishing this.

Chart 4.17. Performance Techniques for the Crawl Stroke and Sidestroke Open Turns

Techniques	Illustration	Performance Errors
Crawl Stroke A. Roll on one side, with lead arm extended toward wall.		A. Failing to roll on side.
B. Bend lead arm upon contact; begin to tuck legs.		B. Failing to bend arm upon contact with wall.
C. Swing legs under body; swing upper body in opposite direction; inhale.		C. Failing to tuck legs enough. Failing to breathe. Raising head too high.
D. Submerge 12–15 inches; legs and arms bent.		D. Failing to sink down well underwater.
E. Remain on side; extend arms and extend legs.		E. Extending legs before arms are extended.
F. Push off in streamlined position (arms over ears).		F. Failing to tuck head. Pushing off on stomach.
G. Gradually roll over to stomach; begin flutter kick.		G. Failing to begin kick while underwater.

Chart 4.17—continued

Techniques	Illustration	Performance Errors
Sidestroke H. Exactly the same as the crawl stroke open turn.	H.1	
1. Roll on one side, lead arm extended toward wall.		H. 1. Failing to roll on side.
2. Bend lead arm upon contact; begin to tuck legs.	H.2	2. Failing to bend arm upon contact with wall.
3. Swing legs under body; swing upper body in opposite direction; inhale.	H.3	3. Failing to tuck legs enough. Failing to breathe. Raising head too high.
4. Submerge 12–15 inches; legs and arms bent.	H.4	4. Failing to sink down well under water.
5. Remain on side; extend arms and extend legs.	H.5	5. Extending legs before arms are extended.
6. Push off in streamlined position (arms over ears).	H.6	6. Failing to tuck head. Pushing off on stomach.
7. After brief glide, pull arm closest to surface down to thigh or, if wishing to swim on same side as before, roll over to other side after push-off.	H.7	7. Pulling through with leading arm. Pulling through with both arms during glide after push-off.
I. Alternate turn.		
1. Reach to contact wall with trailing hand, rather than leading arm. Bend trailing arm. Turn around by dropping shoulder of leading arm, tucking knees and hips.	I.1	I. 1. Failing to bend arm on contact. Failing to tuck tightly.
2. Submerge and push off on proper side. Pull uppermost arm down while underwater.	I.2	2. Failing to submerge. Pulling through with leading arm or with both arms.

Chart 4.18. Performance Techniques for the Backstroke Open Turn

Techniques	Illustration	Performance Errors
A. Contact the wall with leading hand directly in front of its shoulder.	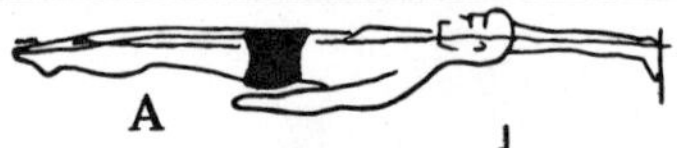	A. Placing the hand too far outside of shoulder.
B. Bend leading arm, begin to tuck knees. Drop shoulder of leading hand, causing slight body roll toward that side.	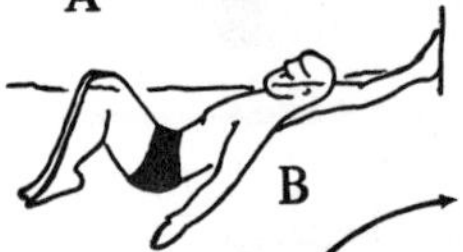	B. Failing to roll toward proper side.
C. Swing tucked legs to wall as upper part of body goes in opposite direction.		C. Failing to tuck tightly.
D. Inhale, submerge 12–15 inches. Place feet on wall, arms bent alongside head.	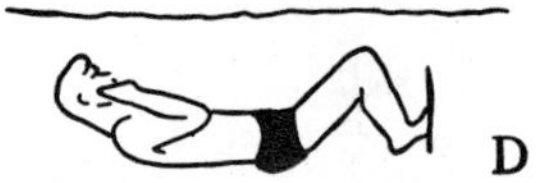	D. Failing to submerge deeply enough.
E. Extend arms, push off under water in a streamlined position.		E. Pushing off on top of the water. Pushing off before arms are extended.
F. Begin flutter kick before surface is reached.	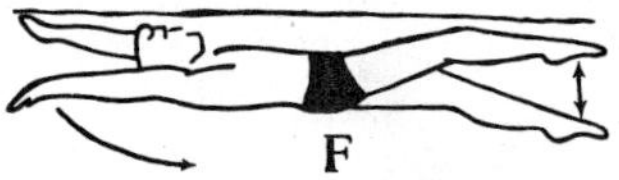	F. Failing to begin kick as momentum decreases.

Chart 4.19. Performance Techniques for the Breaststroke Open Turn

Techniques	Illustration	Performance Errors
A. Contact wall with both hands at same time on same plane.	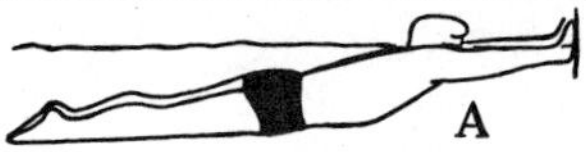	A. Failing to touch wall as rules prescribe (both hands touch simultaneously on same plane).
B. Bend arms; tuck knees.		B. Failing to get close to wall.
C. Push body (head leading) to one side or the other. Inhale.		C. Raising head too high. Failing to tuck head before turning.
D. Submerge 15–20 inches. Place bent arms under chest and face. Roll over on stomach.		D. Failing to get body deep enough before push off.

Chart 4.19—*continued*

Techniques	Illustration	Performance Errors
E. Extend arms and legs as push-off is performed. Attain streamlined position.	E	E. Completing push-off from wall before arms are extended.
F. Incline body upward to surface.	F	F. Having body inclined downward (feet higher than head).

SURFACE DIVING

Surface diving appeals greatly to younger swimmers, but not so much to adults. Experience has shown that most adults will not surface dive voluntarily, but since these skills are part of ARC and YMCA courses, everyone should know how to do them. We are continually amazed at the number of aquatic instructor candidates who cannot do these dives correctly; being able to get underwater with acceptable form is a requirement they all had to pass at one time or another.

The Feet-first, Tuck, and Pike Surface Dives

Charts 4.20, 4.21, and 4.22 present descriptions and diagrams of these dives.

There are no special techniques for teaching any of the surface dives. For the pike and tuck dives, forward momentum before the body is bent at the waist is most important. An easy way to begin to learn the dives is to have the swimmers push off the wall and attempt to dive before they lose their momentum.

UNDERWATER SWIMMING

Like the surface dives, underwater swimming is more popular with the younger set than with the older swimmers. However, swimmers of any age may have to locate a submerged object at some time or pass an ARC or YMCA course, and underwater swimming is essential for such activities as skin diving, spear fishing, and scuba diving. This skill is good for confidence-building and for increasing the breathing capacity. Swimmers must remember that they will travel further underwater if they glide as long as possible between strokes and the feet remain slightly higher than the head.

There is no really required form for underwater swimming; whatever works best is recommended. Before submerging the swimmer should take two or three deep breaths to expel some of the carbon dioxide in the lungs. An instructor must never permit swimmers to take more than four deep breaths before swimming under water. An excessive amount may cause the swimmer to "black out" underwater. A modified breaststroke (see Chart 4.23) is usually employed underwater.

Underwater swimming techniques are usually taught by having the swimmer duck underwater close to the pool side and pushing off from the side with arms extended. As the glide speed slackens, students should pull and push vigorously with the arms and glide again. Students practice these movements until the most satisfactory kick and timing have been determined. Instructors should take care that students are allowed (1) no more than two or three pulls at one submersion, and (2) no more than three or four individual trials in any one day.

Chart 4.20. Performance Techniques for the Feet-first Surface Dive

Techniques	Illustration	Performance Errors
A. Tread water, allowing feet to go directly under body. Extend arms sideward from the body and parallel to surface, palms down.		A. Failing to extend arms sideward, with palms down.
B. Press downward to the thighs at the same time a vigorous kick is given (causing chest to rise well out of the water).		B. Failing to press and kick efficiently enough to raise chest out of water.
C. Allow weight above surface to begin to force body downward.		C. Moving arms sideward or upward.
D. After head submerges, force extended arms (palms upward) toward the surface. To obtain additional depth, fin with the hands while they are overhead.		D. Forcing hands upward too soon (thus causing them to come out of the water). Thrusting arms upward (rather than pulling with arms extended.
E. When desired depth is reached, tuck body and extend both arms and legs. Swim underwater to desired locale.		E. Failing to tuck chin when assuming horizontal position.

Chart 4.21. Performance Techniques for the Tuck Surface Dive

Techniques	Illustration	Performance Errors
A. Gain momentum (usually by performing one or two breaststrokes.		A. Failing to achieve momentum.
B. Bring chin to chest, bend body to right angle at hips, tuck arms to chest.		B. Failing to lower the head and bend enough at the hips.
C. Bend at knees and at hips to place body in tight tuck.		C. Failing to assume a tight tuck position.

Chart 4.21—*continued*

Techniques	Illustration	Performance Errors
D. Extend legs vigorously by pushing toes upward. Arms extended downward. Legs straight and together, toes pointed.	D	D. Failing to keep legs straight, together, and toes pointed after extension. Throwing feet backward (arching back) instead of upward.
E. Let weight of the legs cause body to sink. Use breaststroke pull to attain greater depth if needed. Keep one arm extended overhead if water is less than 10 ft. deep.	E	E. Failing to let weight of legs force body down. Failing to use arm movements to attain desired depth.
F. When desired depth is reached, tuck body or arch back to get it to horizontal position. Swim underwater to desired locale.	F	F. Failing to lower the chin toward the chest when assuming the horizontal position.

Diving From Board

Again, diving from either the low or high board is of most interest to the younger swimmers. If adults do not want to dive, we customarily do not press the issue. However, if at all possible, we try to encourage all younger swimmers to dive, because experience shows that this is a skill that is socially desirable. Diving from the board is discussed in great detail in Chapter 5; especially, see pages 100–02 for comments dealing with the instruction of novice divers.

CLOTHING INFLATION

Whether or not clothing inflation is a useful skill is debatable, but the trend is to ignore it in classes. A person fifty yards or less from safety would certainly not remove clothing, as it presents no burden if survival floating or slow underwater-recovery strokes are used. The ability to inflate clothing was once considered an important precaution in a lake or the ocean, where safety could be a great distance away. But because of the danger of hypothermia (see Chapter 3), it is better to keep clothing on; the layer of water between the skin and clothing stays slightly warmer than the surrounding water.

Clothing inflation skills are also very difficult to master. Our experience has shown that poor swimmers find it very hard to remove and then inflate their clothes. These poor swimmers lack the skills and confidence needed to tread water or survival float for the necessary period.

Chart 4.22. Performance Techniques for the Pike Surface Dive

Techniques	Illustration	Performance Errors
A. Achieve momentum with breaststroke movements.	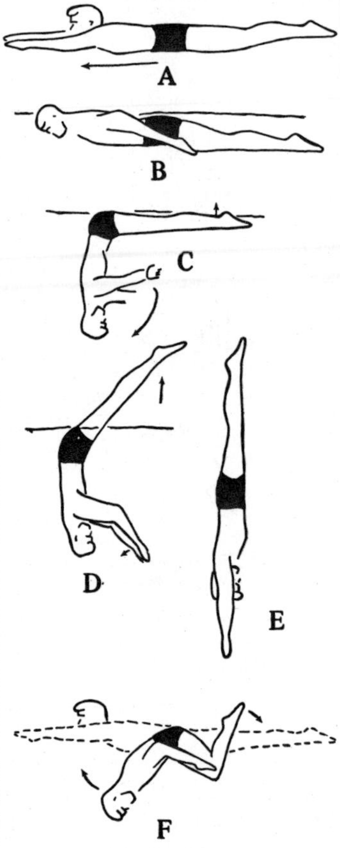	A. Failing to achieve momentum.
B. Pull arms all the way back to the thighs.		B. Failing to pull arms clear back to the thighs.
C. Bend the body at right angles at the hips.		C. Putting body at more or less than a right angle. Failing to keep legs straight.
D. Pull the extended arms (palms facing head) downward toward the head. Raise legs upward without knee bend, but with toes pointed.		D. Failing to use arms to obtain leverage so as to raise the legs. Failing to keep legs straight or toes pointed.
E. Use weight of legs to cause body to sink. Use breaststroke pull to attain greater depth.		E. Failing to permit legs to force body down. Failing to use arm movements to attain desired depth.
F. When desired depth is reached, tuck body or arch back to get it to horizontal position. Swim underwater to desired locale.		F. Failing to lower the chin toward the chest when assuming the horizontal position.

Chart 4.23. Performance Techniques for Underwater Swimming

Techniques	Illustration	Performance Errors
A. Extend arms forward, then pull and push them completely back to the thighs. Tuck chin toward chest. Keep feet at slightly higher level than head. (Some swimmers prefer to have a continuous, wide, slow flutter kick while the arm movement is being done).	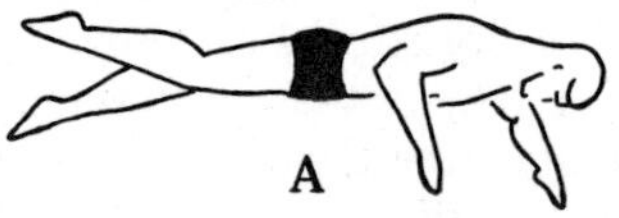	A. Failing to keep head low, chin tucked.

Chart 4.23—*continued*

Techniques	Illustration	Performance Errors
B. Glide. (Some swimmers prefer to deliver a short series of flutter kicks during the glide, or to continue the wide, slow flutter kick).		B. Failing to glide.
C. Gently recover arms to forward extended position. (Some swimmers prefer to deliver a breaststroke or scissors kick as the arms are recovering, or to continue the wide, slow flutter kick.)		C. Recovering the arms too vigorously (thus retarding momentum).
D. Glide with arms extended. (Some swimmers may prefer to continue the wide, slow flutter kick.)		D. Failing to glide.

All swimmers should have experience in survival floating while clothed, with inflation of a shirt while it is being worn (Chart 4.24A and 4.24B) and with swimming distances with the various strokes. Good swimmers can be taught the other skills in Chart 4.24, but should always be reminded that these techniques will seldom be used in a real-life situation.

Chart 4.24. Performance Techniques for Clothing Inflation

Techniques	Illustration	Performance Errors
Shirt A. After survival floating a bit to reduce panic, blow air inside shirt. Button top button, open the shirt between second and third buttons and blow air inside.		A. Failing to lean forward when blowing into the shirt.
B. When sufficient air has entered, rebutton shirt and float face down (as in survival floating). *Note:* T-shirts are virtually impossible to inflate, and some short-sleeved blouses are unsatisfactory. The swimmer may have to hold the collar tight if a button is missing.		B. Assuming a backleaning position (causing air to escape between buttons).

Chart 4.24—*continued*

Techniques	Illustrations	Performance Errors
Remove Shoes C. Tuck shirttails in or tie them in front of waist. Float face downward, slowly untie knots in one shoe. Remove it, repeat with other shoe. *Note:* Some experts favor removing shoes first. We think it is better to attain some degree of calmness and buoyancy before attempting this.	 C	C. Failing to tuck or tie shirttails (causing air to escape around the waist). Failing to keep face down in water.
Pants D. After reinflating the shirt if needed, unfasten pants at the waist. Slide them down to the knees.	 D	D. Removing pants with hurried motions (causing pant legs to cling to body).
E. If breath is needed, take one before removing one pant leg. Remove other pant leg. *Note:* Some experts favor removing one pant leg, then tying a knot in it before removing the other pant leg.	 E	E. Letting both pant legs drop to ankles, thus "tying up" legs. Pulling one pant leg inside out while removing it.
F. Using air trapped in the shirt to float in a vertical position, zip or button pants at waist.	 F	F. Failing to remain in upright position.
G. Tie overhand knot at end of each pant leg.	 G	G. Tying the knot too high or too low on the leg.
H. Spread pants (zipper-side down) at water's surface.	 H	H. Failing to have zipper down.

Chart 4.24—*continued*

Techniques	Illustrations	Performance Errors
I. Inflate by one of these methods:		
1. Holding waistband open. "Push" air into pants. Repeat until they are inflated.	I.1	**I.** 1. Failing to have hand above the water when starting to "push" air. Not keeping waistband below water.
2. Holding waistband open, submerge, blow air into pants. Repeat until they are inflated.	I.2	2. Not keeping waistband below surface of water.
3. Holding pants behind head, sling them over and downward. Repeat if needed.	I.3	3. Not keeping waistband open so as to catch the air.
J. Keeping waistband below water's surface, put one leg (or one arm) through crotch.	J	**J.** Putting too much weight on pants, thus squeezing air through the cloth.
Air Pillow		
K. Using inflated pants, float on back, slowly unbutton shirt or blouse.	K	**K.** Failing to use inflated pants. Failing to move slowly.
L. Slowly remove one sleeve. Tie a single overhand knot just above the slit near the cuff.	L	**L.** Failing to tie knot just above the slit. Failing to move slowly.
M. Slowly remove other sleeve. Tie knot above slit.	M	**M.** Failing to tie knot just above slit. Failing to move slowly.
N. Spread shirt or blouse out (back side up); gather all edges underneath.	N	**N.** Failing to grasp all edges.
O. Submerge, blow air into pillow.	O P	**O.** Failing to keep loose edges of shirt underwater. Failing to submerge in order to blow up into the pillow.
P. Hang on, letting pillow act as the support.		**P.** Applying too much body weight, thus causing air to escape.

Chart 4.24—*continued*

Techniques	Illustration	Performance Errors
Air Chest or Belt Q. If shift or skirt is worn, float on back. Grasp hemline, raise it 1–2 feet above water.	Q	Q. Failing to raise hemline of skirt out of water.
R. Trap air as hemline is returned to water surface. Repeat two or three times if necessary. Float. *Note:* If shift is worn, be sure collar is closed or else air will escape.	R	R. Failing to keep hemline below water surface (thus permitting air to escape).
S. If shirt is worn, remove it.	S.1	
1. Using inflated pants, float on back, slowly unbutton shirt or blouse.		S. 1. Failing to use inflated pants. Failing to move slowly.
2. Slowly remove one sleeve. Tie a single overhand knot just above the slit near the cuff.	S.2	2. Failing to tie knot just above the slit. Failing to move slowly.
3. Slowly remove other sleeve. Tie knot above slit.	S.3	3. Failing to tie knot just above slit. Failing to move slowly.
4. Put shirt on "backside-front," buttoning behind neck.	S.4	4. Having shirt inside out (pockets on inside).
5. Grasp the shirttails, and raise them 1–2 feet above the water. Trap air as the tails are lowered to the water. Repeat two or three times if necessary.	S.5	5. Failing to get sufficient air into shirt.
6. Tie the tails behind back or tuck into undergarments. Float.	S.6	6. Failing to tuck or tie shirt-tails.

The first step in clothing inflation is survival floating. This enables the swimmer to avoid the panic which is so prevalent in cases such as this. After achieving some stability (both of mind and body) the swimmer then decides what article of clothing to inflate. We recommend that swimmers be taught the skills shown in Chart 4.24, in the order presented.

When teaching clothing inflation, plan to take a whole period of class time (at least thirty-five minutes) so that students practice what they see demonstrated. Emphasize that clothes brought from home should be clean; even so, there will be enough thread and lint from them to require extra filtration work. As they enter the water clothed (preferably jumping from the three-meter board), students should swim a distance with their clothes on. They will discover that the crawl or trudgen strokes (arm recovery over water) are less desirable than the sidestroke, elementary backstroke, breaststroke, or inverted breaststroke (arm recovery underwater). While the students are practicing the skills, do not let them touch the sides or pool bottom. Finally, when all have inflated both pieces of clothing, have them attempt to force all of the air out by climbing on top of the clothes. The students will actually see the folly of trying to use clothes as rafts.

CLASS ASSIGNMENTS

1. Teach an intermediate swimmer as many of the skills outlined in the chapter as possible. Keep a daily account of the progress, focusing attention on which teaching strategies (whole, part-whole-part, reciprocal) work best.

2. Talk to an experienced swimming instructor. Would he or she agree with the standards and skills outlined for intermediates and advanced swimmers? What are the hardest strokes to teach intermediates?

3. Talk to an experienced instructor. What are the chief problems in teaching intermediates, ages seven to twelve? thirteen to nineteen? adults?

4. Using the analysis sheets in Appendix B, evaluate a partner on his or her performance in the various strokes. Discuss the results, demonstrate the correct techniques, and attempt to eliminate all errors.

BEHAVIORAL OBJECTIVES

Almost all instructors will teach intermediates or advanced swimmers at some time. Therefore, we expect our students to be able to respond correctly (based on material in this chapter) to questions calling for brief written answers and to meet the standards indicated for the intermediate and advanced skills listed.

1. Be able to explain in writing a logical teaching strategy (beginning with the whole method, and then going to the whole-part-whole method), for teaching the sidestroke, breaststroke, butterfly stroke, single trudgen stroke. The strategy must be consistent with the principles and examples given in this text.

2. Be able to demonstrate the following strokes and skills (a successful demonstration is one with none of the performance errors noted in the charts): (a) sidestroke (both sides), (b) overarm sidestroke, (c) breaststroke, (d) butterfly stroke, (e) back crawl stroke, (f) single trudgen stroke, (g) double trudgen stroke, (h) trudgen crawl stroke, (i) inverted breaststroke (plus variation), (j) open turns (crawl, back, breast), (k) surface dives (tuck, pike, feet-first), (l) underwater swim (thirty feet), (m) clothing inflation (pants, shirt), (n) 200-yard medley swim in five and a half minutes or less.

REFERENCES

American National Red Cross. *Swimming and Water Safety.* Washington, D.C.: American National Red Cross, 1968, pp. 52–88, 92–96, 121–24.
——. *Swimming and Water Safety Courses: Instructor's Manual.* Washington, D.C.: American National Red Cross, 1974, pp. 55–78.
Arnold, Lloyd C., and Freeman, Robert W. *Progressive Swimming and Springboard Diving Program.* New York: National YMCA Program Materials, 1972, pp. 48–62.
Canadian Red Cross Society. *National Instructor Guide and Reference.* Toronto: Canadian Red Cross Society, 1977, pp. 56–76, 95–100, 177–79.

FILMS

American National Red Cross. *Backstroke. Butterfly. Breast Stroke. Sidestroke.* Super 8 mm cartridges. See local ARC office.
——. *Skilled Swimming I. Skilled Swimming II.* 16 mm, color, sound. See local ARC office.
Back Crawl Stroke, Side Stroke, Elementary Backstroke. Inverted Breast Stroke, Breast Stroke, Butterfly Stroke. Wolverine Sports, Ann Arbor, Michigan 48104.
Freestyle and Backstroke Technique. Breast Stroke and Butterfly Techniques. Starts, Turns, and Progressive Drills. Athletic Institute, 200 N. Castlewood Drive, North Palm Beach, Florida 33408.

FILM STRIPS

Backstroke. Butterfly. Breaststroke. Turns and Starts. Sidestroke. Super 8 mm cartridges. Mariner III, Box 38246, Hollywood, California 90038.
Illustrated American Swimming Techniques. Youngbluth Company, P.O. Box 186, Homestead, Florida 33030.

CHAPTER 5

Performing and Teaching Springboard Diving Skills

Springboard diving is a skill that requires coordination. The diver develops grace, control of muscle, and balance, as well as a gratifying leisure-time activity.

THE DIVING TEACHER

The novice diver usually wants to learn a forward dive and a back dive first. A beginning instructor must be prepared to give advice, and it is desirable, though not absolutely essential, that you be able to demonstrate correct dives.

A coach in a park and recreation department, for a voluntary organization, or for a community club team also should be able to give basic instruction in technique to an unskilled candidate for membership on a team. At first, as a novice instructor, you may not have extensive knowledge of springboard diving yourself, but the ability to impart the basics to students will prepare them for more difficult dives. Also, you should become acquainted with textbooks that provide detailed descriptions of advanced dives.

Only three of the more than sixty recognized dives are described in this chapter. These descriptions will help to set a pattern for teaching, but you should refer to other sources for additional skills that will better prepare your divers.

ESSENTIAL QUALITIES OF A BEGINNING DIVER

Learning will progress faster when the novice possesses certain qualities. Objectives are likely to be unattainable when these qualities are lacking. The novice must have a definite desire to learn, a willingness to attempt, confidence in the instructor, a satisfactory degree of neuromuscular control and sense of timing, and courage to continue despite discomfort. He or she must be persistent and attentive to instructions, able to think through what is to be attempted, and relate to performance. The diver's sense of balance, derived from the semicircular canals of the ear, should be reasonably good so that he or she can feel the interaction of body and movement in space. The diver should have enough flexibility to stretch, reach, and twist fluidly and easily.

FUNDAMENTALS OF SPRINGBOARD DIVING

Certain basic knowledge is essential to success in springboard diving. The learner must know and correctly apply physical principles pertaining to the use of the springboard, to the control and manipulation of body parts while moving in space, and to the relationship of thought and action.

In addition, divers should refer to the rules established for competitive diving. These rules have been written by a joint committee representing collegiate, scholastic, and amateur athletic organizations; they appear in rule books published by the National Collegiate Athletic Bureau and the United States Amateur Athletic Union. Of course, not all divers aspire to compete, but the techniques described provide a direction and method for learning the correct execution of each dive. Though basic techniques remain unaltered, specifics are often refined and new dives often created, so it is wise to have at hand a current copy of the competitive diving rule book.

Dive Groups

The large number of possible dives can be organized into five groups.

The diver may leave (a) leave the board while facing forward, (b) facing backward, (c) diving forward, (d) or diving backward, and (e) may incorporate a twist in the dive. Hence, dives are classified into five groups (Chart 5.1).

Chart 5.1. The Five Groups of Dives

A. Forward dive

Facing the water on takeoff and diving forward.

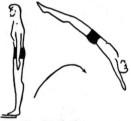

B. Back dive

Facing the board on takeoff and diving backward.

C. Reverse dive

Facing the water on takeoff and diving backward.

D. Inward dive

Facing the board on takeoff and diving forward.

Chart 5.1—*continued*

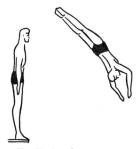

E. Twist dive

Including a twist in any one of the four preceding
types of dive.
Example: a forward dive with one-half twist.

In performing a dive within any one of the five groups, the diver may be in (a) layout (straight)
position; (b) pike (jackknife) position; or (c) tuck position. Chart 5.2 shows these positions. Some twist
dives may be performed in (d) free position in which a combination of tuck, pike, or layout is used
(Chart 5.2).

Chart 5.2. The Four Dive Positions

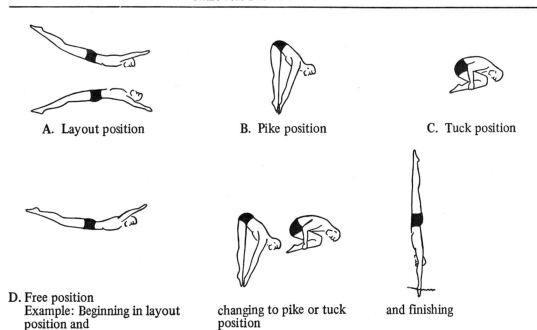

A. Layout position   B. Pike position   C. Tuck position

D. Free position
    Example: Beginning in layout   changing to pike or tuck   and finishing
    position and   position

Action of the Board

The board is a springing device that is used to propel the diver into the air for subsequent entry, either feet- or head-first, into the water. Although termed a "board" because of its original construction of solid or laminated wood, it is commonly constructed of metal or fiberglass. It is anchored to a support at its shore-end base, and at about its midpoint rests upon a fulcrum which, when moved, increases or decreases the flexibility of the board. The diving end projects over the water; the common heights of the board over the water surface are one meter (39.37 inches) for the low board and three meters (118.11 inches) for the high board.

When the impact of weight depresses the board, it must return to its original point of rest and beyond, casting the weight up and out. The learner has two tasks: first, to sense and adjust to the depression and lift of the board so that the diver and the board are one; and second, to accommodate body movements to the nonhorizontal plane of the board as it is depressed. Remember the body is lifted and propelled upward as the board returns to normal. Chart 5.3A illustrates how the amount of depression of the board may alter the angle at which the diver is propelled from the board unless he or she adjusts by increasing the lean backward to compensate for any greater depression of the board downward.

Varying weights depress the board to a greater or lesser degree. For each diver, there is an amount of board flexibility which is best and one should adjust the movable fulcrum to obtain it. The farther the fulcrum is toward the water, the lesser is the flexibility and the faster is the board action; the farther the fulcrum is moved away from the water, the greater is the flexibility and the slower the board action. Chart 5.3B shows that when the fulcrum is moved outward the amount of flexibility is as the heavy diver wants it to be, but is unsuitable for the light diver, and when the fulcrum is moved inward, the amount of flexibility is too great for the heavy diver but satisfactory for the light diver.

Chart 5.3. Effects of Body Weight and Fulcrum Position on Board Action

A. Relationship of Body Weight to the Depression of the Board	B. Relationship of Fulcrum Position to the Flexibility of the Board

The position of the board when it is at rest.

The position of the board when it has been depressed by a light diver.

The position of the board when it has been depressed by a heavy diver.

The farther the fulcrum is moved outward, the less is the flexibility.

The less the fulcrum is moved outward, the greater is the flexibility.

Coordination of the Arms and Legs During Takeoff

In the performance of a dive, arms and legs must act together in a coordinated movement or series of movements. For example, when the diver's arms are swinging upward during takeoff from the board, the hips, knees, and ankles are extending at the same time.

Line of Upward Flight

During the early rise from the board, the line of lift is in a straight body line with the top of the head leading the rise. Then the leading point may be transferred to the chest and hips as in a back dive in layout position, or to the hips as in a forward dive in pike position (Chart 5.4).

Chart 5.4. Leading Points During Upward Flight

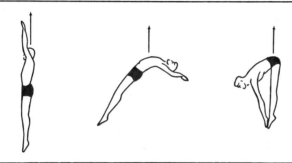

Line of Fall

The line of fall should be nearly vertical, or such as to insure water-entry within 6 feet of the end of the board.

Center of Balance

As a diver moves in the air, his or her total weight will have a center of balance at some point. That center will not be the same in all dives. In the performance of dives in layout or pike position, the hips are the center of balance, like the hub of a wheel or the fulcrum of a teeter-totter. In tuck position dives, the center of the compact mass is approximately at the lower ribs (Chart 5.5).

Chart 5.5. Center of Balance and Rate of Rotation

Arms, head, and legs are used to help to maintain balance. Poor control over the position or action of these parts will disturb balance (e.g., having one arm in a different position than the other, bending the knees, raising or lowering the head). Deliberate changes in the position of any of these parts will effect desired changes in position (e.g., lowering one arm helps in the performance of a twist, and bringing the legs into tuck position makes somersaulting easier).

TEACHING THE NOVICE DIVER

The teacher is the catalyst that causes desired results. He or she must know what to teach and how to teach effectively, must understand the feelings of the learner, must know the capabilities and the limitations of the learner, and must know the mechanics related to the skill, the teaching aids which may be employed to advantage, the appropriate progressions to use, and the performance faults that are common to the novice.

Safety Precautions

Not only do instructors need to be certain that they have not made themselves vulnerable to liability, they also have the moral obligation to do all that should be done to protect the diver.

Safety in Equipment and Facilities. The diving board must be of proper construction, without flaw resulting from use, securely anchored and without sharp edges or protruding screws or bolts. The board should be placed at least seven feet from the nearest wall and fifteen feet from an adjacent board. The water should be clear and at least twelve feet in depth. When possible, the diving area should be separated from the swimming area. Printed notices relevant to use of diving equipment, and warnings pertinent to use at the diver's risk, should be posted prominently.

Safety in Instruction. The instructor must give clear and complete safety instructions and must stringently enforce safety regulations. Repetition of instructions from time to time is advisable, but, above all, it is important that the instructor be able to establish that each learner has been present at some time when instructions were given, to avoid a charge of negligence. The instructor must be present during the entire class time. He or she must not compel a diver to unwillingly do something that the diver is afraid to do.

Health Precautions

Sudden entry into the water affects and effects pressures within the body. Air may be compressed, and water may intrude into sinus cavities and eustachian tube, especially when the diving entry is feet-first. Discomfort is a mild effect, but when water is contaminated or when the diver has a mouth or nose infection, which may be carried into sinus or inner ear areas, the effect is likely to be serious. Water may penetrate from the outer ear to the inner ear if the eardrum is ruptured; hence, no one with a ruptured eardrum should dive.

Additional precautions are helpful to anyone who practices the more complex dives to an appreciable extent, and especially important to the diver with a physical problem like susceptibility to sinus infection. These precautions include sealing the nostrils with waterproof adhesive tape or wearing a firm nose clip for feet-first dives, and inserting lamb's wool in the outer ear to protect the eardrums. The diver should not practice when he or she has an infection and must avoid diving in contaminated water.

Teaching Aids

Devices and methods to implement effective teaching may be categorized as kinesthetic, visual, auditory, and drill aids. Table 5.2 indicates some of them.

Table 5.1. Safety Procedures for Using the Trampoline or Diving Board

Trampoline and Tumbling Belt	Diving Board
The learner practices on a trampoline with a padded frame.	The learner keeps hands extended in front of the head after he or she has entered the water head-first.
Mount the trampoline by stepping from the frame to the bed.	Keep knees slightly flexed when contacting the bottom on any feet-first dive.
Dismount by stepping from the frame to the floor.	Abstain from diving when a swimmer is in the area.
Practice in bare feet.	
Kill the bounce on the trampoline by flexing knees (especially when landing off balance).	Take care not to follow too closely after a preceding diver.
Practice only when an instructor is present and when the instructor has provided capable spotters (usually four).	Bounce the board only once rather than two or more times in succession.
Learn how to spot for others.	Stop practice before becoming overtired.
Use a safety belt when learning new skills.	Bend at the hips, knees, and ankles on contact with the board to kill the bounce when landing off balance or when leaving the board without diving.

Table 5.2. Teaching Aids

Category of Teaching Aid	Uses by Instructors
Kinesthetic	Have the learner use a tumbling belt, twisting belt, or trampoline. Manipulate the learner's arms. Walk on the deck beside the learner, in front of him or her (for the learner to mimic the actions), or behind (with hands on the learner's hips), in order to impart technique and rhythm. Place the hands behind the learner's hips in order to guide the learner, who places his or her hands overhead and leans off-balance in the back dive.
Visual	Show motion pictures, loop films, film strips, or utilize television instant-replay. Use diagrams, which may be predrawn or drawn on the blackboard in the presence of the learner. Use photographs, figure drawings, and still pictures in series. Have the learner view himself or herself in a mirror during deck practice. Give demonstrations or have expert divers give them.
Auditory	Show motion pictures with accompanying comment or description on a sound track. Play taped comments in conjunction with television instant-replay of the learner's performance. Make comments before and after the learner's dive attempt. Give sound signals while the learner is in flight.

Table 5.2—*continued*

Category of Teaching Aid	Uses by Instructors
Drill	Have the learner walk and spring on the deck to learn the approach and hurdle.
	Have the learner perform head-first and feet-first entries from the deck, with emphasis on a straight body line and pointed toes.
	Have the learner spring upward from the board and make a one-half or full pivot before entering the water feet first.
	Have the learner bounce the board *lightly* to sense the rhythm.
	Have the learner wear a short-sleeved sweatshirt for the learning of new dives.
	Have the learner dive over a lightweight stick or bamboo pole held approximately 2 feet outward from the end of the board and approximately 6 feet above the surface of the water, to teach the learner not to spring too far outward.

What Dives to Teach First?

There is no absolute order in which dives should be taught. Decision will be based upon such factors as the total number of dives to be taught, the elements common to two or more dives, the preferences and aversions of the learner, the ability of the instructor to demonstrate, and the previous experience of the learner. Table 5.3 shows a possible order for the presentation of the more common dives, based upon different criteria.

Table 5.3. Order of Teaching Common Dives

Dive	Authors' Suggestion	Learners' Preference	Similar Facing Position	Similar Dive Position
Forward, layout	1	1	1	1
Forward, pike	2	2	2	5
Back, layout	3	6	6	3
Forward, one-half twist, layout	4	3	3	2
Forward single or one-and-one-half somersault, tuck	5	4	4	7
Inward, pike	6	5	7	6
Reverse, layout	7	7	5	4

FORWARD DIVE COMPONENTS

A dissection of each dive reveals that it is composed of distinct but interrelated parts. It is important that these elements be seen as occurring in series and with effects transmitted from one to the next in order as when the first in a row of dominoes is pushed against the next in line. Error in the execution of one dive-part tends to produce error in the next part.

When a forward dive is performed with a running approach, the components are the starting position, the approach, the hurdle, the takeoff, the flight, and the entry.

If the diver elects to perform these dives from a standing position at the diving end of the board, the parts are the starting position, the takeoff, the flight, and the entry.

Chart 5.6. Running Forward Dive Components

| Starting position | Approach | Hurdle | Takeoff | Flight | Entry |

Starting Position

The starting position is, as the name implies, the position taken by the diver at the beginning of the dive. This is the time when both muscle and mind are placed in states of balance and readiness.

Running Dives. The starting position for the forward dive with running approach and hurdle, is a standing position at the shore end of the board facing the water. The body position resembles the military position of attention, with weight somewhat forward on the balls of the feet rather than on the heels. The mental position should be one of alertness, confidence, and with mind fixed upon the mechanics of the dive to be performed.

Standing Dives. The starting position for the standing forward dive is the same as for the running dive, except that the position is taken at the diving end of the board rather than the shore end and that the arms may be extended overhead.

Approach

The running approach for the forward dive is more correctly described as a walk than as a run. Movement that is faster than a rapid walk imparts excessive forward body motion and restricts the attainment of appropriate height in the hurdle and takeoff. The approach is comprised of three or more steps and should be performed in a graceful and forceful manner. Muscular control, but not effort, should be evident. The arm swing in conjunction with leg action should be free and natural. The head should be erect and move in a straight line during the run, and not side-to-side as it would during an improperly balanced approach.

Hurdle

The hurdle for running forward and reverse dives is a leap from one foot, followed by a landing on both feet simultaneously on the end of the board. The final step of the running approach places the foot of one leg in position for a subsequent extension of knee, ankle, and toes of that leg in an upward and forward spring from the board. At the same time, the knee of the other leg is raised to hip level or higher, with the foot in vertical line below the knee. While the diver is in the air, both legs are brought together and straight, with toes pointed toward the board. The toes are raised prior to impact of the balls of the feet upon the board.

The actions of the arms and legs are synchronized. As the spring off one foot is effected, the arms swing forward and upward. They move sideward, backward, and downward as the body drops to the board just before takeoff.

The diver lands on the end of the board with the balls of the feet. As the board is depressed by the impact, the ankles and knees are flexed as needed to eliminate jarring and to prepare the diver to spring as the board whips upward.

The hurdle affects the takeoff and the flight. The height of the hurdle will have some effect on the degree of depression of the board and subsequent height of takeoff; excessive length or distance of hurdle is likely to result in excessive forward movement (outward from the board) on the takeoff. The distance of the hurdle should be approximately equal to the height of the hurdle, and height determined by the maximum lift the diver is able to obtain when springing, in an erect position, from one leg.

Takeoff

The nature of the takeoff and its height determine, to a large degree, the quality and appearance of the dive. In intricate dives, like multiple somersaults and twist dives, the takeoff must be high enough to provide the time for the component movements to be completed prior to entry into the water.

Running Dives. At the completion of the hurdle, the board is at its lowest point of depression and the diver's arms are at the lowest point of the downward arm swing. As the board springs upward, the diver must coordinate the forward and upward lift of the arms with the extension of the knees, ankles, and toes in timing with the rise of the board. Actions must be neither too early nor too late and must appear to be flowing rather than with explosive effort; he or she must use the board rather than fight it.

The teacher of diving must emphasize three additional specific points with reference to takeoff. First, the diver must practice the takeoff from standing position in order to sense the force and timing of the board's action and to adjust body actions to that force and timing. A single bounce of the board serves this purpose (repeated as an individual action and with the reassumption of the starting position between each two bounces); continuous bouncing of the board is hazardous and should be prohibited emphatically.

Second, the bounce and takeoff may be followed, in practice, by entry into the water or by return to the board feet-first. In the latter case, the diver must be taught to recontact the board with knees slightly flexed to "kill" the action of the board and permit the diver to regain a balanced standing position.

Third, since all boards differ to a greater or lesser degree, any diver should adjust to the board and to fulcrum positions before performing the dives for pleasure or in competition. Takeoff trials may show that performing certain dives on that particular board will be especially difficult.

Standing Dives. After assuming the starting position for standing forward and reverse dives, the diver usually will lower the arms to the sides. To execute the takeoff, the diver extends the ankles and rises to the toes as he or she raises the arms forward, upward, and backward. The diver bends at the hips, knees, and ankles as the arms continue to circle backward and downward. These combined actions place him or her in a position to spring upward as the arms are brought forward and upward. The hips, knees, and ankles are extended to place the body in a straight position as the diver rises upward.

The diver must take care that, in an endeavor to depress the board to obtain greater lift and height, he or she does not lift one or both feet above the board (crow hop) and pound them down upon the board prior to takeoff.

Flight

Forward
dive

Entry

The approach, hurdle, and takeoff receive scant attention from the casual observer and only limited attention from the competitive-diving judge. It is the dive itself (what happens while the diver is in the air and how he or she enters the water) that commands the attention of untrained observer and judge alike.

Running Dives. If the approach, hurdle, and takeoff have been satisfactory, the quality of dive execution will depend upon the mastery of techniques (as described for specific dives later in this chapter) and a fluid, controlled performance.

Standing Dives. Again, if the starting position and takeoff are well done, the quality of execution of standing dives will depend on the diver's technique, fluidity, and control.

Entry for all dives is made with the body fully controlled until submersion is complete—the legs should be straight and together, the toes pointed, the head erect, and the arms extended in advance of the head (head-first entry) or along the sides (feet-first entry).

The dive is not complete at the water surface, but at the pool bottom. Moreover, a smooth water surface cannot be distinguished by the diver when performing the more complex dives and, therefore, the surface should be made more easily discernible by splashing or by creation of air bubbles (from submerged air hose or dry ice) that rise and burst at the surface.

Timing of the entry is important. The entry is the final, and often the strongest, impression that the observer has of the dive. If splash is created or if the legs bend at the knees when contact is made with the water, a favorable impression of what has gone before is impaired, and appraisal may be affected to a disproportionate degree.

Entry should be accomplished in longitudinal alignment with the board and within six feet of the end of the board. The line of entry should be approximately vertical, but because the motion of the dive propels the diver outward, the head will enter slightly outward from a vertical alignment with the feet; the farther the takeoff and flight carries the diver outward from the board, the greater the divergence from vertical needs to be.

A dive is short when the diver's body fails to approach the vertical position and long when the body progresses beyond the normal angle of entry (Chart 5.7).

Chart 5.7. Short and Long Forward Dives

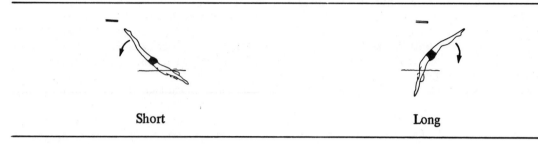

Short   Long

THE FORWARD DIVE IN LAYOUT POSITION

The novice who is learning to dive from the springboard probably will begin with a standing dive. Learning the approach and hurdle will be postponed until the standing dive has been mastered.

The diver should already know the techniques for performance of the plunge dive from a deck (Chapter 3). These techniques can be adapted to the springboard dive. From standing position, the plain dive is less complex and easier to perform than either the swan dive or the jackknife and is likely to be the first taught (Chart 5.8).

Chart 5.8. Forward Dives

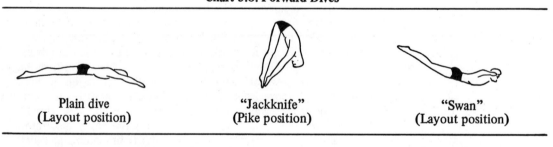

Plain dive   "Jackknife"   "Swan"
(Layout position)   (Pike position)   (Layout position)

When the learner has mastered the performance of the plain front dive, the instructor and learner will decide whether the next dive to be taught and learned will be the forward dive (layout), or forward dive (pike), or back dive.

When one or more forward dives from standing position have been learned, the next likely objective will be the mastery of the techniques of approach and hurdle and the performance of each of those dives following an approach and hurdle.

Before teaching the forward dive in layout position, you must first make certain that the diver has learned essential basics. The plunge dive from the deck must be reviewed, with emphasis on using the arms and legs to effect the spring, and with attention to the correct position in flight and at entry. The diver should be taught the coordination of arm and board actions as he or she takes a single gentle spring at the end of the board and returns to the board feet first, and should be taught to spring upward from the board and enter the water feet first.

Chart 5.9. Performance Techniques for the Forward Dive in Layout Position

Techniques	Illustration	Performance Errors	Illustration
A. Take off from the board in a line of flight upward and slightly outward from end of board.	 A	A. *Standing Dive.* The swing of the arms is not used to implement legspring of the takeoff (1). The feet are lifted above the board (crow hop) during the first part of takeoff (2). *Running Dive.* The approach steps are too long, too fast. The approach is a rapid run rather than walk (3). Forward body-lean is excessive (3). During the approach and hurdle, the head is inclined downward with eyes looking straight at end of the board rather than held erect with eyes looking down (4). In contacting the board following the hurdle, the knees bend excessively, body weight does not depress the board and, after a brief pause, the dive is made as from a standing position (5). *Standing and Running Dives.* Prior to takeoff, the feet are pounded down on the board. The diver does not wait for and utilize lift of the board.	 
B. Make the hips the pivot point as feet are permitted to continue to rise upward over the board and to a position overhead. Cause the head and upper part of body to rise more slowly than legs, until head is in a vertical position below the hips and feet, as the hips are lifted or permitted to rise upward.	B	B. On take-off, the body has excessive forward lean (1). The back is arched in order to raise heels upward (2 and 4). In flight, the feet are raised too rapidly or too much (3).	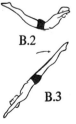

Chart 5.9—continued

Techniques	Illustration	Performance Errors	Illustration

Raise the arms upward in front of the body and directly overhead as the body rises; move the arms to sideward extension when approaching the peak of upward flight; hold them in sideward position until shortly before entry, and then bring them together in advance of the head and with arms pressed against the ears.

During the upward rise, hold the head in normal (erect) position; at the peak of the rise and during most of downward flight, raise head slightly; shortly before entry, return head to normal position.

B

In flight, the feet are not raised to sufficient height. The body is too rigid; smooth adjustment is difficult. The hips are placed in partial pike position (4).

B.4

The head is too low; chin is depressed toward chest (5).

B.5

At entry, the head is held in raised position and impact is taken on face (6).

B.6

The back is arched prior to entry and impact is taken on face and chest (7).

The knees flop over on entry (8).

The arms are not maintained in an extended position on entry (9).

B.7

The point of aim for completion of the dive is the water surface rather than below.

The diver arches the back and endeavors to surface as soon as the head enters the water (10).

B.8

B.9

C. Because the body in flight moves somewhat outward from the board, effect entry into the water before the body reaches a true vertical alignment.

C

B.10

As progress is made from the simple to the more complex and by means of logical, connected steps (Chart 5.10), you should anticipate the probable errors in the learner's performance, teach techniques that will minimize errors, and help the learner to eliminate them when they do occur. Appropriate kinesthetic, visual, auditory, and drill aids (Table 5.2) should be used to speed learning. As the learner makes the first dive attempts from the board, you should anticipate that the board action may throw the diver's legs upward and over and cause a somersault.

THE FORWARD DIVE IN PIKE POSITION

Because several different dives are performed in the pike position, mastery of the forward dive with pike facilitates learning of the dives that are related by position.

In executing a plain forward dive, beginners often bend at the hips to adjust balance and entry. Many instructors suggest that, for this reason, the forward dive in pike position should be taught before

Chart 5.10. Teaching Progression for the Forward Dive in Layout Position

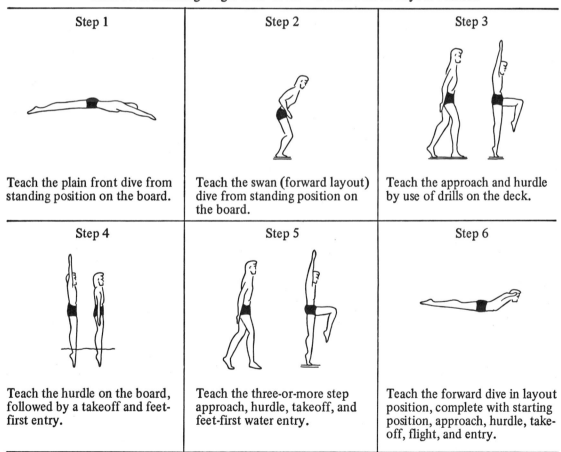

Step 1	Step 2	Step 3
Teach the plain front dive from standing position on the board.	Teach the swan (forward layout) dive from standing position on the board.	Teach the approach and hurdle by use of drills on the deck.
Step 4	**Step 5**	**Step 6**
Teach the hurdle on the board, followed by a takeoff and feet-first entry.	Teach the three-or-more step approach, hurdle, takeoff, and feet-first water entry.	Teach the forward dive in layout position, complete with starting position, approach, hurdle, takeoff, flight, and entry.

the forward dive in layout position and after a plain front dive. The instructor should experiment by teaching the plain front dive and the layout dive to some learners and the plain dive and pike dive to others, and then arrive at his or her own decision on what works best. Chart 5.11 presents the performance techniques that should be emphasized in teaching the forward dive in pike position.

Chart 5.11. Performance Techniques for the Forward Dive in Pike Position

Techniques	Illustration	Performance Errors	Illustration
A. Take off from the board with body straight as it rises almost directly upward from the board. Extend the arms and point them upward in an extension of body line.	A	A. *Standing dive.* The swing of the arms is not used to aid leg spring on takeoff. The dive is performed with arms overhead (1). The feet are lifted from board (crow hop) during the spring before take-off (2) *Running dive.* The approach steps are too long, too fast (3). During the approach and hurdle, the head is inclined downward with eyes looking straight at end of the board (4). In contacting the board after the hurdle, the knees bend excessively (5). *Standing and Running Dives.* Prior to takeoff, the feet are pounded down on the board. The diver does not utilize lift of the board. On takeoff, body has excessive forward lean (6).	A.1 A.2 A.3 A.4 A.5 A.6
B. As body nears the peak of the upward flight, permit the hips to continue to rise, bend at the hips, and bring fingers slightly forward, and then downward to toes or to grasp legs at the calves or ankles as the legs are brought forward to meet the hands. Keep the legs straight and without bend at the knees.	B	B. The pike position is assumed immediately after takeoff (1). The feet are brought up to hands rather than hands down to feet (2). The hands are brought vertically downward rather than slightly forward and downward.	B.1 B.2

Chart 5.11—*continued*

Techniques	Illustration	Performance Errors	Illustration
		The knees are flexed to enable the hands to reach for the feet; the ankles are flexed and toes are extended (3). The back is humped to attain a pike position (4). The body is too rigid (thus, smooth adjustment is difficult).	B.3 B.4
C. At the beginning of downward fall, straighten hips and lift legs upward without knee bend until almost directly above the body. Extend the arms to point downward and place head between extended arms. Because the direction of motion of the body in flight is somewhat outward from the end of the board, effect entry before the body reaches true vertical alignment.	C	C. The chin is depressed toward chest (1). The pike position is held too long (thus, impact is taken on the back) (2). At entry, the head is held in raised position and impact is taken on the face (3). The back is arched prior to entry and impact is taken on face and chest (4). The knees bend (flop over) on entry (5). On entry, the arms are not maintained in extended position (6). The point of aim for completion of the dive is at the water surface rather than below. The diver arches the back, extends the wrists, elevates the arms and begins to surface as soon as the head enters the water (7).	C.1 C.2 C.3 C.4 C.5 C.6 C.7

To be sure that the proper foundation is laid, you should have the learners review the plunge dive from the deck, teach or review the coordination of arm and board actions in a single gentle spring with return to the board feet first, and teach or review the coordination of arm and board actions in a single vigorous spring from a standing position on the board and with entry into the water feet first. The next steps in teaching should be as shown in Chart 5.12.

Chart 5.12. Teaching Progression for the Forward Dive in Pike Position

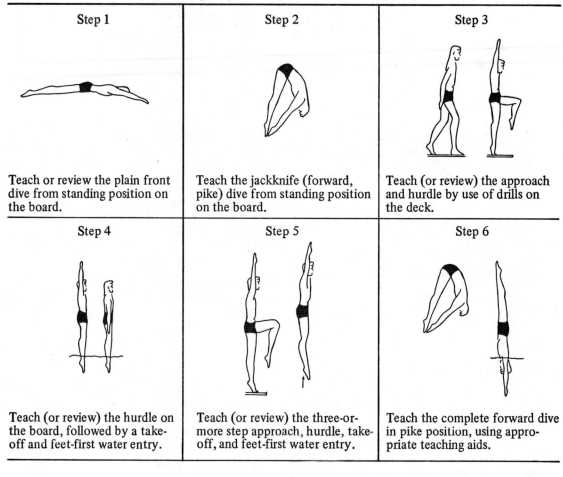

Step 1	Step 2	Step 3
Teach or review the plain front dive from standing position on the board.	Teach the jackknife (forward, pike) dive from standing position on the board.	Teach (or review) the approach and hurdle by use of drills on the deck.
Step 4	Step 5	Step 6
Teach (or review) the hurdle on the board, followed by a take-off and feet-first water entry.	Teach (or review) the three-or-more step approach, hurdle, take-off, and feet-first water entry.	Teach the complete forward dive in pike position, using appropriate teaching aids.

BACKWARD DIVE COMPONENTS

The components of backward dives are the starting position, the takeoff, the flight, and the entry. A major distinguishing characteristic of these dives is that the starting position is taken at the diving end of the board and facing the shore end of the board. In general, the same techniques of takeoff, flight, and entry apply to the backward dive as have been described for the forward dive from the standing position.

Starting Position

Because the dive in competition does not start officially until the diver is in position (arms lowered, feet at end of board), there is no specific method of turning. However, most divers walk to the diving end of the board and place one foot at the end of the board. He or she then pivots on that foot to turn away from the water, in the direction of the pivot foot. As the diver pivots, the arms are raised perpendicular to the body. As the pivot is completed, the other foot is placed in position. Although the diver may then extend the arms overhead, the almost universal practice is to slowly lower the arms to the sides (Chart 5.13).

Chart 5.13. Assumption of the Starting Position for Back Dives

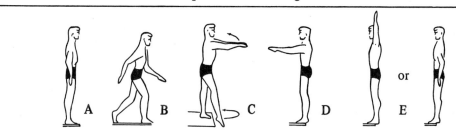

Takeoff

To execute the takeoff, the diver extends the ankles and rises to the toes as the arms are raised forward, upward, and backward. He or she bends at the hips, knees, and ankles as the arms continue to circle backward and downward; these combined actions place the diver in position to spring upward as the arms are brought forward and upward and the hips, knees, and ankles extended to place the body in a straight position (Chart 5.14).

Crow hopping is the lifting of one or both feet from the board after the board is depressed and the subsequent pounding or pressing of the feet down on the board. It is a habit the instructor must prevent the learner from acquiring. Not only is it a telltale sign of inexperience, but its use in competition will require the diving judges to subtract points from the evaluation.

Chart 5.14. Takeoff for Back Dives

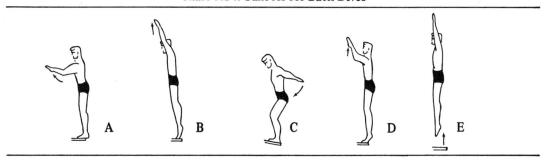

Flight

Because the back dive is performed without the advantage that the hurdle contributes to other dives, it must be completed in less time and with less height. The temptation to hurry the performance will be great, and if the diver succumbs to that urge, the quality of flight will suffer accordingly.

Entry

The techniques of entry for the back dives are essentially the same as for the forward dives. Chart 5.15 shows entries may result from technical errors in takeoff and flight. These errors are the result of the body not rotating properly around its center of gravity. Too much upward swing or dropping the head back will result in a "long" dive, i.e., the legs will go past the desired vertical entry position. Conversely, too little spring or not dropping the head enough will prevent proper rotation, thus causing a "short" dive.

Chart 5.15. Short and Long Back Dives

Short back dive   Long back dive

THE BACK DIVE IN LAYOUT POSITION

The back dive, in addition to being one required of the competitive diver, is one that most novices want to learn. It involves some degree of daring, but performance techniques are relatively simple.

Such difficulty as may be attached to learning of the back dive is due primarily to the back-down position of the diver and, consequently, to the inability to see the water during most of the time consumed in the performance of the dive. Performance is sure to be faulty when the learner loses confidence during the dive and fails to do as he or she has been told. The learner must have the mind set to follow exactly the directions given by the instructor. Chart 5.16 shows techniques for performing the dive and indicates performance errors that may occur.

Practice of the back dive from the deck is unwise because a long dive (where the diver's legs go over too far) may direct the diver into the wall. Although space is rather inadequate to accommodate both learner and teacher, instruction should take place on the diving board. Chart 5.17 illustrates an effective teaching progression.

WRITTEN ASSIGNMENTS

1. Prepare a thirty-minute lesson plan for the presentation of one dive. Include objectives, materials, and equipment needed; safety precautions, teaching aids, methods for group organization and control, information to be given and leading questions, and the time schedule for the period.

Chart 5.16. Performance Techniques for the Back Dive in Layout Position

Techniques	Illustration	Performance Errors	Illustration
A. At takeoff, have the body in a straight line and extend arms overhead. In a continuing flowing movement, drift the arms from overhead position to a position sideward and slightly backward, and extend them sideward from the body. Elevate the chest to lead the rise. Press the hips upward and press the shoulders backward. Assume a slight arch in the back.	A	A. The backward lean on takeoff is excessive (1); entry is back first (2) or stomach first (3). The back arch assumed is too great; the learner tends to somersault. The body does not stretch for height on takeoff. Time to complete the dive is too limited. The chest and hips do not press upward as arms are placed in position sideward from shoulders; there is little force to cause the body to invert to head-down position.	A.1 A.2 A.3
B. Permit the hips to continue to rise and become the pivot point until the straight legs rise into a position overhead.	B C	B. The upward press of hips is too great (thus, the entry is long) (A.3). The knees bend during flight (1). The hips bend during flight (2).	B.1 B.2
C. During the early part of the downward flight, tilt the head backward to permit sight of the water.	D	C. The arms are not precisely level and identical in position, the head is turned to one side, so that the body tends to twist (1).	C.1
D. Before entry is made, bring the arms from sideward position to a position of full extension in advance of the head, and return the head to normal (erect) position.		D. The chin is pressed to the chest, the upper back is bowed, and arms are raised upward as confidence is lost, so that entry is back first (1).	D.1

Chart 5.17. Teaching Progression for the Back Dive in Layout Position

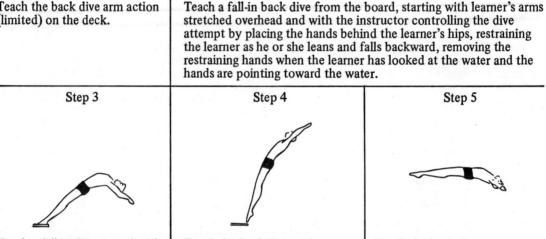

Step 1	Step 2
Teach the back dive arm action (limited) on the deck.	Teach a fall-in back dive from the board, starting with learner's arms stretched overhead and with the instructor controlling the dive attempt by placing the hands behind the learner's hips, restraining the learner as he or she leans and falls backward, removing the restraining hands when the learner has looked at the water and the hands are pointing toward the water.

Step 3	Step 4	Step 5
Teach a fall-in dive started with learner's arms stretched overhead and completed without instructor's assistance.	Teach the back dive with learner's arms stretched overhead and with gentle spring from the board.	Teach the back dive, starting with learner's arms at his sides and following with correct arm and leg action and conventional takeoff.

2. Prepare a report on the use of visual aids in teaching diving.

3. Using the analysis sheets in Appendix B, evaluate a diver's performance on the dives shown in this chapter. Discuss the results, demonstrate the correct techniques, and attempt to eliminate all errors.

BEHAVIORAL OBJECTIVES

Because many swimming instructors will also teach basic springboard diving, we expect our students to be able to respond correctly (based on material in this chapter) to questions calling for brief written answers or diagrams, as indicated below.

1. Discuss the attributes a beginning diver should have.
2. Diagram four dive groups (do not include the twist group).
3. Diagram the layout, pike, and tuck dive positions.

4. Discuss at least one of the safety precautions to be taken by the diving instructor.
5. Discuss at least two teaching aids that may be used when instructing divers.
6. Name, in order of occurrence, the parts of a running springboard dive.
7. Discuss diving entries, including what may affect them, the meaning of "long" and "short," and the position of the body immediately prior to entry.
8. Indicate four performance errors of which a learner may be guilty for any one dive described in this chapter.
9. Give a description of correct performance of any one dive described in this chapter.

REFERENCES

Amateur Athletic Union. *Official Handbook: Swimming, Diving, Water Polo.* New York: Amateur Athletic Union, 1979.

American National Red Cross. *Swimming and Water Safety.* Washington, D.C.: American National Red Cross, 1968, Chapter 8.

Barone, Marian. *Beginning Diving.* Palo Alto, Calif.: National Press, 1973.

Batterman, Charles. *The Techniques of Springboard Diving.* Cambridge, Mass.: MIT Press, 1977.

Madura, John P., and Kise, Brian J. "Basic Training Techniques for Springboard Diving." *JOPER,* October 1976, pp. 70-74.

Wilson, Robert N., and Cramer, John L. "Coaching Safe Springboard Diving." *JOPER,* April 1974, pp. 71-73.

CHAPTER 6

Performing and Teaching Lifesaving Skills

In this chapter we discuss the content of the two standard lifesaving courses taught in the United States by the American Red Cross and the YMCA. All skills required for either course are covered, as well as others we feel have special application to lifesavers. You will note that we require our students to perform any of the skills with a partner of approximately equal size. The reason for this is obvious, when you consider that males are usually stronger and less buoyant—and thus the most difficult to help.

You, and your students, should not confuse the lifesaving course with lifeguarding. This chapter is designed to develop the personal safety skills of swimmers. Many of the techniques shown are used by lifeguards, but the lifesaving student will use them only if qualified professional help is not available.

Since most readers will already have completed an advanced lifesaving course, the description of lifesaving techniques will be relatively brief. But we hope to remind you of the correct form. Complete descriptions of all techniques are given in the publications by the ARC, YMCA, and Lanoue, and represent the final word in relation to a specific course.

BASIC THOUGHTS BEFORE TEACHING A LIFESAVING CLASS

A certain amount of thinking must be done before teaching any class, and lifesaving is no exception. An instructor must first decide who to accept. It is obvious that all certified lifesavers should be strong swimmers. But, in the beginning of every class, some weak swimmers vow that they will be able to swim much better in a short time. True—but will they be improved enough? It is much better to reject, or later fail, the weak swimmers than it is to pass them. They conceivably may be in a situation they cannot handle. Some instructors permit only strong swimmers to begin their classes. Skills such as self-rescue and equipment rescue, would undoubtedly be of value to weak swimmers, but they should not attempt assists, carries, releases, and other, more difficult lifesaving actions.

ARC requires that before starting the advanced lifesaving course, the person should be able to swim 500 yards without stopping. Many prospective lifesavers consider this requirement too stringent and claim that they are just "temporarily" out of shape. It is true that after a good lifesaving class all persons could swim 500 yards with little or no trouble—but would they retain their physical condition? We feel that anyone who cannot swim this distance on the first day of lifesaving class is not yet ready for the class.

On the other hand, it must be admitted that this class could represent the first aquatic course in some time and that the student could swim the distance after a few practice sessions. If permitted to remain, the student could learn a great deal and be much safer in the water. If there are not too many in the class, one solution to this problem might be as follows: let all enrollees remain, but give the 500-yard test within a week after the first session. Anyone who fails must then leave the class.

In lifesaving classes, little stress is placed on performing the strokes with correct form. If a student uses a scissors kick for the breaststroke in the tired swimmer's carry, nothing is said. In lifesaving, strength of movement and ability to complete the task is emphasized. However, do not let an incorrect stroke go without comment. Many lifesavers do not know the correct form for certain strokes (the breaststroke, especially). As an instructor of an advanced swimmer or instructor-trainer course, you will quickly find that possession of a lifesaving certificate does not mean that the student swims all strokes correctly, or even strongly.

Most lifesaving classes are composed of both boys and girls. This may lead to some social problems, but not if the instructor takes preventive action first. Sometimes a student (or parent) will complain that another student is using the hands more than necessary during the class. The best way to forestall any problems in this area is to tell the whole class at the beginning that at the first sign of any misconduct the person responsible will be asked to leave. This usually prevents all problems; if not, make good on your promise.

As the course continues, there will be more skill on the part of the students—and more struggling by the victims. This can be dangerous, so it is wise to establish some sort of a warning system when one of the partners wants to cease the struggle. Usually, a pinch system is agreed upon; that is, when pinched twice in rapid succession by a partner, separate immediately.

GENERAL APPROACHES TO TEACHING A LIFESAVING CLASS

Teaching lifesaving skills is really no different than teaching other aquatic skills. The instructor should first explain the skill to be learned and then demonstrate it both on land and in the water. Most authorities recommend that students practice first on land, then in the water. Practice, obviously, must occur under the watchful eye of the instructor ready to correct mistakes. Each session should include a review of skills previously learned, preferably in some new situation. Several suggestions throughout this chapter illustrate different practice situations; use them to add variety to your instruction.

The skills should be practiced in logical combinations. For example, a better combination for one session is approach stroking, underwater approach, the armpit, the level-off, and the cross-chest carry than the front surface approach, the rear approach, and the underwater approach. By practicing in logical combinations, the student sees how the separate skills conjoin to form effective means of rescue.

A lifesaving course should include a lot of swimming. It should be a vigorous course from the start. The early classes should begin with swimming lengths, featuring those strokes and adaptations that are part of lifesaving. In the middle and later stages of the course, carrying or towing the partner will increase endurance because of the extra weight to be moved. We have found that swimming lengths in one big circle (faster swimmers to the inside, slower ones nearer the edge) is better than swimming in assigned lanes. There is no excuse for stopping when a large circle is used. Swimming lengths with fins or towing rescue tubes, can buoys, or ring buoys will simulate a realistic situation, and help condition students. Pulling and kicking lengths is good, because it forces swimmers to work on all parts of their strokes.

In the early parts of the course, much stress should be put on fast approach stroking. If the group is young or in especially poor physical condition, then one or two days of slow swimming would be acceptable, but why let students swim slowly when they will not be doing so in a real situation? People learn by practicing correctly. You can set time standards for your pool in approach stroking, carrying, or almost any other phase of the course. This is an incentive for students and may be used for grading purposes if desired. For example, all lifesavers should be able to swim 100 yards of approach stroking (using acceptable form) in less than two minutes. In the later stages of the course, approach stroking is less important as a conditioning device when compared to towing a struggling victim.

Short, unannounced exams are a legitimate part of the course. You know from experience that it is easier to teach something if students have studied beforehand. Why not see to it that your students have studied by outlining the next session, and then occasionally seeing if they have studied? This has obvious uses in grading, but there really is a more utilitarian use—encouraging preparedness.

The Red Cross and the YMCA have outlined a daily lesson plan for teaching lifesaving courses (see References). These plans have been developed by experienced instructors. We recommend that you follow one plan or the other until you have gained experience in teaching lifesaving. Even then, you may not want to deviate from these tested plans.

Another decision to make before starting the course is whether you will enter the water yourself for testing purposes. Some instructors refuse because they cannot observe the class as easily, or because they just cannot stand the physical rigors of the testing situation. Other instructors feel that this is the only way to be certain that the victim struggles enough to make it a good examination. However, bringing in some outside victims will provide victims who truly struggle and will enable the instructor to watch and to evaluate.

ESSENTIAL LIFESAVING SKILLS

An advanced lifesaving course can be divided into twelve elements, as listed. The titles and sequence vary, but the YMCA and ARC courses are substantially the same.

1. Personal safety and self-rescue
2. Reaching and equipment rescues
3. Swimming skills for lifesaving
4. Swimming assists
5. Approaches and level-offs
6. Carries and tows
7. Defenses, releases, and escapes
8. Search and rescue
9. Removing victim from water
10. Resuscitation
11. First aid
12. Small craft safety (ARC only)

These twelve categories are examined in this chapter. Unless specifically indicated, all skills shown are required in either the ARC or YMCA lifesaving course. To obtain a certificate, students in our regular lifesaving classes must pass the final skill and written examination required by either the ARC or YMCA.

We have also included some skills that are not required in the standard courses. We think they are of value and teach them in our classes, but they are not part of the examination for certified aquatic workers. Specific behavioral objectives objectives for all skills will be found at the end of the chapter.

PERSONAL SAFETY AND SELF-RESCUE SKILLS

Personal safety skills are based on common sense, so many instructors choose not to spend valuable class time teaching them. But, these skills are necessary for the lifesaver—they can be learned quickly and should be practiced frequently. In chapter 3 we described survival floating, floating on the back, the elementary backstroke, the use of personal flotation devices, treading water, swimming, and release of cramps. The ARC lifesaving course requires that the last three skills be done while wearing clothes. Clothing inflation methods were discussed in Chapter 4. All of the personal safety skills are required in the YMCA and ARC courses in lifesaving, except use of personal flotation devices, which only ARC requires.

REACHING AND EQUIPMENT RESCUE

There is a saying in lifesaving courses that the preferred sequence of rescue is *"Reach* first, *throw* if you can, and then *go* if you must." This point must be repeated continually because, to many, the glamorous part of lifesaving is plunging in and effecting a personal rescue. It is also the most dangerous. Therefore, reaching for a victim or throwing something are much better forms of rescue. Although not usually stressed at this point in a lifesaving course, the teaching of the principle of "keep your eyes on the victim" must begin at this time.

Reaching assists may be less heroic, but they are the best and safest kind of rescue. Literally anything can be used—a towel, stick, board, piece of clothing, arms. Chart 6.1 discusses the reaching and wading assists.

Throwing a ring buoy accurately, whether or not it has an attached line, is difficult for most lifesavers. Chart 6.2 shows how the ring buoy should be used. A one-gallon plastic jug, with an inch of water in the bottom, can be used as a rescue device also.

Chart 6.1. Performance Techniques for Reaching Assists

Techniques	Illustration	Performance Errors
A. Keep center of gravity low and and behind edge of dock, deck or shore. B. Keep weight back as far as possible.		A. Placing center of gravity too high. B. Placing weight on forward foot.
C. Rescuers face opposite directions as they grasp each other's forearms. Spread legs; keep body leaning in direction of safety. D. Wade to shoulder depth. Grasp victim's wrist.		C. Failing to spread legs and plant feet firmly (thus, being pulled off balance). Failing to have body leaning back toward safety. D. Failing to have firm grip on pool or dock side.

Unless indicated otherwise, all skills depicted in the charts in this chapter are required in both the ARC and the YMCA courses. Because requirements vary, consultation with the latest publications of the organization is recommended.

Chart 6.2. Performance Techniques for Throwing the Ring Buoy or Heaving Jug

Techniques	Illustration (Right-handed Thrower)	Performance Errors
A. Keep hand virtually flat so that rope can easily leave the hand.		A. Grasping rope tightly.
B. Foot opposite throwing arm is forward. Grasp buoy in throwing hand, hold rope in other. Step on end of rope with foot opposite throwing arm. Use underhand throw (unless deck railing interferes).		B. Reversing foot position. Failing to step on rope end, thus permitting entire rope to be drawn into water.
C. Release buoy at eye level. Follow through with throwing arm.		C. Releasing buoy too soon (resulting in low throw) or too high (resulting in too short a throw).
D. Aim so that buoy hits beyond the victim.		D. Throwing in front of victim; throwing downstream or downwind from victim.
E. Throw up-current, let buoy drift down to victim.		E. Throwing downcurrent, causing buoy to be carried out of reach.
F. Tell victim to put one arm through hole in center. Slowly reel line in, keeping weight on rear foot.		F. Jerking the line, causing the victim to lose grasp.

The proper technique for advancing a free-floating support into position for a rescue depends on the equipment and the swimmer. The rescuer should either push or pull the support until he or she comes close to (but not next to) the victim. The victim is told to grab one end of the support but not to climb onto it. Talking continuously to the victim will tend be reassuring and cause cooperation. During the return, the rescuer will usually use the breaststroke kick or a scissors kick. During the tow, the rescuer must watch the victim to make certain that all is well.

Both clothing and rescueboards are very effective in helping victims. Chart 6.3 depicts effective techniques for both.

A rescue tube is an invaluable piece of equipment. It can be towed quickly to a victim. Then it can be used either for a reaching assist or as a free-floating support. Chart 6.4 depicts this essential rescue device.

Essentially, teaching these skills is a matter of explanation, demonstration, and supervised practice. For some items, continual daily practice is needed. We hope that most lifesavers will "reach" or "throw" before they "go." Yet, in most lifesaving courses only about 2 percent of the time is spent on these forms of rescue. It is no wonder that students forget that they are to reach, then throw. After the first

Chart 6.3. Performance Techniques for the Use of Clothing and Rescueboards as Free-Floating Supports

Techniques	Illustration	Performance Errors
A. Place inflated clothing under legs (or arm) of victim. If two rescuers available, one supports victim while other inflates clothes.	 A	A. Forcing air out of the clothing by putting all of victim's weight upon the inflated article.
B. Grasp forearms of victim; use surfboard as support.	 B	B. Failing to grasp victim securely.
C. Use a rescueboard to bring victim ashore.		
1. Turn board upside down. Get victim on side of board opposite rescuer. Grasp victim's forearm with one hand, the far side of the board with the other.	 C.1	C. 1. Failing to turn board upside down before grasping victim.
2. Roll board toward self, pulling victim on top of it.	 C.2	2. Failing to grasp the victim's forearm tightly enough.
3. Turn victim so legs are atop the board. Paddle to safety.	 C.3	3. Failing to place victim completely on top of the board.

Chart 6.4. Performance Techniques for the Rescue Tube

Techniques	Illustration	Performance Errors
Throwing Tube A. With tube buckled and non-throwing hand grasping shoulder strap, throw underhand to victim.	 A	A. Rescuer being pulled into water because weight not kept back on hind foot.
Swim, Extend, Tow B. Wearing unbuckled tube, enter water with lifesaving jump. If run from beach, carry tube by grasping it in middle. C. Swim to victim.	 B C	B. Improper form for strike jump. Dragging tube on beach before entering water. C. Improper form for approach stroking.

Chart 6.4—*continued*

Techniques	Illustration	Performance Errors
D. Extend tube, then tow victim to safety. Can grasp near end of tube or tow with shoulder strap.	D	D. Failing to observe victim at all times.
Tube as Support E. Victim leans over tube slightly and brings it to chest as rescuer swims behind.	E F	E. Victim grasps tubes with hands, not close to chest.
F. Grasp ends of tube, firmly pull together behind back of victim. Snap buckle to close belt.		F. Failing to snap buckle together on first attempt.
G. Tow as before, with victim on back.	G	G. Failing to watch victim.

two sessions, these skills are not usually practiced! The best way to ingrain these rescues into the minds of lifesavers is to have a daily practice session on at least one of the skills. At first, the instructor will have to direct this practice, but soon the students will do it as a part of the daily warmup.

Learning reaching, wading, and free-floating rescues is easiest with a partner. After explanation and demonstration, the class divides into two groups; the members of one group act as the victims. All possible situations should be practiced. The instructor can have a number of warm-up situations to suggest. Sample warm-ups are:

1. Partner is four feet from side in water eight feet deep. Jump in, grab gutter with one hand, and extend leg to victim; pull to safety. Or, dive in, push partner (from behind) to safety.
2. Partner is directly under end of one-meter board. Standing as close to partner as possible, throw the rescue tube; pull to safety.
3. Partner is in middle of pool. Grab the nearest loose kickboard and use it for the rescue.

Start with a short underhand throw (ten feet) and limited follow-through in learning to throw the ring buoy or heaving jug. After gaining accuracy, practice throwing to a partner who moves farther away. Because most pools or beaches have only two to three buoys at the most, it is difficult for everyone to get adequate practice. The instructor can designate one couple to practice five throws each before a class and another to practice five throws after the class. Thus, four students per day will practice throwing the buoy. However the available equipment is used, remember that students cannot get too much practice on this skill. When an uneven number of students are in class, the odd person can practice throwing the buoy while the others are practicing tows, releases, or other rescue skills. Throwing *must* be practiced, or the lifesaver may forget to do it in a dangerous situation.

SWIMMING SKILLS FOR LIFESAVING

Swimming skills are the foundation for the lifesaving course, and must be taught early and well. Swimming exercises can be used as warm-up throughout the course.

In lifesaving swimming, the rescuer should enter the water with a jump or a shallow dive. Because the cardinal rule is to keep the eyes on the victim, a jump is preferred. But the jump has a serious disadvantage: it takes longer to reach the victim because of no forward momentum. Both entry forms should be learned. Chart 6.5 discusses these forms of entry.

Chart 6.5. Performance Techniques for Lifesaving Takeoffs

Techniques	Illustration	Performance Errors
Stride Jump A. Leap outward with head and hips forward of legs, legs spread, arms well away from body, eyes on victim. B. Upon contact with water, squeeze legs and then press down with arms. Keep head above water; keep eyes on victim.	 A B	A. Entering water in erect position, without any forward lean. B. Permitting head to go underwater, losing sight of victim.
Shallow Water Dive C. Lean off-balance forward. Keep eyes on victim as long as possible. D. Thrust arms forward vigorously; lower the head at last possible moment; enter water at slight angle downward. E. Come to surface as soon as possible. Begin approach stroking.	C D E	C. Failing to keep eyes on victim. D. Failing to watch victim as long as possible. Entering water at a steep angle. E. Remaining under water longer than necessary.

Approach stroking is the means of reaching the victim. The crawl stroke or breast stroke are both effective, but two requirements must always be fulfilled—to keep your eye on the victim and arrive quickly with energy to spare. The crawl stroke, with head up, is usually considered the best stroke for this purpose. It is faster and not as tiring to the rescuer. Keeping the head up while swimming this stroke does not call for drastic alterations; the feet usually will kick deeper in the water because the back is arched, but this is of no great consequence. The breaststroke is usually the second-preferred stroke; it is a slower stroke, though for swimmers with a poor flutter kick it could be faster.

The quick reverse is a skill taught only in lifesaving classes. The consequences of doing it poorly are grave, because the victim will surely grasp the rescuer if he can. The correct procedure is shown in Chart 6.6.

When towing a victim, an inverted scissors kick is almost always used. The usual scissors kick tends to become tangled in the legs of the victim during a cross-chest carry; for this reason the inverted kick may be used.

Chart 6.6. Performance Techniques for the Quick Reverses

Techniques	Illustration	Performance Errors
Front Reverse A. Approach within 3 feet of victim. Stop forward momentum.	A	A. Getting too close (thus, permitting victim to grab rescuer). Failing to stop (thus, drifting into victim). Stopping too far away (thus, having to swim closer).
B. Shift body weight by leaning back, tucking legs ahead of hips. Extend legs into position for scissors or breaststroke kicks. Extend one arm backward, ready for pulling.	B	B. Making contact before legs and arm are ready to propel rescuer toward safety.
Rear Reverse C. Approach within 2 feet of victim. Stop forward momentum.	C	C. Getting too close. Failing to stop (thus, drifting into victim). Stopping too far away (thus, having to swim closer).
D. Shift body weight by leaning back. Prepare legs to deliver scissors or breaststroke kicks. Prepare one arm to pull toward safety.	D	D. Making contact before legs and arm are ready to propel rescuer toward safety.

The modified breaststroke necessary for lifesaving is nothing more than a "heads up, back arched" position. This eliminates any appreciable glide, but does provide visibility and stability for the tired swimmer carry, and, during approach stroking, helps the rescuer to keep his or her eyes on the victim.

A rescuer may sometimes tow a victim on the back; this calls for the strongest possible kick. It can be done several ways, as long as the rescuer is partially "sitting up" and looking at the victim at all times. This body position will naturally cause the body to bend at the hips and the kick to be deeper than usual.

Chart 6.7 depicts the modifications necessary in the sidestroke, breaststroke, and supine kicking.

The swimming skills necessary to lifesaving can be taught and practiced in the following sequence: entry, approach stroking, quick reverse, towing. Once the first two skills are learned, they can be practiced. Then the third can be added, and so on. The main teaching progression should be the usual pattern of explanation, demonstration, practice under supervision, and review.

One of the best ways to add meaning to this whole sequence of skills is to time students for various segments. For example, any lifesaver should be able to enter the water and approach stroke for sixty feet within thirty seconds. Standards for your particular lake or pool can be set up or records can be kept

Chart 6.7. Lifesaving Performance Techniques for Sidestroke, Breaststroke, and Supine Kick

Techniques	Illustration	Performance Errors
Sidestroke A. Use the sidestroke shallow arm pull and the inverted scissors kick.	A	A. Bringing top leg forward (as in the regular scissors kick).
Breaststroke B. Arch back so that head is completely out of water at all times.	B	B. Failing to have head up far enough to permit the eyes to always remain on victim.
Supine Kick C. Use either a scissors, whip or wedge kick. Have feet much deeper than usual. Keep eyes on victim.	C	C. Entangling feet with those of victim. Taking eyes off victim.

(e.g., best time ever recorded, best average time by a particular class, best time for each sex, best time using breaststroke). The same procedure could be followed for the towing drill, either with or without a victim.

An excellent conditioning method, which also is a good drill because it features work on one skill at a time, is width swimming in deep water as follows:

1. Groups A and B on opposite sides in deep water, instructor in middle on shore or diving board.
2. Instructor gives specific directions to each group: "Group A—feet-first surface dive, swim under water to other side, Group B—breaststroke approach stroking," or "Group A—towing an imaginary victim with inverted scissors kick, Group B—pike surface dive and underwater swim."
3. Each group leaves its base at the same time and as they near each other, performs as directed.
4. Repeat, with appropriate variations, for two minutes at first, gradually going up to five minutes. As the group becomes strong, have them tread water at each side instead of grabbing pool or dock.

This drill may also illustrate poor teaching. As students become tired, they tend to perform the surface dives or strokes improperly or fail to swim underwater the required distance. Some instructors overlook these matters, concentrating instead on the conditioning aspects of the drill. If there are sound reasons why strokes or dives should be done in a particular manner, then it is poor teaching to let violations occur without telling the swimmer. Working the group to exhaustion is not the way to perfect skills.

SWIMMING ASSISTS

Even though a rescuer has to enter the water to assist a victim, he or she still should try to avoid the more ostentatious holds and carries. The less physical contact made with the victim, the safer the rescuer is. Even more important, if the victim can get to safety without being towed or carried, a valuable lesson has been learned—if the swimmer doesn't panic the dangerous and embarrassing predicament can be avoided next time.

One frequently overlooked method of assisting a swimmer to safety is pushing or shoving. Frequently, a swimmer is within six feet from the pool edge or shallow water. It really doesn't make much sense to use the tired swimmer carry or the chin pull for such a short distance if an easier and equally safe method can be used. The pushing technique is done exactly as its name implies—the rescuer places his or her hands on the hips, upper body, or arm of the victim and pushes toward safety. The pushing technique is especially effective in pools where there is a solid bottom for the rescuer to push-off from, and a definite pool edge for the victim to grab.

The easiest way to help a victim in deep water consists of some sort of support and propulsion by the rescuer. Regardless of whether the armpit assist (YMCA) or the arm assists (ARC) are used, the rescuer should encourage the swimmer to kick and move the arms. Two rescuers should be involved, if possible. These techniques are shown in Chart 6.8.

Chart 6.8. Performance Techniques for Swimming Assists

Techniques	Illustration	Performance Errors
Armpit Assist (Front) (YMCA Only) A. With swimmer on stomach, rescuer places hand under near armpit. Swimmer is towed to safety.	 A	A. Failing to achieve sufficient momentum (inducing panic in swimmer). Lifting swimmer's shoulder out of water. Failing to verbally encourage swimmer.
Arm Assist (Front) B. Rescuer grasps (thumb up) back of upper arm (near armpit) of swimmer. Assist by pushing swimmer.	 B	B. Placing rescuer's hand on top of swimmer's arm. Failing to achieve sufficient momentum. Failing to verbally encourage swimmer.
Arm Assist (Back) C. Same as arm assist (front) except that swimmer is on back. Assist by pushing swimmer (ARC) or towing (YMCA).	 C	C. Placing rescuer's hand on top of swimmer's arm. Failing to achieve sufficient momentum. Failing to verbally encourage swimmer.
Arm Assist (Two Rescuers) D. Same as B or C above, one rescuer at each armpit. (Called tandem tow by YMCA).	 D	D. Same as B or C above.

Chart 6.8—*continued*

Techniques	Illustration	Performance Errors
Leg Support Assist (YMCA Only) E. With victim on back, place his or her calves on rescuer's shoulders. Victim crosses ankles behind rescuer's head. Rescuer swims breaststroke, pushing victim toward safety. *Note:* Use in calm water only.	E	E. Not having victim completely on his or her back before placing legs on rescuer's shoulder.

The tired swimmer carry is really a pushing movement, and thus can be classified as a swimming assist. As Chart 6.9 shows, the rescuer approaches the victim from the front and begins a continual stream of encouraging words as soon as possible. Interspersing these comments ("Let me help you a bit," "This won't take very long") with directions ("Put your hands on my shoulders," "Look at the sky," "Keep your arms straight") the rescuer swims smoothly to the victim and makes contact. The rescuer usually must make a wide turn in order to head for safety. It is easier to swim if the victim's legs are split on either side of the rescuer's body; but for the beginning lifesaver, this is not advisable because it can lead to a body scissors if the victim becomes panicky.

Lanoue (1963, pp. 47–50) argued that the traditional tired swimmer carry is not a very effective way of performing the task. In the traditional method, the temptation is great for the victim to press down on the rescuer's shoulders. Lanoue pointed out that in rough water, where breathing is difficult, a terrific physical strain is placed on the rescuer unless the rescuer and victim both hold their heads high. He further said that if the victim should get water in his mouth, the natural reaction is going to be to hug the rescuer tightly. Therefore, Lanoue advocated a position where the rescuer pushes the victim but does not allow the victim to make contact except with the feet. Chart 6.9 also depicts Lanoue's variation of the tired swimmer carry.

Chart 6.9. Performance Techniques for the Tired Swimmer Carry

Techniques	Illustration	Performance Errors
Traditional A. Approach victim and begin reassuring talk.	A	A. Failing to talk before making contact with victim.
B. Tell victim to put head back, place hands on rescuer's shoulders, look at sky, put both legs to one side of rescuer, keep arms straight. *Note:* Victim's legs can be spread if desired, one on each side of rescuer.	B	B. Permitting victim to sit in water, or raise head, or lay head back too far, or bend arms.

Chart 6.9—*continued*

Techniques	Illustration	Performance Errors
C. Continue to swim (breast-stroke) and talk.	C	C. Swimming a stroke that causes victim's hands to slip from rescuer's shoulders. (e.g., crawl stroke, sidestroke) Surging ahead with a powerful stroke, and then dropping back so as to cause loss of contact.
D. Change direction of victim by grasping one elbow, continue stroking with other hand.	D	D. Turning in wrong direction. Turning too sharply causing loss of momentum.
Variation (Lanoue) E. Approach victim and begin reassuring talk.	E	E. Failing to talk before making contact with victim.
F. Tell victim to put head back. arms at side, thrust chest toward sky, look at sky.	F	F. Permitting victim to sit in water, or raise head, or lay head back too far, or bend arms.
G. Grasp victim's ankles; kick two or three times to gain momentum. (If distance is short, continue kicking until safety is reached.)	G	G. Failing to gain momentum.
H. Place victim's toes inside waistband of suit, bend his or her knees slightly (or place toes in shoulder straps). Keep eyes on victim.	H	H. Failing to place toes securely to prevent loss of contact. Failing to keep eyes on victim.
I. Use drownproofing technique for traveling a distance.	I	I. Submerging excessively (inducing panic because victim thinks he or she is sinking).

At least two problems may arise when using the tired swimmer assist. If a great distance is involved, the rescuer may become tired; thus, the YMCA advocates a tired swimmer support. Also, the victim may decide he or she does not like to be on the back, and suddenly grab the rescuer tightly around the neck and clamp the legs in a body scissors around the rescuer's waist. If safety is close at hand, the rescuer should attempt to continue swimming without trying to release the hold. Chart 6.10 depicts both the tired swimmer support and the front head-hold body scissors assist.

Chart 6.10. Performance Techniques for the Tired Swimmer Support and the Front Head-Hold Body Scissors Assist

Techniques	Illustration	Performance Errors
Tired Swimmer Support (YMCA Only) A. Rescuer moves to vertical position, has victim lay back in water and slide arms to extended overhead position (underwater). Victim's legs rise toward surface, lodging in armpits of rescuer. B. Rescuer lays on back, uses kick (scissors, inverted breast) and easy hand scull in order to keep both persons afloat.	A B	A. Failure to talk calmly and give clear instructions to victim. B. Failure of victim to lay back completely.
Front Head-Hold Body Scissors Assist (YMCA Only) C. Rescuer keeps face above water, stroke and kick fast, swim toward safety. If rescuer cannot receive sufficient air, a release from the hold must be effected.	C	C. Failure to attempt to swim toward safety first, before trying to release hold.

Since the first responsibility of the instructor is to teach the skills advocated by the organization (ARC, YMCA, or other), the traditional methods of assisting the tired swimmer must be taught. However, it is our opinion that the shoving method and Lanoue's technique for the tired swimmer carry should be practiced, if only to make lifesavers aware that there are several ways to achieve a particular objective. If time permits, the students should be given an opportunity to swim a distance (say, 300 yards) and see which of the tired swimmer methods is less tiring. Lanoue says that ". . . under average conditions, the rescuer, who is exhausted at a few hundred yards with standard techniques, will be quite comfortable after half a mile using this different technique." (Lanoue, 1963, p. 49). Is he right? If the distance to be covered is great, it is important for the lifesaver to know.

Many drills can be used to aid learners in perfecting the tired swimmer carry. Some of these are summarized in Chart 6.11. In addition, each instructor probably will develop his or her own.

Chart 6.11. Practicing the Tired Swimmer Carry

Techniques	Illustration	Purpose
A. In deep water, two students face one another and place their hands on each other's shoulders. At the signal each tries to force the other's head underwater.		A. Develops kicking power and endurance.
B. Swim 100–200 yards in non-stop circle formation, carrying a tired swimmer.		B. Develops ability to turn without losing contact.
C. Swim 50–100 yards in a non-stop circle formation, carrying a tired swimmer. Rescuer must talk almost all the time. If talking stops for more than 10 seconds, victim applies front head-hold and body scissors. Rescuer must release hold and continue.		C. Develops habit of continual talking. Develops endurance.
D. Swim 100–200 yards (circle formation, nonstop). Victim presses down on rescuer's shoulders as rescuer swims and talks.		D. Develops endurance.

All techniques can be made more difficult either by increasing distances, using nonfloaters, or using partners who weigh considerably more than the rescuers.

APPROACHES AND LEVEL-OFFS

The two most important things to stress in this category are:

1. The approach is designed to put the rescuer in position for a level-off which is moving a victim from a vertical position to a horizontal one from which he or she can be assisted, towed, or carried to safety. The level-off, though technically not a part of the approach, is for all practical purposes the final result in this category.
2. The rear and front surface approaches must include a satisfactory reverse.

The rear approach is preferred over all others, for the obvious reason that the rescuer cannot be easily grabbed by the swimmer. After approaching to within two feet of the person, the rescuer reverses (described earlier in Chart 6.6C and 6.6D), applies a level-off, and carries the person in this fashion until shifting to one of the regular carries. Chart 6.12 summarizes the rear approach, ending in one of the level-offs.

For the chin pull or grasp described in ARC or YMCA texts, the cupped hand of the rescuer is placed on the chin of the victim. The rescuer tilts the victim's head back and goes to a carry once the

Chart 6.12. Performance Techniques for the Rear Approach and Alternate Level-offs

Techniques	Illustration	Performance Errors
A. Approach within 2 feet of victim. Perform quick reverse. (See Chart 6.6C and 6.6D.)	 A	A. Approaching too closely. Failing to stop (thus, drifting into victim). Stopping too far away.
B. *Armpit level-off.* Rescuer reaches with forward arm, grasps underneath upper arm (near armpit) of swimmer. Talk to swimmer reassuringly. Tow swimmer to safety or go to a regular carry.	 B	B. Grasping top of upper arm. Failure to talk to swimmer.
C. Chin pull. Quickly put arm closest to victim over his shoulder.	 C.1	C. Failing to move quickly.
1. Grasp chin with two fingers above point of chin, two fingers below.		1. Placing more than two fingers above point of chin. Placing fewer than two fingers (thus choking victim).
2. Deliver several vigorous and quick kicks. Momentum will level body in water.	 C.2	2. Failing to achieve momentum.
3. Shift to a regular carry after victim is leveled.	 C.3	3. Continuing to carry victim with chin pull. Failing to continue kicking while shifting to carry.
D. *Two-hand level-off.* When attempting to level off non-buoyant or heavy person, submerge, grasp victim's armpits, kick vigorously to surface. Assume towing position.	 D	D. Trying to lift person too high out of water.

level-off position has been reached. If more control is desired, the victim's head may be held tightly against the rescuer's shoulder (Chart 6.13A).

However, what happens if the victim tries to escape? If he or she rolls *away* from the cupped hand, the rescuer can probably maintain control (Chart 6.13B). But if the victim rolls *toward* the cupped hand, the rescuer cannot stop the escape (Chart 6.13C). Thus, the traditional chin pull normally used on struggling victims is dangerous because of its potential lack of control.

An alternative method of the chin pull is to proceed as before, but for the rescuer to bend his or her arm so that the head of the victim can be clamped between the rescuer's upper and lower arms (Chart 6.13D). This hold prevents the victim from escaping. It is tiring for the rescuer to maintain for more than one or two minutes, but it does ensure that the victim remains under control until level-off.

The front surface approach, in its regular version, is used when the victim is semiconscious and barely staying afloat in the water. Assuming that the arms are thrust forward at the surface, the rescuer swims to within three feet of the victim, reverses, and grasps him or her. As the leveling kicks are delivered, the victim is rolled on the back, the level-off is applied, and an appropriate carry is performed. Chart 6.14 describes these maneuvers, as well as the upper-arm grasp.

A variation of the front surface approach makes it much easier to perform the task of rolling the victim on the back. The rescuer goes to one side of the victim and grasps the underside of the victim's wrist (right hand of rescuer to right wrist of victim or left to left). Rolling the rescuer's arm over will roll the victim onto the back. Chart 6.14 also shows this variation.

Chart 6.13. Performance Techniques for the Chin Pull

Techniques	Illustration	Performance Errors
Regular A. Place two fingers above point of chin, two fingers below; arm straight. Swim on the side, with eyes on victim.		A. Placing more than two fingers above point of chin (thus, rescuer's fingers in victim's mouth); placing less than two fingers (thus, choking victim).
B. Victim usually cannot escape by rolling *away* from rescuer's hand.		B. Failing to roll with the victim.
C. Victim probably can escape by rolling *toward* rescuer's hand.		C. Failing to push away immediately if victim succeeds in turning.
Variation D. Grasp victim's head as before, but clamp the back of his head into the angle formed by upper and lower arm segments of rescuer.		D. Failing to clamp victim's head tightly.

Chart 6.14. Performance Techniques for the Front Approach

Techniques	Illustration	Performance Errors
Wrist Grip (ARC Only) A. Grasp victim's wrist with hand (right on right, left on left) with knuckles of rescuer's hand facing upward and thumb to outside.		A. Grasping wrong wrist.
B. Deliver several kicks, pulling victim to floating position on stomach.		B. Failing to achieve a level position.
C. Move victim's wrist and arm across between self and victim. Rotate own arm to turn thumb downward and then outward to roll victim on his or her back.		C. Failing to move arm diagonally enough (thus, victim will not roll over).
D. After victim rolls on back, apply level-off and appropriate carry.		D. Releasing grip on victim's wrist before chin pull is applied.
Upper-Arm Grasp (YMCA Only) E. With active victim, rescuer reverses, quickly grasps victim's upper arm (thumb up, right hand to right upper arm or vice versa), swim and kick back toward safety.		E. Rescuer places thumbs down while grasping victim's upper arm. Rescuer grabs below elbow rather than upper arm.
F. After both are moving, rescuer rotates his or her arm in order to roll victim on back, then applies proper tow.		F. Failing to roll victim on his or her back as soon as possible.
Variation G. Grasp victim's wrist with hand (right to right or left to left) with back of own hand facing downward and thumb to inside.		G. Grasping top of wrist. Grasping wrong wrist.
H. Deliver several kicks. Level the victim.		H. Failing to achieve level position.

Figure 6.14—*continued*

Techniques	Illustration	Performance Errors
I. Move victim's wrist and arm across between self and victim. Rotate own arm to turn thumb upward, outward, and downward to roll victim onto the back.	 I	I. Not moving arm diagonally enough (thus victim will not roll over).
J. After victim rolls on back, apply level-off and appropriate carry.	 J	J. Releasing grip on victim's wrist before chin pull is applied.

Lanoue (1963, pp. 50-51) suggested a variation of the front surface approach that certainly bears attention. He maintained that making any physical contact with a victim, even if barely conscious, is dangerous. Therefore, Lanoue advocated that until the victim is almost exhausted, it is better to circle and not attempt any kind of hold or carry. If the rescuer can urge the swimmer to safety, so much the better; in a surprisingly large number of cases, the victim will swim to safety and thus eliminate the need for any physical contact. If the victim cannot swim, the rescuer should wait until the victim is nearly exhausted before using either the front surface or the rear approach. Because the victim is so exhausted, the danger of a prolonged physical struggle is greatly lessened.

Our general rule is that a struggling swimmer, whose energy is not yet spent, should not be approached from the front. In such cases, use the rear approach if possible. If not, use the underwater approach. The victim whose strength is weak probably will have his or her hands at the surface, so there is no need for the underwater approach. If the hands are convenient for contact, use the front surface approach. Incidentally, Pia (1976) reports that most drowning and near-drowning victims do not struggle violently before sinking. They make gradually weaker arm movements and disappear below the surface.

The underwater approach is used when the victim is actively struggling to stay afloat. The primary goal is to come up behind the victim. To do this, you usually have to turn the victim around. After approach stroking, the rescuer surface dives. (The feet-first surface dive is best, because there is less forward movement and less risk of the feet being grabbed by the victim.) From an underwater position below the feet, the rescuer swims up to the victim, grabs the knees, and turns him or her around. While the victim is thus facing away, the rescuer slides the hands up the victim until the head breaks water, and quickly goes into a level-off and carry. Chart 6.15 describes the underwater approach.

Recovering a submerged victim calls for a search of the bottom; regardless of whether the head-first or feet-first surface dive is done, the rescuer must scan or feel the bottom. If the water is murky, then the rescuer must come close enough to the bottom so that a hand would touch any body. The task is simpler, of course, for the trained scuba diver—the air tanks let the searcher remain underwater and the face mask makes vision much better.

Once the victim is located, the rescuer swims behind, and by grabbing the upper arm, either pulls or pushes the victim to the surface. If the level-off can be done while the victim is coming to the surface, so much the better. If the bottom is firm, the rescuer should push off from it, but a muddy or unknown bottom presents so many dangers that the rescuer should swim up.

Approaches and level-offs can be learned with partner drills in shallow and then deep water. As long as the rescuer is performing correctly, the victim's role is passive for the first six to ten practices. How-

Chart 6.15. Performance Techniques for the Front Underwater Approach

Techniques	Illustration	Performance Errors
A. Make surface dive 6-10 feet from the victim. Go to a depth below the victim's feet.		A. Diving closer than 6 feet or farther than 10 feet from victim. Failing to dive deeply enough.
B. Grasp victim at knees. Turn around by pushing on one leg and pulling on the other.		B. Failing to notice directly of victim's knees (he or she might have turned around trying to find rescuer).
C. Maintain contact with victim while rising to the surface.		C. Permitting victim to turn around and face rescuer. Lifting victim up toward the surface. Pulling down on victim while rising.
D. Upon reaching surface, go immediately into level-off and appropriate carry.		D. Permitting victim to sink or turn around.

ever, if the rescuer is making mistakes, the victim should react. The instructor should insist on a reaction from the victim when something is wrong; this will make both learners more aware of the correct procedure.

In the standard front surface approach, the turning-over of the victim is not easy. Some "victims" help out by initiating the roll themselves. This should not be allowed; the rescuer should practice until the diagonal pull has been mastered and a resisting victim can be turned over.

When practicing the underwater approach, there are at least four drills that should be used. In each of them, have all the rescuers approach the victims in a wave formation, timed so that they will all surface dive at the same time. Without telling the rescuers, have the victims do as Chart 6.16 suggests.

It is possible to combine the recovery of a submerged victim with underwater swimming. Have both the victim and the rescuer submerge, with the rescuer closing the eyes. After a quick count to five, the rescuer opens the eyes, locates the victim, swims behind, and brings the victim to the surface. The victim should be in different places for each practice—near the surface, over in a corner of the pool, or near a dock piling. Older lifesavers or better swimmers can take longer to hide, but the count of five at first is sufficient for both parties to get practice.

CARRIES AND TOWS

Once the victim has been placed in a level-off position, he or she must be carried or towed to safety. The swimming assists and tired swimmer's carry discussed earlier are methods of doing this. However,

Chart 6.16. Practicing the Front Underwater Approach

Techniques	Illustration	Purpose
A. Victim tries to grab legs of rescuer just after the head-first surface dive has begun. If successful, the victim hangs on tightly.	**A**	A. Make rescuer aware of the dangers of surface diving too close to the victim.
B. Victim turns around just after rescuer surface dives. If rescuer does not notice, the victim will be turned back around. The rescuer will be greeted by a front head-hold as he or she breaks the surface.	**B**	B. Make rescuer realize that the victim might turn around in an attempt to locate the rescuer.
C. After victim has been turned around, he or she tries to turn back as rescuer rises to surface. If successful, rescuer will be greeted by front head-hold.	**C**	C. Emphasize to the rescuer the importance of maintaining contact and using force if necessary to stay behind the victim.
D. Victim does feet-first surface dive just after rescuer has done so. Victim tries to grab the rescuer while both are under water.	**D**	D. Have rescuer realize that this possibility exists, and that any way to get behind the victim is acceptable.

they are not safe to use when the victim is extremely scared or is much larger, heavier, or stronger than the rescuer. Other carries or tows have been developed to propel the victims who cannot be safely assisted otherwise. For a struggling victim, the cross-chest carry with a control hold is the most desirable. The tows and other carries described in this section are useful in certain situations.

In the cross-chest carry, the weight of the victim is carried on the side of the rescuer. For this reason, it is the most tiring of the carries, but is valuable because it provides a strong degree of control. The free arm of the rescuer (that is, the arm not used for the chin pull) is placed diagonally across the chest of the victim with the hand forced firmly into the armpit. Some authorities advocate that the rescuer's arm be at about a seventy-five degree angle (Chart 6.17A) while others maintain that the arm should go diagonally across the victim from the shoulder to armpit (Chart 6.17B). The position in Chart 6.17B affords greater control.

There is also disagreement as to which hand should be used for the cross-chest carry. Some advocate using the same hand for both the chin tilt and the cross-chest carry to make the transition very quickly (Chart 6.17C). This does allow a moment or two of freedom for the victim, during which he or she may begin to struggle again. The more common practice is to retain the chin pull with one hand until the other arm is placed for the cross-chest carry (Chart 6.17D).

Lanoue (1963, pp. 52–54) has a variation of the cross-chest carry that deserves study by lifesavers. He maintained it would be better if the rescuer served as a buoyant raft upon which the victim could float, rather than have the victim as a weight on the hip.

The control tow is not designed as a carry, but sometimes becomes one by necessity. It is used when a victim is struggling so much that the rescuer is afraid of maintaining control. The victim cannot escape

Chart 6.17. Performance Techniques for the Cross-Chest Carry, Control Tows, and Surf Tows

Techniques	Illustration	Performance Errors
Regular A. Place hip under the victim, one arm pressed tightly against victim's chest with the hand pressed against the victim's side near the waist. or B. Place hip under the victim, one arm pressed tightly against victim's chest with the hand pressed against the victim's side at the armpit. C. Same hand may be used for both cross-chest carry and chin pull when changing from one to the other. or D. When going from chin pull to cross-chest carry, hold chin pull until other hand has completed the cross-chest hold. **Lanoue's Variation** E. Float on back, directly under the victim. Victim's head should be just below rescuer's chin. Place one hand on victim's breastbone, clamping securely. Use scissors or inverted breast-stroke kick, plus the hand not holding victim, for propulsion.	A B C D E	A. Failing to securely grasp the victim. Failing to place hip tightly to victim's back. B. Failing to securely grasp the victim. Failing to place the hip tightly to the victim's back. C. Failing to quickly reestablish control of the victim (thus permitting escape). D. Failing to have ability to swim equally well on either side. E. Failing to retain control of victim. Entangling own legs with those of victim.

Chart 6.17—*continued*

Techniques	Illustration	Performance Errors
Control Tow F. After the cross-chest carry is completed, use free hand to grasp wrist of other arm. Clamp victim tightly. Use scissors or breaststroke kick for propulsion.	F	F. Failing to provide momentum because of a weak kick.
Surf Tow **(YMCA Only)** G. Same as cross-chest carry, except that rescuer has both arms under armpits of victim. Used at beaches in rough water.	G	G. Failing to provide momentum because of a weak kick.

from this position if the rescuer is of approximately equal strength. As the victim rolls from side to side, the rescuer tightly clamps his or her arms on the victim's chest and back, and propels them both by kicking. Victims tend to roll greatly; rather than trying to resist this action, the rescuer should roll with the victim. While this puts the victim underwater briefly, it enables the rescuer to remain behind and in control.

Chart 6.17 depicts the regular cross-chest carry, Lanoue's variation, and the control and surf tows.

The hair, head, wrist, and collar tows are all useful, because towing (i.e., pulling a floating person) is less tiring for the rescuer than carrying (i.e., supporting a person's weight). The lack of control is a serious shortcoming of the tows; hence, they are used only on passive victims. Chart 6.18 illustrates the four tows. A fifth, the armpit tow included in the YMCA program, was discussed earlier as the arm assist on the back (Chart 6.8C).

It is wise to have some standards to which the students can compare their performances. It is fairly easy to establish these, using the following procedure:

1. Perform the skill (for example, enter feet-first, swim sixty feet, do the rear approach and then the cross-chest carry back to the starting point).
2. Record the times for at least fifteen students.
3. Judge the good and bad times arbitrarily.
4. Use these standards until a greater sample has been tested.

As mentioned in other sections, it would be wise for you and your students to compare the different methods of performing the cross-chest carry. The degree of ease with which each carry can be done should be determined. If time permits, it would be enlightening for the students to see how far they could carry their partner with each method. Sometime, the lives of two people could depend on this knowledge.

Students should practice often with struggling, not passive, victims. If a victim does not struggle, the lifesaver might just as well tow a log. Require the victims to struggle and, if they do not, have them repeat the performance.

Chart 6.18. Performance Techniques for the Hair, Head, Wrist, and Collar Tows

Techniques	Illustration	Performance Errors
Hair Tow A. Take free hand and place it (fingers spread) on top of victim's head. B. Hand is moved forward until hairline is reached. C. Curl fingers to make a fist (include greatest possible amount of hair in grasp). D. Tow victim smoothly, being sure wrist is held down and arm is straight. Eyes kept on victim.	A B C D	A. Failing to place hand on the top of victim's head. B. Failing to move hand forward. C. Grabbing hair at front of victim's head (without performing techniques A and B). D. Failing to hold wrist down (thus, tilting victim's head forward and putting mouth in the water). Failing to hold arm straight (thus permitting victim to reach underneath and grab rescuer's legs).
Head Tow **(YMCA Only)** E. Place hands on each cheek of victim, palms in; fingers curled around victim's chin (middle finger on edge of jawbone), heels of hands close to ears and thumbs pressing in strong contact with forehead above eyebrows. Swim on the back, eyes on victim, using scissors or breast-stroke kick.	E	E. Failing to tilt victim's head backward so his mouth is out of water. Swimming in a near-vertical position. Failing to achieve sufficient momentum with the kick.
Wrist Tow **(ARC Only)** F. After level-off, rescuer grasps victim's wrist, gradually straightening both arms (rescuer, victim) as legs and other arm provide propulsion.	F	F. Failure to keep arms of rescuer, victim straight. Failure to tow victim face up.

Chart 6.18—*continued*

Techniques	Illustration	Performance Errors
Rescuer rotates victim's wrist to ensure face is out of the water. **Collar Tow** G. Grasp rear of victim's collar; tow as in hair carry.	G	G. Inserting more fingers than necessary (thus causing choking).

A teaching method useful for showing the value of the recommended chin pull is to tell victims that if they get a chance they should roll out of the chin tilt at *any* time during the course. If the victim does not become aware of such a chance, you should call it to his or her attention. (The rescuer will certainly know!) By continual awareness of the danger of the usual chin pull, rescuers will soon become skilled in the use of the recommended method and be safer.

DEFENSES, RELEASES, AND ESCAPES

We hope the rescuer will not have to use defenses, releases, and escapes. However, lifesavers must realize that anyone, no matter how weak on land, can be a "tiger" when struggling in the water. Letting the victim become tired before the rescuer makes physical contact is theoretically sound, but a lifesaver might find himself grabbed or held by a victim. Knowing how to deal with such unexpected situations is essential.

Blocking, with one or two hands, is used to prevent close contact with the victim. As shown in Chart 6.19, the technique involves putting one hand on the chest of the victim. It is possible to use one foot (Chart 6.19B) as a blocking device, but this prevents the rescuer from using a kick to back away if needed. The YMCA technique indicates that the rescuer can stay at the surface or go underwater to block, while the ARC advocates going underwater (Chart 6.19C). Each has advantages: staying at the surface enables the rescuer to breathe and to see clearly what the victim is doing, while going under removes the victim's temptation to continue grabbing for the rescuer.

The block and carry is a natural extension of the block. If the distance to safety is short, the rescuer can let the victim maintain the hold on the arm and tow him or her to safety (Chart 6.19D). This technique has much to recommend it if the distance is short and the victim is smaller than the rescuer. It has obvious drawbacks if these conditions are not met.

The block and turn, and the front parry are techniques used to free the rescuer from the victim's grasp and place him or her in a control position. Both are shown in Chart 6.20.

The push-away release from a front head-hold is advocated by ARC. The rescuer deliberately sinks underwater and pushes on the victim's hips. If the rescuer's thumbs are forced into the abdomen and the heels of the hand pushed vigorously against the victim's hips, the victim will release the hold quite readily. Using the thumbs is not mentioned by ARC, but we have found it most effective.

Both ARC and YMCA advocate releasing or escaping from a front head-hold by pushing up on the victim's arms while ducking under the water. Then, the rescuer should turn the victim to secure a control tow or carry.

Chart 6.19. Performance Techniques for the Block and Block and Carry

Techniques	Illustration	Performance Errors
Block A. Place fully extended arm at the base of the victim's throat and hold the victim away. B. Place one foot against chest of victim and hold victim off. C. Using extended arm, go under water to hold victim off.		A. Permitting victim to approach too closely. Failing to keep blocking arm fully extended. B. Kicking the victim, rather than placing foot on chest. C. Failing to keep blocking arm fully extended.
Block and Carry (ARC Only) D. Swim toward safety as victim retains grip on one arm.		D. Permitting victim to "climb the arm," forcing the rescuer underwater. Failing to keep blocking arm fully extended.

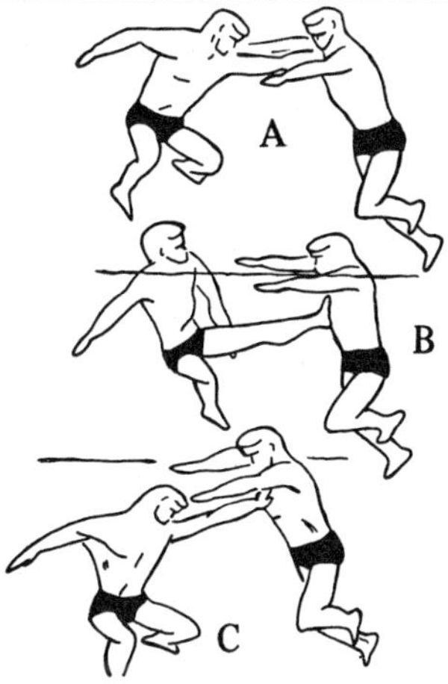

Chart 6.20. Performance Techniques for the Block and Turn and Front Parry

Techniques	Illustration	Performance Errors
Block and Turn A. Reach with free hand to just above closest elbow; fork grip (thumb to inside) used to grip victim. B. Lift up on victim's arm and push it across to opposite side; arm that has been seized is forced down and thus freed from grasp of victim. C. Maintain grip until level-off is secured.		A. Grasping victim's arm below elbow. Failing to grasp victim with proper fork grip. B. Failing to lift victim's arm up before pushing it to opposite side. C. Releasing grip on victim's upper arm before level-off is applied.

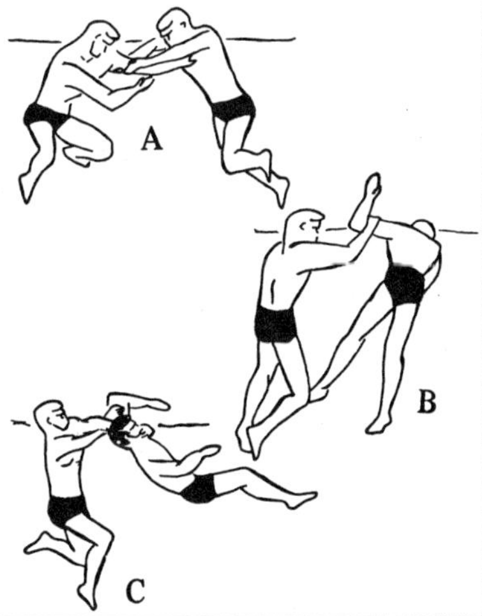

Chart 6.20—*continued*

Techniques	Illustration	Performance Errors
Front Parry (YMCA Only) D. Use both hands to contact victim's arms near armpits. Lift victim slightly, at the same time chin is tucked.		D. Failing to tuck chin (thus giving victim opportunity to grab rescuer's head).
E. Maintain grip on one of victim's arms. Go behind the victim, and apply chin pull.		E. Failing to maintain grip on one of victim's arms.

If the victim has secured a front head-hold with a body scissors the rescuer is in the worst position. Releasing and escaping, as advocated by the YMCA, involves forcing the victim's head underwater and eventually placing him or her in a control tow.

Chart 6.21 depicts all of these maneuvers.

Releasing a double grip on one arm is done differently by the two groups. The YMCA prefers life-savers to hold the victim underwater, and then turn him or her around with pressure on the chin or armpit. ARC advocates using a one-foot push away. Finally, ARC teaches an escape from a double grip. All three of these maneuvers are shown in Chart 6.22.

Releasing and escaping from a rear head-hold can be done various ways, either using leverage created by applying pressure to the victim's arms or by surprise somersaults. Chart 6.23 depicts these maneuvers.

When dealing with two drowning victims who are grasping each other, both the ARC and YMCA maintain that if the distance is short and it is feasible, the rescuer should hair carry one victim and tow them both to safety.

However, when this cannot be done ARC advises a technique for separating them. (The question always arises—should the victims be separated? This cannot be answered in any text. It depends on the rescuer, the distance to safety, and other factors. It is obvious that if they are separated, one has a much greater chance of reaching safety than the other. You could argue that if they were separated, one might be able to reach safety. Common sense would tell the rescuer to try to rescue the weaker of the two swimmers.) In the ARC technique, the rescuer swims up behind one victim, separates him or her from the other, and tows one to safety. Chart 6.24 describes this method.

It is important to remind students that a real victim may not react in precisely the same fashion described in this text. The lifesaver's job will be to break the hold and maneuver to attain the control position. To perform this task successfully, lifesavers should have a number of practice sessions in which the victim acts in an unexpected way. For example, the victim can grip one wrist and then suddenly go to the other one. Certain holds can be applied at random, such as grabbing the rescuer's right wrist and, after the rescuer is set to react to this, go to a front head-hold.

Chart 6.21. Performance Techniques for Releases and Escapes from Front Head-Hold

Techniques	Illustration	Performance Errors
Front Head-Hold Pushaway Release (ARC) A. Deliberately sink and place hands on the victim's hips.		A. Attempting to remain on face of water.
B. Pull head down and forward (tuck chin). Push vigorously against victim's hips.		B. Failing to tuck the chin.
C. Maintain control of victim. Roll victim over.		C. Losing contact with victim, either before or after rolling over.
D. Come to surface and apply level-off.		D. Failing to apply level-off before victim regains hold.
Front Head-Hold Escape (ARC) or Release (YMCA) E. Rescuer submerges with victim, hands (thumbs inside) grasping upper arms of victim as the chin is tucked and shoulders hunched. Rescuer forcefully pushes up on victim's arms, thus slipping down out of grasp. Rescuer escapes by backing away quickly (ARC).		E. Failing to submerge victim before beginning to free self. Failing to back away to avoid regrasp by victim.
F. After ducking out of grip, rescuer moves behind victim and applics control tow (YMCA).		F. Failing to immediately get behind victim.
Front Head-Hold—Body Scissors Release (YMCA) G. Rescuer raises head, begins rapid breaststroke. Reach behind victim's head, grasp hair, pull it underwater.		G. Failure to submerge face of victim.

Chart 6.21—*continued*

Techniques	Illustration	Performance Errors
H. Continue to swim. When victim relaxes grip, release head and push his or her right shoulder under rescuer's right armpit (or vice versa).		H. Failure to quickly begin to turn victim on his or her back.
I. Victim now turned with back to rescuer. Rescuer grasps own wrist with free hand, thus placing victim in control tow.		I. Failure to quickly secure victim in control tow.

Chart 6.22. Performance Techniques for the Release and Escape from Double Grip on One Arm

Techniques	Illustrations	Performance Errors
Double Grip on One Arm Release (YMCA Only)		
A. Rescuer pushes victim downward simultaneously kicking to raise self up.		A. Failing to cause victim to sink.
B. Forcefully swing free hand across victim's neck, grasping either his or her chin or armpit. Hold victim underwater.		B. Failing to keep victim face down underwater.
C. Victim now face down underwater. When grip on rescuer's arm released, place victim in control.		C. Permitting victim to escape, rather than being placed under control.
Release (ARC Only)		
D. Reach across with free hand and grasp top wrist of victim. At same time, press down on other wrist, forcing victim underwater.		D. Failing to grasp correct wrist. Failing to force victim underwater.
E. Bring foot (same side of body as free hand) up and over victim's shoulder). Place it on chest of victim.		E. Failing to bring foot outside the shoulder.

Chart 6.22—*continued*

Techniques	Illustration	Performance Errors
F. Straighten the leg as victim releases grip. Maintain grip on victim's wrist.	F	F. Kicking the victim (rather than pushing him or her away). Losing contact with victim.
G. Kick to gain momentum, turn victim around and apply chin pull (preferred) or arm-pit assist.	G	G. Failing to obtain sufficient momentum. Failing to turn victim around before applying hold.
Escape (ARC Only) H. After submerging the victim, rescuer reaches across with his or her free hand, grasps fist of seized arm, and quickly and vigorously pulls upward. *Variation:* Rescuer pulls grasped arm downward if victim has "knuckles-up" grip.	H	H. Failing to submerge victim. Failing to pull upward with with enough force. Failing to back away after arm is released.

Chart 6.23. Performance Techniques for Rear Head-Hold Releases and Escapes

Techniques	Illustration	Performance Errors
Rear Pivot Release (YMCA Only) A. Grab a bite of air, tuck chin and turn it to one side.	A B	A. Failing to grab bite of air and/or tuck chin.
B. Drop shoulder, continue to turn in direction of chin rotation.		B. Failing to drop shoulder, thus hindering twist.
C. Twist around to face victim.	C	C. Failing to turn all the way.

Chart 6.23—*continued*

Techniques	Illustration	Performance Errors
D. Place hands on upper arm of victim, push vigorously up and to one side. (Rescuer is now behind the victim.) Apply control tow. *Note:* In rear pivot breakaway, rescuer backs away rather than applying control tow.	D	D. Failing to push on upper arms of victim.
Rear Head-Hold Release (ARC Only) E. Grab a bite of air. Tuck chin in and turn it to one side.	E	E. Failing to grab a bite of air and/or tuck chin.
F. Place on hand (thumb on top) over victim's lower hand. Place other hand (fork grip, thumb to inside) above elbow of victim's same arm.	F G	F. Failing to grasp proper hand of victim. Failure to grasp victim's elbow.
G. Twist victim's arm downward and inward. Duck head, turn away from victim's arm.		G. Failing to apply sufficient pressure to force victim to release hold.
H. Continue twisting, as victim is pulled forward. End with victim's arm in hammerlock.	H	H. Failing to continue pressure until hammerlock position attained.
I. Retain grip on wrist until chin pull is applied.	I	I. Failing to retain hammerlock means victim is free to try another hold.
Rear Head-Hold Escape (ARC Only) J. Submerge with victim, hands (thumbs inside) grasping upper arms of victim. As the chin is tucked and shoulders hunched, forcefully push up on victim's arms, thus slipping down out of grasp. Swim away quickly.	J	J. Failing to submerge victim before beginning to free self. Failing to swim away to avoid regrasp by victim.

Chart 6.23—*continued*

Techniques	Illustration	Performance Errors
Rear Headlock Somersault Release (YMCA Only) K. After chin tuck and bite of air, twist into victim by dropping chin and shoulder and forcing near arm (elbow first) between victim and self. Example: right chin thrust and drop, right shoulder drop, right elbow and arm forced between bodies. L. Lift hand of near arm out of water and place on face of victim, meanwhile placing other hand underneath victim's knees. M. Push back on victim's face, then lift up on his or her legs. This causes victim to backward somersault, thus releasing hold. Move to control hold.	K L M	K. Forcing the near arm hand first, not elbow first. L. Failure to place one hand underneath victim's knees. Placing hand of near arm on victim's cheek rather than on face. M. Lifting up on victim's legs before pushing back on his or her face.
Rear Head-Hold—Pullover Release (YMCA Only) N. After tucking chin and getting air, reach overhead and grab victim behind the neck with both hands. O. Forcefully bend forward at waist, pulling victim over rescuer's head into a forward somersault. Move into a control tow.	N O	N. Failure to securely grasp behind victim's neck. O. Failure to bend forward with enough force and surprise.
Rear Head-Hold with Body Scissors (YMCA Only) P. After tucking chin and getting air, bend at waist and grab victim's top foot, place an elbow on the calf or shin of the same leg.	P	P. Failing to secure a firm grip on the victim's foot.

Chart 6.23—*continued*

Techniques	Illustration	Performance Errors
Q. Simultaneously lift upward on the foot and press downward on the calf or shin. When the leg has been released, move to any of the rear head-hold releases.	 Q	Q. Lifting up on victim's foot but failing to press down on calf or shin.

Chart 6.24. Performance Techniques for Rescuing and Separating Two Drowning Persons

Techniques	Illustration	Performance Errors
YMCA Method: Rescue Both Persons A. Get behind one victim, grasp chin or upper arm, tow both toward safety.	 A	A. Attempting to swim a great distance towing two victims.
ARC Method: Separate the Two, Rescue One B. Get behind one victim, place cupped hands over victim's chin.	 B	B. Failing to get secure hold on the chin.
C. Press down on victim's shoulders; place one foot on chest of the other victim. *Note:* If one victim has grasped the other from behind, then rescuer must place foot on the upper back of the other victim.	 C	C. Failing to submerge the victims. Failing to securely place the foot in position.
D. Press to straighten leg, separate the victims. Continue with chin pull on the one victim.	 D	D. Kicking the second victim, rather than pressing against him or her with one foot.

Another way for the rescuer to develop the ability to react quickly is to have him or her swim into a situation about which nothing is known. For example, have the victims about five feet apart, hanging on to the trough or treading water in a straight line. One rescuer starts to swim parallel to this group with the eyes *closed*. A designated victim (unknown to the rescuer) will grab the rescuer. When contact is made, the rescuer must open the eyes and react in an acceptable manner. Acceptable reactions are not always like the textbook reactions. As an instructor, you must see that the lifesaver can properly do the skills required by the organization. But in "ad lib" situations, any method short of injuring the victim to gain the control hold is acceptable.

The instructor must continually stress that the holds used in the class are dangerous and that the students must be careful when they are practicing. Accidents will happen, but negligence on the part of the instructor will be difficult to disprove if a neck is injured or a shoulder dislocated.

UNDERWATER SEARCH AND RESCUE

Underwater searches are best conducted with scuba equipment, but such gear can seldom be used to rescue a victim who has disappeared but could be resuscitated. Thus, lifesavers must be able to employ less effective but quicker means of searching.

Search drills are nothing more than formations or patterns whereby every square foot of the bottom is examined. There is no universal pattern for use in every instance, but a formation that covers all of the bottom must be employed. Chart 6.25 illustrates the basic principles of searching the bottom and diagrams the commonly used formations.

Chart 6.25. Principles and Formations for Searching the Bottom

Techniques	Illustration	Performance Errors
Principles A. Rescuer(s) in line with object on shore (and with each other).		A. Failing to take a sighting (thus perhaps overlooking part of the bottom).
B. Rescuer(s) wade as far as possible. All dive together. Dive within 1 foot of bottom.		B. Failing to dive within 1 foot of the bottom.
C. Take preestablished number (two or three) of strokes underwater. Come straight up.		C. Failing to take same number of strokes may cause some part to be overlooked.
D. Back up 3–4 feet, dive again and continue search.		D. Failing to back up for next dive may mean overlooking area just beyond previous dive.

Chart 6.25—continued

Common Formations

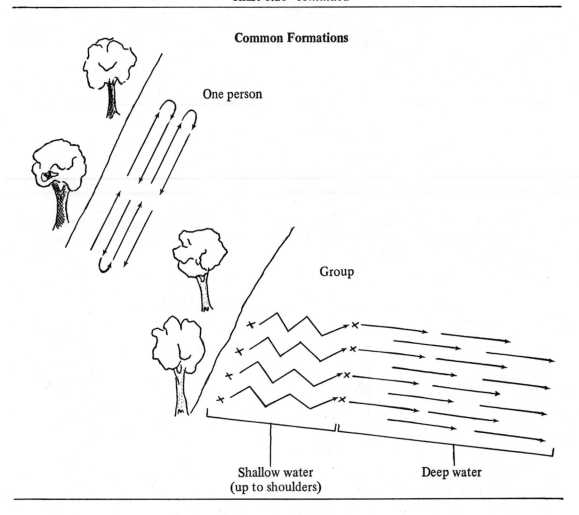

One person

Group

Shallow water
(up to shoulders)

Deep water

The use of mask, fins, and snorkel is covered in the ARC course. Each learner's mask and fins should be checked to ensure proper fit before the class enters the water. Students should be shown how to defog the face mask by rubbing the inside with water or saliva, how to put it on (face is covered first, then the strap is stretched to the back of the head), and how to check for leaks. A mask filled with water can be emptied underwater by tilting the head and pressing the top side of the mask to the face while exhaling slowly through the nose. As the swimmer goes into deeper water, pressure on the ears or face mask may be relieved by exhaling slightly through the nose.

Backward walking with fins is recommended on land, but it would be better never to wear fins out of the water. Once in the water, kicking with a long, wide, slow flutter kick is recommended.

The snorkel mouthpiece is inserted so that it is gripped with the teeth. The snorkel should be kept vertical to the surface. Clearing it after surfacing requires a forceful exhalation through the mouth.

Basic principles of searching using fins, mask, and snorkel are described in Chart 6.26.

Recovering objects is merely a matter of placing an object, such as a brick, on the hip and pushing off the bottom. If a person is found, the rescuer swims to a point behind the victim's head, grasps him or her in a chin pull, head carry, or by the wrist, and swims to the surface. A push-off from the bottom should not be attempted unless the bottom is known to be firm and clean.

Much practice is needed in these skills because most swimmers are not too familiar with this equipment. Because masks, fins, and snorkels are usually limited in number, we recommend that these skills be taught early in the course so that practice is not confined to one or two sessions. These skills should be reviewed in daily practice drills.

Chart 6.26. Performance Techniques for Searching with Mask, Fins, and Snorkel

Techniques	Illustration	Performance Errors
A. When entering water with face mask, use the lifesaving jump or front or back somersault from the deck. Hands must hold mask firmly to face.		A. Failing to use one or both hands to hold face mask in place.
B. Swimming at surface is similar to prone glide with arms at side.		B. Moving too fast (thus causing segments of bottom to be overlooked).
C. Surface dive, using any type. Hands may be used if needed to hold mask firmly to face.		C. Failing to back up before surface diving (thus causing part of bottom to be unsearched).
D. Underwater searching is done with kick for propulsion.		D. Failing to sweep eyes over area ahead of rescuer.
E. When surfacing, stop just before surface, look up, extend arms.		E. Failing to see if surface is clear before emerging.

REMOVING A VICTIM FROM THE WATER

Lifts and carries are more valuable than many lifesavers believe. They may need to be performed quickly so resuscitation efforts can begin in time. If uninjured and not in need of resuscitation, the victim should rest briefly in shallow water and leave under his or her own power.

The pool lift is a technique whereby one rescuer can lift the victim to the deck or boat to continue resuscitation. It is important to remove the victim as quickly as possible, without causing injury. Chart 6.27 shows the accepted form for the pool (or boat) lift. When a neck injury is suspected, as is often the case in a diving accident, the victim is not moved until some means of rigid support is available. Maneuvers to meet this situation are also shown in Chart 6.27.

Chart 6.27. Performance Techniques for Removing a Victim from the Water

Techniques	Illustration	Performance Errors
Pool, Dock, or Boat Lift A. Place hands of victim one atop the other and cover them with one of rescuer's own hands. Maintain pressure on victim's hands while climbing out of the water.		A. Permitting hands of victim to slip back into the water.
B. Grasp wrists of victim, lift straight up until victim's waist is even with deck.		B. Failing to lift straight up will cause victim's stomach to be scraped.
C. Fold top half of victim's body over onto deck. (If victim is unconscious, cross one arm underneath the head to avoid letting it drop on the deck.)		C. Failing to raise top half of victim's body out of the water. Failing to exercise caution when lowering upper half of body to the deck.
D. Hold top part of victim's body while pulling near leg of victim toward the deck.		D. Permitting top half of body to slide back into the water.
Suspected Neck or Spine Injury E. Being very careful not to move victim unless absolutely necessary, float long rigid object (preferably, a spine board) underneath victim.		E. Failing to use great care in placing the object under victim's body.
F. After strapping body, limbs and head in immobile position, carefully remove victim from water. Keep warm and treat for shock until trained personnel arrive.		F. Failing to strap all body segments to board.
Team Lift (ARC Only) G. First and second rescuers grasp hands underneath victim's shoulders. Third rescuer supports feet. Walk in unison toward safety.		G. Failing of one rescuer to give directions to group.

Chart 6.27—*continued*

Techniques	Illustration	Performance Errors
Shallow Water Assist (ARC Only) H. Rescuer puts one arm behind victim's back for support, ducks and grasps victim's near arm firmly as it encircles rescuer's neck. Walk slowly toward safety.	H	H. Lifting victim's near arm around rescuer's shoulder rather than ducking under arm.

When the victim must be removed from a lake or river, one or more of three carries are commonly used. The drag to the beach (although technically not a carry) is preferable because it is the quickest. The saddleback carry is used when a heavy victim must be carried a distance, while the fireman's carry is employed when the victim is of equal or less weight than the rescuer. Chart 6.28 depicts these methods.

Chart 6.28. Performance Techniques for Carrying a Victim from the Water

Techniques	Illustration	Performance Errors
Drag to the Beach A. Stand behind victim, clasp hands over his chest. Walk backward, dragging heels of victim on ground.	A	A. Permitting hips or legs of victim to drag.
Saddleback Carry B. Face head of victim with hips at right angles to victim's body.	B	B. Having stomach to victim's side, rather than hip.
C. Reach with outside hand, grasp underside of victim's far wrist.	C	C. Failing to reach with outside hand. Failing to grasp underside of wrist.
D. Lift victim's wrist around back of head; at same time turn so that back is toward victim's stomach.	D	D. Failing to face away from victim in order to turn back toward him.

Chart 6.28—*continued*

Techniques	Illustration	Performance Errors
E. Other hand slides across victim's back to support head. Release grip at wrist and encircle legs just above knees.	 E	E. Failing to keep victim's face out of water.
Fireman's Carry (YMCA Only) F. Face victim with one hand under the neck and the other over the near leg and under the far knee.	 F	F. Failing to reach over the near leg before grasping the far leg. Extending arm between victim's legs from below instead of from above.
G. Duck under water. Roll victim onto near shoulder.	 G	G. Failing to submerge completely under the water.
H. Stand. Grasp near wrist of victim, securely holding victim to the rescuer's shoulders.	 H	H. Failing to properly position victim before standing.

Lowering the victim to the ground is not easy. If done too quickly, injury may result; if done too slowly, valuable time is wasted. Chart 6.29 shows how the victim is lowered to the ground in the drag, the saddleback, and the fireman's carry.

Carrying a victim is obviously much easier when two or three rescuers are available. Chart 6.30 illustrates techniques for two- and three-rescuer carries.

There are no special teaching devices to use in this area, but lifts, carries, and let-downs should be part of the daily practice.

RESUSCITATION

The techniques of mouth-to-mouth resuscitation were discussed in Chapter 3. Everyone should master this technique. The chest pressure–arm lift method may be necessary on occasions when mouth-to-mouth resiscitation is impossible because of facial injuries. It should be clearly understood that mouth-to-mouth resuscitation is the emergency procedure recommended by all United States health groups. Of course, if a mechanical resuscitator and a trained operator are available, they should be used.

Cardio-pulmonary resuscitation (CPR) is not advocated unless special training has been received. CPR is essential in certain cases, and should be a part of all lifesaving courses, if a certified instructor and extra sessions are possible.

Chart 6.29. Performance Techniques for Lowering a Victim to the Ground

Techniques	Illustration	Performance Errors
Drag Carry A. Lower victim to ground, stepping over the body with one foot. This places victim on stomach.	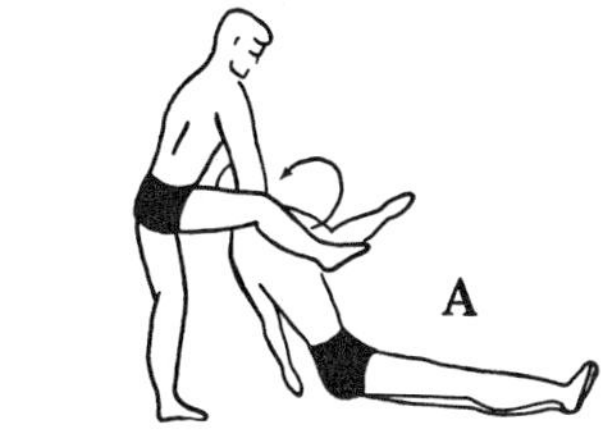	A. Failing to roll victim over as he or she is placed on the ground.
Saddleback Carry B. Kneel, slowly lean back. Victim is gently lowered to ground.	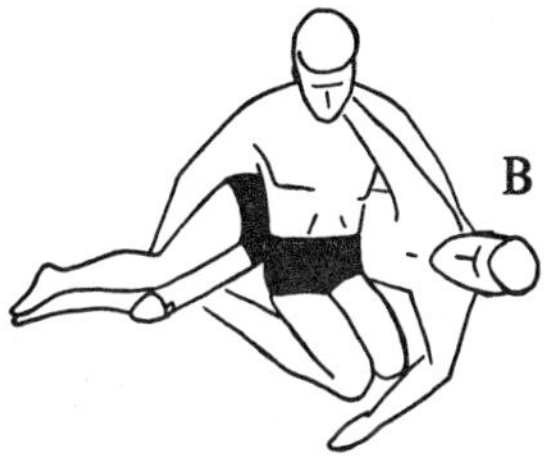	B. Permitting victim to drop to ground.
Fireman's Carry (YMCA Only) C. Kneel on knee opposite the shoulder on which the victim is carried. Other leg is bent at right angles, foot securely placed on the ground. D. Victim is placed in sitting position on knee of rescuer. Victim is gently lowered to ground on his or her back or side.	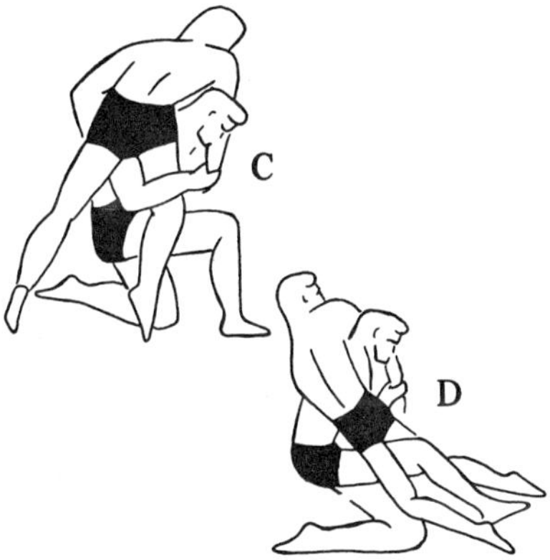	C. Kneeling on wrong knee. Failing to place other leg in secure position. D. Failing to retain tight grip on victim. Failing to lower victim slowly.

Chart 6.30. Performance Techniques for the Two- and Three-Rescuer Carries

Techniques	Illustration	Performance Errors
Two-Rescuer Carry (YMCA Only) A. Victim is carried feet-first— one rescuer supporting the knees, the other supporting the upper back. Kneel to lower victim gently to the ground.	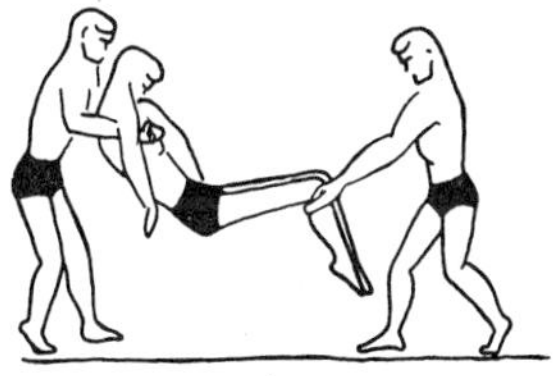	A. Supporting victim under shoulders and/or the lower legs. Failing to place the victim on the ground gently.

Chart 6.30—*continued*

Techniques	Illustration	Performance Errors
Three-Rescuer Carry (YMCA Only) B. One rescuer supports the legs as shown; the other two clasp each other's arms and support the victim at the abdomen and shoulders. Victim is lowered to ground by kneeling and gently placing him or her on the ground (chest first).	**B**	B. Failing to securely grasp arms with fellow rescuer. Failing to place victim on the ground gently.

Chest Pressure–Arm Lift Resuscitation

The chest pressure–arm lift method of resuscitation is used when the mouth-to-mouth method cannot be used. A victim (e.g., a pregnant woman) may need to be on the back. This method does not force as much oxygen into the blood as the mouth-to-mouth method, but it has been used successfully in hundreds of cases. Red Cross directions for the pressure-arm lift method are described in Chart 6.31.

Performing resuscitation as soon as possible is crucial to survival. Resuscitation in deep water is a skill acquired by lifeguards, but lifesavers should realize that resuscitation must start as soon as shallow

Chart 6.31. Manual Method of Artificial Respiration

Chest Pressure–Arm Lift

Place the victim in a face-up position and put something under the shoulders to raise them and allow the head to drop backward. Turn victim's head to side.

Kneel at the victim's head, grasp the wrists, cross them, rock forward and press the hands over the lower chest (Figure 1). This should cause air to flow out.

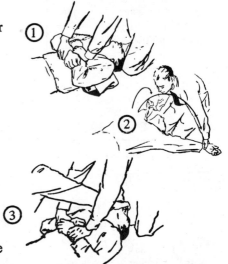

Immediately release this pressure by rocking back, pulling the arms outward and upward over the victim's head and backward as far as possible (Figure 2). This should cause air to rush in.

Repeat this cycle about 12 times per minute, checking the mouth frequently for obstructions.

If a second rescuer is available, have him or her hold the victim's head so that the jaw is jutting out (Figure 3). The helper should be alert to detect the presence of any stomach contents in the mouth and keep the mouth as clean as possible at all times.

Illustrations and excerpt from *Standard First Aid and Personal Safety*, copyright © 1973, 1979 by the American National Red Cross, reproduced with permission.

water or the side of a pool, dock, boat, or raft, or any other solid object is reached. Chart 6.32 indicates how this might be done.

An effective deep water resuscitation method that can be performed while moving to safety is the mouth-to-snorkel technique, Jim Waterfield and Jim Gabel, scuba instructors at the Philadelphia Mid-City YMCA, developed this technique in 1961. Mouth-to-snorkel resuscitation is easy to learn, effective, and essential if one rescuer must tow a nonbreathing victim any distance at all. The YMCA includes this as a part of their lifesaving course. Chart 6.33 illustrates this technique.

Chart 6.32. Artificial Resuscitation in the Water

  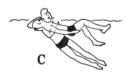

Chart 6.33. Performance Techniques for Mouth-to-Snorkel Breathing

Techniques	Illustration	Performance Errors
A. Starting with the chin pull, hold the victim's head against his or her chest. The free hand controls the snorkel.		A. Failing to control victim's head.
B. Water is cleared from the snorkel by letting it run out. The snorkel is then kept clear by bending the tube end up, or by holding it in the teeth.		B. Failing to keep water out of snorkel after clearing it.
C. Release fingers from the chin pull to receive the snorkel mouthpiece between the middle and ring fingers, while keeping control of the victim's head.		C. Failing to control victim's head.
D. Press the snorkel flange over the victim's mouth, making sure to press tightly all around the flange.		D. Snorkel mouthpiece not tightly sealed around victim's mouth.

Chart 6.33—*continued*

Techniques	Illustration	Performance Errors
E. The victim's nose is sealed with the rescuer's thumb, against the index finger of the hand. (The index finger, pressing against the victim's nostrils, may provide an adequate seal.)		E. Nose is not sealed shut.
F. Blow forcefully into the tube end of the snorkel, then remove mouth to allow rescuer's air to leave victim's lungs.		F. Exhaled air not permitted to escape.
G. Swimming on his or her back, with propulsion provided by kick, tow the victim while giving mouth-to-snorkel artificial respiration.		

Source: Albert Pierce, *Deep Water Rescue Breathing.* Used with permission.

When a victim has been revived, he or she should be kept quiet until regular breathing resumes. The rescuer should warm the victim with blankets or coats, and should watch for signs of shock (pallor, rapid pulse, nausea, vomiting, irregular breathing, and cold, clammy skin). Although this may be difficult to enforce at times, the victim should rest for at least thirty minutes before getting to his or her feet.

An excellent source of information on resuscitation is Chapter 11 in Charles Silvia's book, *Lifesaving and Water Safety Today,* which contains an interesting history, the medical background of resuscitation, and explanations and illustrations of many techniques and mechanical apparatus. Chapter 8 in CNCA's *Lifeguard Training* and Chapter 11 in *National Instructor Guide and Reference,* by the Canadian Red Cross Society, are also good sources.

The most important fact to emphasize to students is that resuscitation must be started as soon as possible and continued as long as possible. In a swimming rescue the victim must be moved to safety as quickly as possible. Students often fail to realize that resuscitative measures must begin immediately. Recovery statistics like those listed in Table 6.1 should be given to students to impress them with the need for immediate resuscitative efforts.

Movies like *Pulse of Life* (available from most ARC or state health departments) are excellent introductions to resuscitation methods. Teachers may also use loop films, such as *Mouth-to-Mouth, Mouth-to-Nose-Breathing* (ARC) on an individual basis. ARC recommends that students do not practice mouth-to-mouth resuscitation on each other; we feel that, from a hygenic standpoint, this admonition makes sense. The use of ResusciAnne (a training manikin available through most ARC offices, state health departments, and university physical education departments) is strongly advocated. This lifelike dummy enables each person to actually practice mouth-to-mouth resuscitation in an acceptably hygienic manner. Mouth-to-mouth resuscitation is too important to be left to a movie or a lecture. Usually lifesaving students practice resuscitation only once or twice. But this knowledge is so potentially valuable that we feel it should be practiced several times during any lifesaving course.

Table 6.1. Recovery Statistics

After breathing has stopped and artificial respiration is begun the *chances of recovery* (averages only, as individuals differ) are:

1 minute after breathing has stopped . . . . 98 out of 100
2 minutes after breathing has stopped . . . . 92 out of 100
3 minutes after breathing has stopped . . . . 72 out of 100
4 minutes after breathing has stopped . . . . 50 out of 100
5 minutes after breathing has stopped . . . . 25 out of 100
6 minutes after breathing has stopped . . . . 11 out of 100
7 minutes after breathing has stopped . . . . 8 out of 100
8 minutes after breathing has stopped . . . . 5 out of 100
9 minutes after breathing has stopped . . . . 2 out of 100
10 minutes after breathing has stopped . . . . 1 out of 100
11 minutes after breathing has stopped . . . . 1 out of 1000
12 minutes after breathing has stopped . . . . 1 out of 10,000

Adapted from Canadian Red Cross Society, *National Instructor Guide and Reference,* p. 132.

First Aid

Both ARC and YMCA include in their student manuals specific information on aquatic first aid. Many lifesaving instructors, pleading lack of time or lack of expertise, do not cover first aid. Even though lifesaving courses are not designed to train lifeguards, first aid for common aquatic accidents should be taught to all who will be in or near the water. At the very least, students should be made aware of proper procedures for dealing with:

1. Bleeding
2. Shock
3. Head, neck, and spinal injuries
4. Burns
5. Heat exhaustion, cramps, stroke
6. Heart attack
7. Epilepsy

ARC's *Lifesaving: Rescue and Water Safety,* Chapter 12, has very good first aid material, as does the Canadian Red Cross Society's *National Instructor Guide and Reference.*

SMALL CRAFT SAFETY

Some lifesaving courses are taught without the use of rowboat or canoe. If at least one of these craft is available, it should be used. If there truly is no craft, then it is still possible to show the movie *Oars and Paddles* (available from ARC). The movie should be followed with at least an explanation of the following material and then a rescreening of the film.

Chart 6.34 depicts the techniques to be followed when entering, changing positions, or leaving a small craft. It also shows the preferred manner for sculling.

Entering and leaving a craft while it is in deep water is much more difficult than it sounds. The lifesaver needs to return to the craft after making his rescue. Chart 6.35 describes possible methods.

Chart 6.34. Performance Techniques for Small Craft Skills

Techniques	Illustration	Performance Errors
Entering A. Grasp gunwales (sides) as first step is made in center of craft. Knees bent, center of gravity low. B. Assist another person by extending a hand while seated.	A B	A. Failing to step in center of craft. B. Failing to assist another person.
C. Assist another person to enter a canoe by bracing the craft with a paddle (or holding dock).	C	C. Failing to either brace the craft or hold it onto the dock.
Leaving D. Leave a craft by reversing the above procedures.	D (see A, B, C)	D. See A, B, C above.
Changing Positions E. Grasp gunwales; keep center of gravity low.	E	E. Failing to keep center of gravity low.
Sculling F. Hold oar at 45° angle to water, submerged to its throat and flat to water's surface; wrist is straight and arm bent.	F	F. Failing to achieve proper angle of oar.
G. Drop wrist, causing blade to push against water as it moves sideward.	G	G. Failing to exert pushing force against water.
H. Raise the wrist, causing same edge of blade to push against water as it moves back to original position.		H. Failing to exert pushing force against water.
Hand Paddling I. Sitting in bottom, use hand as paddle.	I	I. Leaning too far to the side while paddling.

ARC only.

Chart 6.35. Performance Techniques for Leaving and Entering a Craft in Deep Water

Techniques	Illustration	Performance Errors
Leaving Boat or Canoe A. Put one hand on gunwale; leap over. Retain grip to prevent craft from being pushed away. **Entering Boat or Canoe** B. Climb over stern of boat; if motor interferes, enter at corner of stern. C. In canoe, depress gunwale with stomach; grasp far gunwale. D. Put as much weight on far hand as possible; lift legs and slide inside. **Entering Swamped Boat or Canoe** E. Depress one gunwale no more than necessary; slide in on stomach. F. Roll over; sit in middle and paddle with hands.		A. Failing to retain grip on gunwale. B. Failing to enter boat without tipping it. C. Depressing gunwale so much that water enters the canoe. D. Failing to shift weight to far hand. E. Depressing gunwale so much that canoe tips. F. Failing to sit in middle while paddling.

ARC only.

A capsize routine involves deliberately swamping a boat or canoe and then maneuvering it to safety. Once the craft is swamped, the swimmer enters it, sits in the bottom, and hand-paddles to safety. Lifesavers should realize that a boat or canoe seldom sinks to the bottom. They should attempt to maintain contact with the craft and use it as a raft.

Lifesavers should know that the essential principle of a boat or canoe rescue of a victim is the same as in a swimming rescue—keep the eyes on the victim. This means rowing the boat stern first if there is only a short way to go or glancing frequently over the shoulder if rowing bow first. The rescuer may extend an oar or paddle to the victim, or stand and throw a ring buoy. Once a victim has been brought to the craft, the steps outlined in Chart 6.36 are followed.

Chart 6.36. Procedures to Follow When Victim Reaches Boat or Canoe

Techniques	Illustration	Performance Errors
Boat Rescue A. If needed, begin resuscitation immediately.	A	A. Failing to begin resuscitation immediately.
B. If possible, get victim into boat for resuscitation. Injuries may prevent this.	B	B. Failing to determine if victim is injured.
C. If victim has strength, let him or her hang onto transom and be pulled to safety. or	C	C. Rowing too vigorously (thus, causing victim to lose grasp).
D. Lift victim into boat using pool lift.	D	D. Failing to brace self to prevent falling or being pulled into water.
E. Keep victim warm. Check for shock.		E. Failing to observe first aid precautions.
Canoe Rescue F. If needed, begin resuscitation immediately. If possible, get victim into canoe (using pool lift).	F (see A and B)	F. Failing to begin resuscitation immediately.
G. Victim enters canoe by grasping gunwale and climbing; rescuer must sit and lean to other side.	G	G. Failing to counter-balance victim's weight by leaning to other side of canoe.

ARC only.

There is no substitute for actual experience with small craft, but sometimes they are just not available. As stated earlier, showing a film and assigning text readings is always possible. The references suggest other aids for the students.

CLASS ASSIGNMENTS

1. Observe a local lifesaving class in action and talk to the instructor.
   a. Are all students skilled and strong enough to become lifesavers?

b. What seem to be their weakest skills?

c. How many "dropouts" have there been?

d. What skills are the hardest to teach?

2. Have a friend (who has no lifesaving experience) grab you with various holds. Can you release them? (Be certain that you have arranged a pinch system beforehand.)

3. Talk to local lifeguards. Make a table showing answers to these questions:

How many lifeguards were interviewed? _____

How many rescues had they made within the past year? _____

How many were reaching rescues? _____

How many were throwing rescues? _____

How many were boat or canoe rescues? _____

How many were swimming rescues? _____

How many rescues were in pools? _____ Lakes? _____ Ocean? _____

How many rescues demanded application of releases? _____ Holds? _____ Carries of more than ten feet? _____

BEHAVIORAL OBJECTIVES

While only certain aquatic instructors will teach lifesaving skills, we expect our students to be able to respond correctly (based on material in this chapter) to questions calling for brief written answers, and to meet the standards indicated for lifesaving skills.

1. Accurately reflect the authors' thoughts in regard to these items that should be considered before teaching a lifesaving class:

    a. Inclusion of swimmers who are unable to swim 500 yards in the class

    b. Emphasis on form in the various strokes

    c. Possible solution to the problem of "wandering hands"

    d. Value of a "pinch" system of communication

2. Accurately reflect the thoughts of the authors in regard to these techniques used in teaching the class:

    a. The use of approaches, holds, releases, and tows as logical teaching assignments.

    b. One method of conditioning the class (other than solo swimming of a certain distance)

    c. The value of quizzes

    d. One reason why the instructor should enter the water for testing purposes

    e. One reason why the instructor should not enter the water for testing purposes

3. Perform any or all of the following skill tests, meeting the standards shown.

Test	Skill	Conditions	Standards
A	1. Throw ring buoy	Victim 25 feet away	1. Throw buoy or line within reach of victim two out of three times
B	2. Approach from rear	Male victim of equal weight, deep water	2. Correct form as described in text
	3. Reverse		3. See 2
	4. Chin pull (traditional)		4. See 2

Test	Skill	Conditions	Standards
C	5. Approach swim from front	Struggling male victim of equal weight, deep water	5. See 2
	6. Surface dive (any type)		6. See 2
	7. Underwater approach		7. See 2
	8. Chin pull (variation)		8. See 2
D	9. Tired swimmer's carry (variation)	Partner of same sex, carry 100 feet (including one turn), end in deep water	9. See 2
	10. Pool lift		10. See 2
E	11. Release rear head-hold	Struggling male victim of equal size, deep water	11. See 2
	12. Shove to safety	8 feet from safety	12. Victim reaches safety with one push
F	13. Release double grip on one wrist	Struggling male victim of equal size, deep water	13. See 2
	14. Control carry	Carry 50 feet	14. See 2
G	15. Back press-arm lift resuscitation	Partner of same sex, on deck or beach	15. See 2
H	16. Chest pressure-arm lift resuscitation	Partner of same sex, on deck or beach	16. See 2

REFERENCES

American National Red Cross. *Basic Canoeing.* Washington, D.C.: American National Red Cross, 1963, 1965.

——. *Basic Rowing.* Washington, D.C.: American National Red Cross, 1964.

——. *Lifesaving Rescue and Water Safety.* Washington, D.C.: American National Red Cross, 1974.

——. *Life Saving: Rescue and Water Safety Instructor's Manual.* Washington, D.C.: American National Red Cross, 1974.

Arnold, Charles G., ed. *Aquatic Safety and Lifesaving Programs.* 2nd ed. New York: National YMCA Program Materials, 1979.

Boy Scouts of America. *Aquatics Program.* New Brunswick, N.J.: Boy Scouts of America, 1965.

Canadian Red Cross Society. *National Instructor Guide and Reference.* Toronto: Canadian Red Cross Society, 1977, pp. 107–48.

Council for National Cooperation in Aquatics. *Life Guard Training: Principles and Administration.* 2nd ed., rev. New York: National YMCA Program Materials, 1973.

Lanoue, Fred R. *Drownproofing.* Englewood Cliffs, N.J.: Prentice-Hall, Inc., 1963.

Palm, Jocelyn, ed. *Alert: Aquatic Supervision in Action.* Toronto: Royal Life Saving Society Canada, 1974.

Pia, Frank. "Observations on the Drowning of Non-Swimmers." *Aquatic Management Journal,* Vol. 3, No. 3 (1976–1977), pp. 3–5.

Pierce, Albert. "Deep Water Rescue Breathing." Mimeographed. Yeadon, Pa.

Silvia, Charles E. *Lifesaving and Water Safety Today.* New York: Association Press, 1965.

FILMS

American National Red Cross. *Survival Swimming. Nonswimming Rescues. Swimming Rescues. Special Equipment Rescues. Defenses, Releases and Escapes. Removal from the Water. Preventive Lifeguarding. Snorkeling Skills and Rescue Techniques. Boating Safety and Rescues. Survival for Sportsmen. Oars and Paddles.* Contact local ARC office.

Boy Scouts of America. *Trouble with Ice.* Contact local BSA office.

Drowning Facts and Myths. Water Safety Films, Inc., 3 Boulder Brae Lane, Larchmont, New York 10538.

National Safety Council. *Find a Float.* National Safety Council, 440 No. Michigan Ave., Chicago, Illinois 60611.

On Drowning. Water Safety Films, Inc., 3 Boulder Brae Lane, Larchmont, New York 10538.

Pierce, Albert. *Deep Water Rescue Breathing.* Pierce Productions, 29 Harvard Street, Arlington, Massachusetts 02174.

Pulse of Life. CPR. Multi-Media Standard First Aid. Contact local ARC office.

Safe Handling of Diving Injuries. American Film Producers, Inc., 1540 Broadway, New York, New York 10036.

POSTERS

Universal Drowning Poster. Water Safety Films, Inc., 3 Boulder Brae Lane, Larchmont, New York 10538.

CHAPTER 7

Aquatic Instruction for Preschool Children, Adults, and Special Populations

Swim Programs for Preschool Children
Swim Programs for Adults
Swim Programs for Special Populations

At least three groups require specially adapted aquatic programs. Each group represents a significant number of people who participate in aquatics, and each deserves effective instruction. Programs for preschool children, held in backyard, motel, school, or agency pools, are extremely popular. Adult programs are increasingly more common as comprehensive city recreation programs and retirement community programs are developed. Finally, classes for special populations are no longer always segregated; passage of P.L. 94-142 mandates that all such persons are entitled to instruction in the "least restrictive environment." For some, this means inclusion in regularly scheduled classes.

Members of these three groups may have difficulty in learning all the essential aquatic skills presented in Chapter 3. Nevertheless, that is the goal. With special teaching techniques, you should try to teach each skill given in Chapter 3 after reflecting on the material in this present chapter.

SWIM PROGRAMS FOR PRESCHOOL CHILDREN

Teaching school-age children to swim has always been of paramount importance to parents, instructors, teachers and agencies, but not until the early 1960s was there enthusiasm for enrolling very young children (six months to four years old) in classes. It was once felt that these children were "too young" to learn. However, agency and private pool operators found that these children could learn to swim, and that parents were quite willing to pay for this instruction. Now, nearly every agency, public pool, city recreation program, and private instructor conducts a preschool "learn to swim" program.

Children can learn to move in the water at very early ages, but many instructors continue to be apprehensive about their safety. Most experienced teachers will agree with the following admonition:

Because certain considerations affecting the child's learning and safety require a degree of development not attained by most children before they are three years old, the Council for National Cooperation in Aquatics recommends that the minimum age for organized swimming instruction be set at age three, and that it is imperative that parents be made to realize that even though preschoolers may learn to swim, *no young child,* particularly the preschooler can ever be considered "water safe" and must be carefully supervised when in or around water. (Council for National Cooperation in Aquatics, 1975)

The argument over whether children under three are too young for organized instruction is also controversial from a medical standpoint. Although there is no proof, some physicians advise that the stress of swimming may retard a child's growth, cause psychological damage, or even make a difference in swimming ability in later years. Experienced instructors may not believe these assertions, but all parties agree on the need for proper supervision.

No two preschool swimming programs are the same, because the facilities and instructors vary. Nevertheless, certain basic considerations (Table 7.1) should be taken into account by the beginning aquatic worker.

Table 7.1. Basic Considerations for Preschool Learn-to-Swim Programs

Goals

The main goal is to have fun while making children safer in water. Do not expect to quickly develop correct strokes in children under two years old.

Specific skills and techniques to help meet the goals include:

1. Water adjustment (face in water, etc.)
2. Survival and safety skills (bobbing, floating, resuscitation, reaching assists) if age of students permits
3. Enjoyment (not fear) of the water
4. Educating parents concerning safety procedures and aquatic teaching techniques
5. Developing muscular development, social adjustment, neurological coordination in children

Organization

For safety, strictly adhere to a 1:1 teacher-pupil ratio.

Restrict class size to 5 or fewer students if children between 6 months and 2 years old are enrolled. More students (as many as 10) can be taken if children are older (3-4 years) *and* safety can be ensured.

The chief instructor (trained professional) guides parents or assistant instructors as they work one-to-one with children. In most programs, a parent is usually with the child.

Programs should be short (3-6 weeks) and frequent (2-3 sessions per week). Water temperature (87°-92° preferred) and air temperature (85°-90°) determine length of class period (20-30 minutes).

Instructors (especially parents) must be trained. See Table 7.2.

Facilities and Equipment

The most important items in this category are bright, cheerful environment and high water temperatures (87°F or warmer).

A small pool and shallow water are desirable but often unavailable. Wading pool not desirable but can be used.

Toys (both floatable and sinkable) may be brought from home.

Flotation devices (buoyant belts, small tubes, kickboards, flippers) are commonly used.

Evidence (Thomas, 1976) suggests no appreciable increase in water sanitation problems, but frequent checks are advisable.

Teaching Techniques

Repeat class rules daily.

Prepare information sheet (goals, hints, home practice ideas) for parents.

Instructors should wear brightly colored, tight fitting suits.

Table 7.1–*continued*

Much repetition (e.g., 25 submergings each day, repeated several days) is essential. Learning doesn't mean one successful performance.

Ignore crying at first; it will stop! Persistent crying usually indicates discomfort (coldness, fatigue); don't ignore it.

Remember physical, psychological, and social limitations of students. Examples: easily fatigued; children under 12 months don't imitate easily; won't share toys.

Gabrielson (1972) advocates "total push" method (child is given tasks to perform each day). "Gentle persuasion" is also advocated.

Repeat organized games daily.

Let children warm up (sitting on deck with towel) if needed.

Allow free play time both before and after instruction.

Most children are not fearful, but avoid getting them in situations where you have to rescue them.

Use much reward and praise.

Instructors of preschool children should be gentle and persuasive. Some of the very best teachers are loving, understanding parents who wish to share a learning experience with their children. Since teachers are the key to a successful program, Table 7.2 discusses necessary qualifications and skills.

Table 7.2. Teachers of Preschool Programs

Selecting the Teachers

Most preschool programs require parents to be the teachers. But should they be?

Why parents *should* be teachers:

> Security to the child
> Able to motivate the child
> Usually enjoy the experience while improving their own water skill at same time

Why parents *should not* be teachers:

> May not be trained aquatic instructors (they can't do the skills, and want to use their own teaching techniques)
> May transmit their own fear of water to the child
> May overprotect the child (crying child may prevent them from being as forceful as necessary)

Our conclusion: Parents can be good instructors *if* they are trained. Regardless, the chief instructor must have special training (ARC, YMCA, recognized private program experience) and must supervise training program of all who help.

Training the Teachers

A planned training program (one to three sessions) must be held before the children are present. It should cover the following points:

Table 7.2—*continued*

Topic	Points to Cover
Goals of the program	See Table 7.1.
Safety procedures	Ensure safety at this facility *and* other likely swimming sites (e.g., wading pool at home, lake).
Working with children	Talk at their level. Have patience. Use persuasion. Follow leader's advice but be creative too. Don't expect polished swimmers.
Pool skills	
Water entry	Teacher enters water, then helps child into water
Swimming positions	With child on stomach (later on back), hold (rest) child's head on teacher's upper arm, support body from underneath, walk backward. Talk reassuringly! With child on stomach, walk forward, holding child just below the arm pit, or grasp flotation belt, or grasp suit. Talk reassuringly!
Submerging	Child (lying on stomach) face teacher, who grasps below the armpits. Pull child toward parent, submerging head and upper body as pull made. Begin with one second submersion, increase to 5–10 seconds.
Kicking	Teacher walks backward as child grasps teacher around neck, reach under child's body and move the legs up and down in flutter kick. Keep legs fairly straight.
Towing	Grasp extended arm of child with teacher's extended arms.

There are several excellent books written on teaching tots to swim (see Bibliography). For an overall view of the skills and procedures typical to most preschool programs, see Table 7.3.

In summary, preschool swimming instruction is an aquatic need and will be available in every comprehensive aquatic program. However, trained instructors and a safe environment are the essential guidelines; if these two characteristics cannot be met, forgo the program.

Table 7.3. Typical Skills in Preschool Swim Classes

I. Parent training (See Table 7.2)

II. Beginning preschool class

Skills	Comments
1. Safety in locker and pool area	1. Explain *and* demonstrate safety rules.
2. Entering and leaving pool	2. Stress that students *never* enter water unless teacher is already in. Practice ladder climb, or deck-level entry and exit.
3. Face in water	3. Blow water out of teacher's cupped hands (can practice at home).

Table 7.3–*continued*

Skills	Comments
4. Hanging on to edge	4. Careful! Deck-level pools have a poor gripping surface.
5. Travel along edge	5. Slide hands, not hand-over-hand.
6. Manipulated flutter kick (stomach, back)	6. Emphasize little splash. Keep legs straight, not stiff. Strive for continuous movement.
7. Submerging body parts	7. Submerge mouth first, then face, then head, then body.
8. Floating on stomach and back	8. Start from side, go 1'-2' to teacher; teacher pushes child back to side. Few students like to float on back at first.
9. Human stroke	9. Face in water. Manipulate the arms. Lift head for breath.
10. Kick a distance	10. Lift head for breath.
11. Pick up object under water	11. Teacher holds object just under water, then holds it deeper, and finally puts it on bottom. The child may need help to reach the bottom.
12. Enter water alone by slipping over edge, then by sitting-slide, then by jump	12. Be ready in case their hands slip on side. The child should jump into the water, not into the teacher's arms.

III. Advanced preschool class

Skills	Comments
1. Review safety procedures, skills of entering and leaving pool, face in water, floating, human stroke	1. Concentrate on improving arm strokes.
2. Increase distance travelled (kicking, swimming)	2. Push off from side, travel to parent.
3. Retrieve objects from bottom	3. Move to deeper water.
4. Jump off diving board	4. Can have students grasp pole.
5. Dive from deck	5. Use kneeling, standing, progression.
6. Finning on back	6. Add or permit inverted flutter kick.
7. Turn over from back to stomach, and vice versa	7. Push off, turn over while momentum is present.
8. Reaching assists	8. Explain, show film.
9. Mouth-to-mouth resuscitation	9. Explain, show film.

SWIM PROGRAMS FOR ADULTS

Adults should, in theory, be able to learn to swim easily. They understand concepts, they are motivated, and they have a wealth of experience in all kinds of psychomotor tasks. However, it is common to find that their enthusiasm rapidly wanes because they fail to progress as fast as they wish; their overall prowess has diminished more than they thought! Generally, more drop-outs occur as the students become older, and thus effective organization and teaching strategies by the instructor are a necessity.

As with all swim programs, some basic considerations underlie a successful adult swim program. Table 7.4 describes these considerations.

Table 7.4. Basic Considerations for Adult Learn-to-Swim Programs

Goals

Main goals of adult learn-to-swim programs are:

1. Personal enjoyment
2. Gain safety skills for self and others
3. Improve personal health and fitness

Specific skills and techniques that help meet these goals are:

1. Water adjustment, and corresponding fear reduction; learning at least two effective strokes
2. Survival floating, bobbing, turning over from stomach to back and vice versa, reaching assists, resuscitation
3. Ability to swim distances without undue fatigue

Organization

If possible, hold classes during the school day (less noise, less crowded).

Short (2-3 weeks) series of lessons are preferred, with 3–4 sessions per week. Sessions of 30–40 minutes are recommended.

Peer groups (same general age and ability levels) will attract and retain adults.

Supervised free time in water, before and after class, is desirable. It will be used primarily for swimming widths or lengths.

Permission by personal physician before entering program is desirable, especially for adults older than thirty-nine.

Safety procedures (e.g., CPR and first aid training by all instructors and guards, maximum teacher-pupil ratio of 1:10) must be followed.

Facilities and Equipment

Entry and exit from pool can be major problems. In absence of fixed ladders, put chairs or steps underwater in corners.

At the beginning, adults may be inactive, so warmer water (84°-86°) will be more comfortable.

Flotation devices may be useful and aid relaxation, but also may be embarrassing.

Swim flippers are useful in both learning the flutter kicks and swimming distances.

Motivating Adult Beginning Swimmers

Instructor who is humanistic and low key will have better success, as adults respond well to respect, politeness, and consideration of individuals.

The social aspect may be the most important adult goal; don't neglect it.

Enhancement of self-image is a key motivational device for adult beginners.

Instructor should emphasize values of swimming (e.g., gain lifetime skills, improve sense of well-being, slow the aging process, possible reduce frequency/severity of heart problems, improve general fitness level).

Understanding of adult fears, and means for rectifying them is essential.

Fear	Procedures for Reducing Fears
Water itself	Stress buoyancy skills, flotation devices if needed, survival floating.
Embarrassment	Small and similar grouping, demonstration by peers, self comparison and not comparison with others.

Table 7.4—*continued*

Failure to learn	Stress easy-to-complex progressions, continually compare self with past skill achievements, self-readiness more important than instructor's lesson plan.

Physical problems (vision, lack of strength) might necessitate special adaptations (e.g., wear glasses in water, wear small flotation device).

Early success is greatest motivator! Teach modified backstroke (inverted flutter kick, finning); goal is one width the first day, one length the second.

Teaching Strategies

Stress guided-discovery (e.g., instructor explains, class member demonstrates, adult experiments as instructor guides).

Begin with whole method, work on parts as needed.

Emphasize floating and survival floating skills early in course.

Strive for, but don't expect correct form in all strokes. Help with adaptations if necessary (e.g., extreme body roll to aid breathing in crawl, scissors kick in breaststroke).

Most adults find backstroke and sidestroke are easier to swim than crawl stroke and breaststroke. However, to many, swimming means only the crawl stroke. Attempt all strokes so that those who have problems with crawl stroke don't get discouraged.

Continually emphasize that the goal is easy movement through water, rather than speed or form.

Water exercises will improve aquatic skills as well as aid in conditioning.

Encourage daily distance swimming, gradually increasing yardage.

Don't stress diving; only a few will wish to learn.

Hearing problems of older adults, compounded by poor acoustics in pools, necessitates good volume and diction.

Additional material from Johnson (1978) and Smith (1978)

There are few training programs for teaching instructors of adult swimming. The skills taught to youth (excluding diving and lifesaving) provide the basis for course content. However, a final admonition is in order—adults (including senior citizens) are more interested in self-improvement than in competition. Techniques used with youth (kicking races across pool, holding breath the longest) are usually unappealing. What *is* appealing is a sense of accomplishment in navigating a distance without becoming exhausted!

SWIM PROGRAMS FOR SPECIAL POPULATIONS

Depending upon the criteria, there are approximately 50,000,000 Americans with some physical, mental, or emotional impairment.* The majority (90 percent) of these people have little or no diffi-

*The term "handicapped" is commonly used in the United States; however, it is more accurate to consider those with physical, mental or emotional problems as members of a special population, and thus the term "special population" will be used throughout this chapter to signify persons with various handicaps.

Appreciation is expressed to Dr. Ricardo Chavez, Colorado State University, for suggestions on this section.

culty in participating in regular aquatic programs. Until the last fifteen years, the remaining 10 percent had very little opportunity to participate in swimming programs; for the most part, they were restricted to occasional special programs conducted by interested groups of volunteers.

The tide has turned! With the passage of P.L. 94-142 and Section 504 of the Rehabilitation Act of 1973, the special populations have been given the opportunity to participate in "the least restrictive environment" (the most regularly scheduled program that he or she can benefit from). These laws do not prohibit special programs, but encourage "mainstreaming" (placing persons in a regular class until it is clearly shown that a special class would be more beneficial). Mainstreaming will become the common mode of aquatic instruction in the future.

What of the immediate future? The little research that has been done indicates that the handicapped gain more if they are mainstreamed (McIlwain, 1978). However, not all veteran swimming instructors would agree that mainstreaming is best. Both sides of this issue, followed by our recommendations, are summarized in Table 7.5.

Table 7.5. Advantages and Disadvantages of Mainstreaming of Special Populations

Advantages	P.L. 94-142 states that students should have an opportunity to succeed in regular classes before being moved.
	Programs that include all kinds of special populations as well as normals (reverse mainstreaming) increase awareness and concern of all participants.
	Special populations have problems throughout life; why make them feel different by a separate swimming class?
Disadvantages	Requires more, and specially trained, teachers.
	Without many teachers, a few special people with many normals make it extremely difficult to teach either group.
	Safety considerations for the special population require much time away from teaching.
	Special equipment and facilities needed by special students restrict total swim area.
	Most teachers are not currently qualified (and thus not enthusiastic) about working with special populations.

Our view: Society creates the handicaps, and some who are disabled are not handicapped in their ability to move through, be safe in, and enjoy aquatic sports. As more instructors become qualified, mainstreaming will gain impetus in aquatic programs. Professional aquatic workers will be required to become certified instructors of special groups. Eventually, only the most severely handicapped will be segregated into special classes.

We feel mainstreaming should be encouraged and supported. However, some people, because of their impairments, always will need segregated classes. These special classes are not easy to begin or sustain. Each community's program is unique and depends upon students, helpers, facilities, and community enthusiasm. Table 7.6 gives advice on initiating a program for special populations.

Because of the varied disabilities of the students, specific advice on all the techniques and skills needed by instructors is impossible to provide. Table 7.7 summarizes some skills, but attendance at workshops will always yield several "tricks of the trade," even for experienced instructors.

No textbook can replace actual experience in working with special populations. Since these people are normal in some ways and unique in others, adaptation is the key word. Nevertheless, Table 7.8 attempts to summarize several facts and concepts when working with persons with specific impairments.

Table 7.6. Initiating Programs for Special Populations

Goals

The overall goal is to enable students to enjoy aquatic activity regardless of their physical, mental, or emotional condition. "Programming for individuals with impairments is not designed to isolate them from ongoing programs. Rather, the purpose is to design swimming activities in which they will be able to participate in spite of their impairments." (Reynolds, 1974.)

Specific goals include:

1. Adapting recognized aquatic strokes and skills to the capabilities of the students
2. Ensuring the safety of the student, both now and in the future
3. Creating attitudinal beliefs in the special student, the parents or guardians, and normals that while handicaps are created by society, they are overcome by individuals

Organization*

Determine program needs
    Survey community to determine number of students, available facilities, and potential helpers.
Form sponsoring group
    Advisory Council shall represent every logical group of cross section of community.
    Council must contain at least one doctor.
    Subdivide into groups for specific tasks (Public Relations, Budget, etc.).
    Form plan of action.
    Select overall director.
Select and train personnel
    Director and Council select master teachers and/or assistants.
    Seek help from all community groups (schools, service clubs, medical units, etc.).
    Recruit personnel for both pool and other tasks (e.g., transportation, record keeping).
    Majority of helpers should (ideally) be certified by YMCA, Red Cross, or other organized groups before program begins.
    Inservice training must be continuous, as volunteers come and go. Master teacher should have extra training (e.g., Aquatic Council of AAHPERD course, or equivalent).
Public relations
    Designate director.
    Publicize worthiness of program through planned public relations effort.
    Cooperate with other agencies.

Facilities and Equipment*

Pool
    Get best local site (must consider access to buildings and locker rooms, how students enter water, deck space, pool depth, safety devices, special equipment needed, storage for equipment, acoustics, ventilation, water circulation).
    Obtain small pool if possible.
    Water temperature should be 85°-88° F.
    Make pool bright, cheerful; paint targets, lines, shapes on pool bottom.
Dressing area
    Accessible to wheelchairs.
    On same level as pool.
    Nonslip floor.
    Hand rails.

Table 7.6—*continued*

Funding*

While program might become self-supporting eventually, it is not likely.Contact local groups (United Way, service clubs, foundations, agencies). Government (local, county, state) are more apt to help initially. An ongoing successful program is usually necessary for federal grants.

*Adapted from Project Aquatic Mainstreaming, "Outline for a Successful Program for Mainstreaming Special Populations through Aquatic Programs," 1978; Spannuth, 1974; Gabrielsen, 1975; Rafolovich and Meehan, 1976; American National Red Cross, *Adapted Aquatics,* 1977.

Table 7.7. Teaching Procedures for Working with Special Populations

Beginning the Program

Start small (relatively few number of students).
Be successful (enroll those with greatest chance of success).
Be certain that all students have medical permission.
Start with younger children (ages 6-10).

Course Content

Consider Ersling's (1974) "Spiral Concept," i.e., simple to complex skills that increase self-confidence and feeling of accomplishment as tasks are successfully done. Skills taught in this sequence include:

1. Physical adaptation to water
2. Mobility (non-buoyant)
3. Floating
4. Leg propulsion
5. Arm propulsion
6. Combined arm-leg propulsion
7. Deep-water mobility

Teaching Procedures and Hints

Safety of students is paramount; *never* deviate from 1:1 ratio and observation of safety rules.
Establish consistent regulations for conduct in dressing area and pool.
Overcome fear of the situation; this will take time. Be imaginative, and develop adaptations. Movement exploration techniques are valuable (see Table 7.8).
All swimming activities (diving, underwater, snorkel, etc.) are appropriate.
Low fitness level may hinder learning.
Begin each day with group instruction, then individual work, then free time.
"Games approach" (Miller, 1976) is an excellent technique that works!
Basic concept is that students (of all ages) will overcome fears and progress more rapidly if tasks are fun.
All flotation devices are helpful, but controversial as to their regular use.
Gymnastics mats (5 ft. X 10 ft. X 1 in.) are excellent "floating stations." Useful for support while resting, practicing swimming movement, beginning diving.
Students become very attached to instructor; problems may arise when instructor is absent.

Record Keeping

After student leaves the control of the instructor, record that day's work. Indicate what was done, the progress, the problems, and what to practice next time.
Records are confidential, reviewed only by qualified persons (physical therapist, doctor, director, etc.)

Table 7.8. Teaching Swimming to Those with Specific Impairments

Orthopedic

An essential task is to improve muscle tone.
Stress breath control, floating, and balance.
Be especially careful about water entry and exit.
Beware of skin infections (from braces, etc.).
Modify strokes as much as needed.

Spina Bifida

Must control bladder and bowel function with collecting bags, diapers, etc.
Greater fear of water than those with other impairments.
Stress breath control, front and back crawl, breaststroke, elementary backstroke.
Students can swim distances but do so very slowly.

Cerebral Palsy

A competent instructor, who understands CP, is a necessity.
The main aim is to reduce unwanted movements.
Stress walking in water, breath control, back floating.
Gently force student to make movements; avoid dependency on instructor.

Mentally Retarded

Use multisensory approach—visual, auditory, kinesthetic.
Stress relaxation, repetition, fun, tangible rewards.
Part method is more successful than whole method.
Pre-water orientation (locker room, toilet, shallow and deep water, etc.) is essential.
Class procedures should be consistently followed.
Preschool, developmentally disabled persons especially need help.
Movement education methods are valuable (see below).
AAHPERD text (1969) is an excellent source of information.

Blind

Begin immediately to orient student to surroundings.
Guide students with lane lines, sounding devices, verbal cues, touching body parts.
When diving, have sighted person give "all clear" signal to blind person after he or she requests it.
Head-up swimming permits hearing instructions.
Any stroke (e.g., crawl) where one hand ahead of other is best (prevents ramming head into object).

Deaf

Talk face to face.
Enunciate clearly.
Have prearranged hand signals.

Deaf-Blind

Start swimming instruction as soon as possible, even at home.
Stages of instruction
    Beginning—develop trust relationship with instructor, water.adjustment, back floating (face floating difficult), security, directionality, leg development, stimulation of balance and body positions
    Intermediate—promote independence, face float
    Advanced—gradually teach all skills normally taught to beginners, stressing propulsion with safety
Must have trained leaders who understand special needs of blind-deaf.
Parents should be encouraged to enter water with child, but parent does not take the place of trained instructor.
Age and aquatic experience of child determines methods of teaching skills.

Table 7.8—*continued*

Mentally Ill

Socialization process and development of self-esteem, self-worth, self-confidence are main goals.
Mastery of skills (floating, movement through water) will reduce tension.
Ratio of 1:1 gradually changes until there are several students with one instructor.

Learning Disabled

Common characteristics include average or above intelligence, hyperactivity, perceptual problems,
emotional problems, perseveration (continual repeating of movement).
Swim program should aim more toward alleviation of the particular learning problem rather than
teaching swimming. Water activities then should reflect classroom perceptual skills and academic
programs as much as possible. Swim program should stress:
    Visual discrimination
    Auditory discrimination
    Auditory memory
    Eye-hand and eye-foot coordination
    Spatial awareness
Water adjustment is very stressful.
Initially, use small area of pool, marked off and not used by persons with other impairments.
Movement education concepts and methods are usually successful. For example:

Body Awareness Concepts	Examples
Move through water	Any stroke, glide
Raise and lower body part	Crawl stroke arms
Curling body	Tuck float
Stretch	Prone float
Pairs of limbs	Walk on lane line, one foot on either side

Space Awareness Concepts	
Personal space	Swimming laps, own space to kick
Direction	Catch, press, pull, recovery of arms in a stroke
Level	Underwater swimming
Size of movement	Finning vs. breast stroke arm action

Effort Awareness Concepts	
Strength	Tread water vs. speed swimming
Time	Flutter kick vs. scissors kick
Flow (smoothness)	Breast stroke for speed or distance
Force application (straight, curved, angular)	Arm action (press down vs. press back), dives

Stress individualized goal setting and progress rates.
Develop swimming strokes and skills if student is ready. Normally, great adaptations are not necessary.

Adapted from AAHPERD, 1969; Balch, 1974; Dougherty, 1972; Newman, 1970; Reid, 1976; Thayer, 1976.

CLASS ASSIGNMENTS

1. Observe a preschool swimming class. Focus specifically on one child, paying attention to how he or
   she:
   a. becomes adjusted to the water
   b. responds to comments by the instructor

   c. responds to comments by the parent

   d. reacts when water is splashed on the face

2. Observe a preschool swimming class. Focus specifically on the group, paying attention to:

   a. the safety techniques used

   b. the interaction between the head instructor and the parents

   c. the techniques used by the head instructor to direct the learning environment

3. Teach an adult at least one stroke. Contrast this experience with your prior experience teaching youngsters.

4. Observe a swimming program for a special population. Pay attention to:

   a. the safety techniques used

   b. how the leader directs the learning environment

   c. the stroke adaptations made by various individuals

5. Complete an ARC or YMCA training course for working with special populations.

6. Survey your community for facilities appropriate to each of the special groups mentioned in this chapter.

BEHAVIORAL OBJECTIVES

Because all aquatic instructors will, at one time or another, have preschool children, adults, or persons with special problems in their classes, we expect our students to respond correctly (based on material in this chapter) to questions calling for brief written answers, as indicated below.

1. Discuss the skills to be taught in a preschool children's swimming program, and at least one specific technique to teach each skill.

2. Prepare an outline that would aid parents in teaching a child how to safely swim on the stomach.

3. Construct a chart, showing similarities *or* contrasts, when teaching youngsters and adults these strokes: (a) elementary backstroke, (b) front crawl, (c) sidestroke.

4. Support or reject the concept of mainstreaming in aquatics.

5. Think of a friend who has an impairment. Outline how you would teach him or her to safely swim either on the stomach, side, or back.

REFERENCES

Swimming for Preschool Children

American National Red Cross. *Swimming and Water Safety.* Washington, D.C.: American National Red Cross, 1968.

American Red Cross. *Guide to Parent-Child Method of Teaching Pre-Kindergarten to Swim.* St. Louis: Bi-State Chapter of American Red Cross, 4901 Washington Blvd., St. Louis, Missouri, 63108.

Bory, Eva. *Teaching Your Child to Swim.* New York: Tradewinds Group, 1976.

Council for National Cooperation in Aquatics. *Water Fun for Everyone.* Manassas, Va.: Council for National Cooperation in Aquatics, 1981.

Cowle, Lucille. *Teaching Your Tot to Swim.* New York: Vantage Press, Inc., 1970.

DeBarbadillo, John, and Murphy, Marjorie. *Teaching the Very Young to Swim.* New York: National YMCA Program Materials, 1973.

Gabrielsen, B. W. "Teaching Pre-School Age Children to Swim." *Waters of the World: Use and Conservation.* 1972 CNCA Conference. Manassas, Va.: Council for National Cooperation in Aquatics, 1972, pp. 80–82.

Gabrielsen, M. A.; Spears, Betty; and Gabrielsen, B. W. *Aquatic Handbook.* 2nd ed. Englewood Cliffs, N. J.: Prentice-Hall, Inc. 1968, pp. 50–62.

Haircourt, Roy, *Beginner's Guide to Swimming and Water Safety*. New York: Drake Publishers, Inc., 1972.

Hart, Robert D., "Medical Aspects of Pre-School Aquatic Program." *Aquatics for All*. 1976 CNCA conference, Manassas, Va.: Council for National Cooperation in Aquatics, 1976, pp. 57–59.

Kauffman, Carolyn. *How to Teach Children to Swim*. New York: Cornerstone Library Publications, 1966.

Newman, Virginia Hunt. *Teaching the Infant to Swim*. New York: Harcourt Brace Jovanovich, 1967.

———. *Teaching Young Children to Swim and Dive*. New York: Harcourt Brace Jovanovich, 1969.

Petzel, Pauline. *Teach Your Tot to Swim*. St. Petersburg, Fla.: Great Outdoors Publishing Company, 1975.

Prudden, Bonnie. *Your Baby Can Swim*. New York: Reader's Digest Press, 1977.

Thomas, David G., "Pool Chemistry and Pre-School Swimming Programs," *Aquatics For All*. 1976 CNCA Conference. Manassas, Va.: Council for National Cooperation in Aquatics, 1976, pp. 62–64.

Swimming for Adults

American National Red Cross. *Swimming and Water Safety*. 1st ed. Washington, D.C.: American National Red Cross, 1968, pp. 41–42.

Ferinden, William. *Teaching Swimming*. 4th ed. Linden, N.J.: Remediation Associates, 1975, pp. 123–28.

Gabrielsen, B. W. "Swimming for Adults and Elderly." *Waters of the World: Use and Conservation*. 1972 CNCA Conference. Manassas, Va.: Council for National Cooperation in Aquatics, 1972, pp. 76–79.

Johnson, Ralph L. "Leadership in Adult Aquatics." *New Horizons in Aquatics*. Manassas, Va.: Council for National Cooperation in Aquatics, 1978, pp. 40–45.

Smith, Murray. "Adults as Participants in Aquatic Programs," *New Horizons in Aquatics*. Manassas, Va.: Council for National Cooperation in Aquatics, 1978, pp. 45–50.

Swimming for Special Populations

AAHPERD. *A Practical Guide for Teaching the Mentally Retarded to Swim*. Reston, Va.: AAHPERD, 1969.

American National Red Cross. *Adapted Aquatics*. Washington, D.C.: American National Red Cross, 1977.

Aquatic Council of AAHPERD. Course Outline for Teacher of Handicapped Swimming.

Balch, Roland. "The Handicapped and their Abilities." *Action in Aquatics*. Manassas, Va.: Council for National Cooperation in Aquatics, 1974, pp. 25–30.

Canadian Red Cross Society. *Manual for Teaching Swimming to the Disabled*. Toronto: Canadian Red Cross Society.

Cordellos, Harry C. *Aquatic Recreation for the Blind*. Reston, Va.: AAHPERD, 1976.

Council for National Cooperation in Aquatics and AAHPERD. *Information Sheet: Aquatics for the Impaired, Disabled, and Handicapped*. Mimeographed pamphlet, 1972. Project No. OEG-0-72-5454-233563, Department of Health, Education and Welfare.

Dougherty, Chuck. *Motor Development and Aquatic Activity for the Deaf-Blind Child*. Mimeographed. Paper presented at National Workshop on Project Aquatics, Denver, 1974.

Dunn, John. *Practical Suggestions for Mainstreaming in Aquatics*. Mimeographed. Physical Education Department, Oregon State University, Corvallis, 1975.

Ersling, Walter F. "The Spiral Concept—An Approach in Teaching Swimming to the Developmentally Disabled and Mentally Retarded." *The Physical Educator*, May 1974. pp. 72-74

Gabrielsen, M. A. "Pool Facilities for Impaired and Disabled Persons." *Swiming Pools: A Guide to their Planning, Design and Operation*. Fort Lauderdale: Hoffman Publications, 3rd ed., 1975.

Heckathorn, Jill. *Strokes and Strokes: An Instructor's Manual for Developing Swim Programs for Stroke Victims*. Reston, Va.: AAHPERD, 1980.

Lawrence, Connie C., and Hackett, Layne C., *Water Learning: A New Adventure*. Palo Alto, Calif.: Peek Publications, 1975.

MacIlwain, Lionel. Speech given at Operation Mainstreaming Conference, Denver, February 1978.

Miller, Joan. "The Game Approach: A Teaching Method for Water Programs." *Aquatics for All*. Manassas, Va.: Council for National Cooperation in Aquatics, 1976, pp. 73–77.

Newman, Judy. *Swimming for Children with Physical and Sensory Impairments*. Springfield, Ill.: C.C. Thomas, 1970.

——. "Swimming for the Spina Bifida." *JOHPER*, October 1970, pp. 67–68.

Priest, Louise. "A Look at Attitudes." *New Horizons in Aquatics*. Manassas, Va.: Council for National Cooperation in Aquatics, 1978, pp. 62–63.

Rafalovich, Mary, and Meehan, Dan, "Advanced Training of Volunteers and Professional Personnel." *Aquatics for All*. Manassas, Va.: Council for National Cooperation in Aquatics, 1976, pp. 36–37.

Reid, Ruth. "Movement Education in Aquatics for the Handicapped." *Aquatics for All*. Manassas, Va.: Council for National Cooperation in Aquatics, 1976. pp. 92–97.

Reynolds, Grace D. *A Swimming Program for the Handicapped*. New York: National YMCA Program Materials, 1973.

——. "Adaptive Swimming–New Programs for the Handicapped." *YMCA Today*, Summer 1974, p. 4.

——. "Integration of Community Resources in Programming for Those with Special Needs." *Aquatics for All*. Manassas, Va.: Council for National Cooperation in Aquatics, 1976, pp. 71–73.

Spannuth, John R. "Organization and Administration of Aquatic Programs for the Handicapped." *Action in Aquatics*. Manassas, Va.: Council for National Cooperation in Aquatics, 1974, p. 31.

Thayer, Jenny. "Teaching the Learning Disabled Child in Aquatics." *Aquatics for All*. Manassas, Va.: Council for National Cooperation in Aquatics, 1976, pp. 78–80.

Basic Sources of Information for Special Populations

Orozco, Robert. *Mainstreaming Resources*. National Board of YMCA.

Recreation Center for the Handicapped, 207 Skyline Blvd., San Francisco, California 94132.

Project Aquatics Mainstreaming, YMCA of Southwest Washington, Box 698, Longview, Washington 98632.

Special education category in library indices.

Stein, Julian, adapted physical education specialist, AAHPERD, 1900 Association Drive, Reston, Virginia 22091.

Films for Special Populations

American Red Cross, *Focus on Ability*. Stock No. 321604. Shows basic techniques of dealing with persons who have orthopedic, mental, emotional, or sensory disabilities.

Documentary Films. *Splash*. Documentary Films, Aptos, California 95003.

CHAPTER 8

Evaluation of Swimming Skills

What is Involved in Evaluation?
Basic Considerations
Standards
Recording Achievement
Completing and Submitting Records
Basic Evaluation Procedures

The beginning instructor thinks that teaching a class is comparatively easy, if the printed instructions of the organization are followed. This is generally true. But the evaluation of students is often a different story. Not all organizations outline precise standards to be met by students—and the objectives of some school programs are even more vague.

WHAT IS INVOLVED IN EVALUATION?

To evaluate effectively, every aquatic instructor must first ask, "How good must the student be to pass this course?" This question leads to the practical problem of how much time and effort to devote to teaching and how much to testing. Other questions quickly arise. Where is the information concerning the tests? What record forms are available, and must these forms be used? If so, how are they completed? Assuming that you know what to test on, how can the results be recorded so that you later can tell a student specifically why he did not pass a particular test?

Teaching in a school presents additional problems. Will the ARC or YMCA program be followed, or will a local program be developed? Can objectives for the course be devised that meet the purposes of the course? Can they be clearly understood by the students? What is the difference between an A student and an F student? Will you adhere to a set of grading standards (and run the risk of all students earning the same grade), or will you use the natural curve method? Whichever method you use, what knowledge of elementary statistics will you need to develop the standards and determine letter grades?

We cannot provide the final answers. However, we believe our suggestions will help meet the problem facing you in a particular situation.

BASIC CONSIDERATIONS

Before evaluation can be attempted, the instructor must decide: (1) what standards of achievement are expected and (2) how much time will be devoted to evaluation. Meaningful evaluation will be a difficult, if not impossible, process unless these factors are considered.

The standards of achievement can vary greatly from program to program. The ARC and YMCA have exact listings of skills to be taught. The instructor is authorized to conduct a specific course and all students in this course are expected to have the same minimum level of skill at the completion of the course. But the standard of performance is not always precisely specified; for example, "The student should swim [using various styles or strokes] with proper coordination, breathing, and effective stroking . . . " (ARC, *Swimming and Water Safety Courses,* p. 78). What is "effective stroking?"

The great variety of aquatic skills possessed by students in a physical education class makes it virtually impossible to conduct a "regular" beginners, advanced swimmers, or other course in school situations. If several instructors are available, then several levels of instruction can be given at once. Because this usually is not feasible, the individual instructor develops a local course with local standards. The fact that letter grades must be given complicates matters. The beginning instructor is faced with deciding what skills to teach, how well these skills should be mastered, and then how to grade. This chapter, we hope, will help resolve some of these issues.

How to test must also be considered. Some instructors test throughout the course. Normally, this means teaching a skill on one day and testing each student during the next one or two sessions. When a student has passed all the tests, he has passed the course. Most of the ARC and YMCA courses are taught in this manner; these organizations provide skill sheets (discussed later) which make daily testing feasible. Testing throughout the course is highly motivating for most students; they see that they are making steady progress. It also provides the instructor with a clear picture of the rate of progress for each student in the class.

Other instructors maintain that testing during most class sessions wastes time that could be more profitably spent in practicing or learning new skills. They emphasize that all aquatic courses are designed to ensure a certain level of skill at the conclusion of the course, not in the middle. These instructors assert that two full days of testing at the end of a course will enable all those who should pass to do so.

Most instructors use skill sheets and tests throughout any swimming course they conduct. They feel that the advantages of student motivation outweigh any time that is lost in testing. Whatever the decision, testing must be done with specific standards in mind.

STANDARDS

In an ARC, YMCA, or other organized program, the instructor's primary responsibility is to teach the expected skills and to make certain that the students are qualified according to the standards of that group. Listings of skills and evaluation standards are found in the books described in Table 8.1.

Table 8.1. Texts for Swimming and Rescue-Lifesaving Courses

Course	Student Text	Instructor's Text
Swimming		
ARC	*Swimming and Water Safety,* 1968 edition. Descriptions of swimming strokes, related aquatic skills, diving fundamentals, safety, survival floating, and artificial respiration. Basic text for students in all ARC swimming courses.	*Instructor's Manual: Swimming and Water Safety Courses,* 1968 edition. General information for teaching, and descriptions of the skills and standards of each course. *Manual for the Basic Swimming Instructor,* 1974 edition. Sections 1-7 are virtually the same as Sections 1-6 and 10 of the *Instructor's Manual for Swimming and Water Safety Courses.* One new section, "Game Approach to Teaching Children," is included.

Table 8.1–*continued*

Course	Student Text	Instructor's Text
YMCA	None	*Progressive Swimming and Springboard Diving,* 1972 edition. YMCA instructional methods, training, and testing from beginning swimmer through advanced watermanship, specific comments on administration, and outlines for 10 aquatic lectures.
CRCS	None	*National Instructor Guide and Reference,* 1977 edition. Describes in detail all items in CRCS learn-to-swim programs. Student's common errors and corrections. Evaluation standards are given.

Swimming for special populations

ARC	None	*Adapted Aquatics,* 1977 edition. Considers theory and practice for swimming programs for people with physical or mental handicaps. Includes techniques for specific handicaps and disabilities, program organization, and teaching methods.
		Methods in Adapted Aquatics, 1977 edition. Designed specifically for those enrolling in ARC instructor's course in adapted aquatics.
YMCA	None	*A Swimming Program for the Handicapped.* Detailed discussions of the philosophy, recruitment and training of personnel, teaching strategies, handicaps encountered, and facility requirements for aquatic programs for the handicapped. (Current text under revision.)
CRCS	None	*Manual for Teaching Swimming to the Disabled,* no date. Aims and objectives, values of swimming, types of disabilities, and planning and administering programs.
Other		AAHPERD. *A Practical Guide for Teaching the Mentally Retarded to Swim,* 1969 edition. Methods, progressions, stunts, facilities, and program organization for improving aquatic instruction to the mentally retarded.

Rescue and lifesaving

ARC	*Basic Rescue and Water Safety,* 1974 edition. Basic water safety techniques (e.g., assists, PFDs, boating safety) and basic rescue techniques (clothing inflation, survival floating, search and rescue, recovery of submerged victims) that can be done by nonswimmers and beginners or children over 9.	*Manual for the Basic Swimming Instructor,* 1974 edition. Sections 9–13 outline the basic water safety course. The basic rescue and water safety course content, techniques, etc. is given on pp. 95–109. See text below for additional help when teaching these courses.

Table 8.1—*continued*

Course	Student Text	Instructor's Text
	Lifesaving: Rescue and Water Safety, 1974 edition. Lifesaving skills and techniques for the advanced lifesaving course.	*Instructor's Manual: Lifesaving, Rescue and Water Safety,* 1974 edition. To be used when teaching basic water safety, basic rescue and water safety, and advanced lifesaving courses. Outlines the units, gives teaching suggestions, and indicates the skills (but not the standards) for the final examination.
YMCA	*Aquatic Safety and Lifesaving Program,* 1979 edition. Describes the YMCA safety and lifesaving program. To be used when taking or teaching aquatic safety, advanced aquatic safety, and senior lifesaving courses. Contains text and illustrations of units.	*Aquatic Safety and Lifesaving Programs,* 1979 edition. Text description given in left-hand column. Chapter 16 contains lesson plans for senior lifesaving course.

RECORDING ACHIEVEMENT

None of the organizations require that the instructor keep records as the course is being taught, but it is wise to do so. Both the ARC (see Chart 8.1) and the YMCA (see Chart 8.2) provide helpful guides. The ARC worksheets are more convenient to the instructor. One sheet contains names of all students in class, plus a listing of the skills to be tested, and a box for each skill to be checked as it is successfully done. Some instructors add two more features to their worksheets: (1) space for comments and/or totals; and (2) a key for the code (Examples: P means passed, P– means poor but passing, Ab means absent, etc.).

Chart 8.1 is a reproduction of a Red Cross swimming worksheet. Instructors in school aquatic programs can easily develop similar skill sheets. Posting a copy of the skill sheet where all students can see it will prepare them for the next skills to be taught.

For lifesaving tests, it is possible to develop specific directions which explain what is desired. For example, a test involving the lifesaving entry, approach swim, contact and carry could be done in this fashion.

1. Victim of approximately the same weight as rescuer is in vertical position in deep water, arms at surface, facing shallow end, five feet from deep end.
2. Rescuer enters water at shallow end with lifesaving dive. The stopwatch is started with the first movement of the dive.
3. Rescuer may use any stroke in approach but must not take eyes off victim.
4. The approach distance is sixty feet.
5. The rescuer must
   a. Reverse
   b. Make front surface approach
   c. Level victim
   d. Assume cross-chest carry
       Victim held firmly
       Rescuer's hips placed under victim's back

Chart 8.1. Red Cross Swimming Worksheet

COURSE	GROUP	DATE STARTED	DATE COMPLETED	INSTRUCTOR OR AIDE

- Skills for courses are listed on reverse side.
- Skills may be written in space provided or checked by number.
- Use *Swimming and Water Safety Courses: Instructor's Manual* (Stock No. 321216) for teaching courses.
- Record activity on *Course Record—Swimming/Water Safety* (Form 5722).

GRADE "P." PASSING "INC." INCOMPLETE

PARTICIPANT'S NAME	1	2	3	4	5	6	7	8	9	10	11	12	13	14	15	16	17	18	19	20	
1.																					
2.																					
3.																					
4.																					
5.																					
6.																					
7.																					
8.																					
9.																					
10.																					
11.																					
12.																					
13.																					
14.																					
15.																					
16.																					
17.																					
18.																					
19.																					

Chart 8.2. YMCA Minnow Progress Card

NAME

MINNOW
(Advanced Beginner)

Date Passed

1. Survival Float–3 minutes on front (drownproofing). _____

2. Lifesaving Skills–Reaching and extension assists from shore (pole, towel, etc.). Mouth-to-mouth resuscitation. _____

3. Safety Swim–Jump into deep water, swim 30 feet on front, tread and scull 10 seconds, return to starting point using flutter back scull. _____

4. Endurance Swim–Front dive, swim 60–75 feet front crawl stroke with rotary breathing, return back crawl. _____

Date Started_____Date Completed_____

SEE YOUR SWIMMING TEACHER FOR INSTRUCTIONS.
Be SURE to complete these skills and go on to the next.

Next Program: FISH–Intermediate Swimmer

Source: National YMCA Program Materials. Used by permission.

Victim must not assist with arms or legs

Victim's face must not submerge at any time

6. The watch is stopped as rescuer's head crosses pool line at twenty-foot mark (length of tow is forty feet).

7. An elapsed time greater than sixty seconds is failure. Any error in technique (items 2, 3, 5, 6) means automatic failure.

The ARC requires students to achieve a certain number of points in their final test. Points for the above test item can be assigned as follows (assuming the instructor wishes to assign seven points for excellent performance).

35 seconds or less = 7 points
36–40 seconds = 6 points
41–45 seconds = 5 points
46–49 seconds = 4 points
50–53 seconds = 3 points
54–57 seconds = 2 points
58–60 seconds = 1 point

COMPLETING AND SUBMITTING RECORDS

Completing the records is not a difficult process–if directions are followed. Two copies are submitted, and a third copy retained for your records. Beginning instructors are invariably careless with their own records, but experience will soon show that at least one inquiry (either from the organization or a student) can be expected for each three classes taught.

Instructors should sign each form properly and submit it as soon as possible. For ARC courses, the form is submitted to the local chapter. In YMCA courses, the physical director for the local association receives the form and then sends it to the proper headquarters.

Experienced instructors have adopted several "tricks of the trade." These are explained in Table 8.2.

Table 8.2. Completing and Submitting Records

Item	Suggestions
Allowing a student in your class	It is very important to check the eligibility of each student for each particular course, especially the lifesaving courses that have an age requirement. The problem of what to do with a person who is "almost" the proper age will always arise. Most instructors will allow the person to enroll if the birthday falls before the completion of the course. Some instructors will accept anyone whose birthday falls within three or four weeks of the completion of the course. However, extending the limits invariably causes problems. An underage person cannot be officially passed, and if enrolled, there will be a delay in sending the record or changing the age. In the long run, following the exact requirements is the best procedure for the organization, the student, and the instructor.
Screening the class	Instructors in ARC and YMCA courses are sometimes judged on the number of students they pass during the season. One way to increase this total is to have all students, regardless of swimming ability, begin in the lowest level and quickly earn all awards up to their true level. While this looks good on the records, it is wasteful on three accounts: (1) most of the instructor's time should be spent teaching, not testing; (2) the student is there to learn new skills, not to enhance someone's reputation as a swimming teacher; and (3) it costs money and time to process the records. There is no justification for this practice. A qualified teacher should be able to screen students so that they will start in the proper class and progress normally—not from beginner through advanced swimming in two months.
Using work copy for your records	Keep one copy of the skill sheet on the clipboard and be unconcerned about its wrinkled appearance. It won't be presentable for submission, but can become the third (personal) copy.
Omission of students from final record sheet	Most experienced instructors submit records with few, if any, names of students who have failed the course. This does not imply that there are no students in this category! Since the original sheet (which lists the names of all class members) is used as the guide when making the official record, merely omit the names of those who failed when filling out the copies to be sent in.
Distributing award certificates	If certificates can be given the same day that the class terminates, it minimizes work for the instructor. However, usually there is a delay before the awards are ready for distribution. Experienced instructors soon learn to have each student who will earn a certificate hand in a stamped, self-addressed envelope. After the certificates are returned to the instructor to be signed, it is a simple matter to put them into the envelopes and mail them. It might seem easier and less expensive for the student to call for the certificate at an office, but invariably the awards are not yet ready and this causes consternation to all concerned. Mailing seems to be by far the best answer.

BASIC EVALUATION PROCEDURES

Constructing Behavioral Objectives

It is extremely difficult to transplant a regulation swim program into the average physical education program. The level of skill in a school class is usually so mixed that one instructor cannot properly teach every student. For a homogeneous group, or if there are several instructors for the several skill levels, the ARC program is recommended.

However, most instructors in a physical education program develop their own courses, using either the ARC or YMCA program as their primary sources. In developing a course, the instructor is at an immediate disadvantage because objectives must be developed based on local needs, and the national groups have already decided upon theirs. Objectives refer to those statements which indicate the course content. The listing of skills to be taught (with their standards of evaluation) are in fact a statement of the objectives of the Red Cross and YMCA programs.

The primary objective of the YMCA and ARC is the development of aquatic skills. However, school programs customarily have at least two other objectives—development of attitudes and knowledge. The instructor must decide before the course which objectives to seek, and state them clearly to students.

Quite often the objectives for a unit or course of study are so vague that they do not mean the same thing to all people. For example, one objective of any ARC, YMCA, or school aquatic program is "to swim the breaststroke correctly." Yet, in every lifesaving or water safety instructor class, at least one student performs the breaststroke with a scissors kick, doesn't glide, or pulls the arms past shoulder level. This student was passed by an instructor who apparently didn't know or didn't apply the usual standards for the breaststroke. If the objective was "The student must be able to swim the breaststroke for fifty feet, must use the whip kick, must not pull past the shoulder level, and must glide at least two seconds with the face in the water between strokes," every instructor could probably agree as to what an acceptable stroke should be.

The objective just described is termed "behavioral," because it specifically tells what the behavior of the learner should be after he has learned. The objectives listed at the end of most chapters in this book are behavioral objectives. These objectives should be written so exactingly that all readers will know precisely what we expect of our students. Any student, whether working for a certificate or a grade, wants to know beforehand exactly what must be done to pass the course. The ARC and YMCA have both clearly defined the skills to be taught in their courses, but a list of skills does not necessarily ensure that all instructors will apply the same standards.

Behavioral objectives are not easy to construct because they require careful consideration and precise writing. The objectives in the chapters of this text meet the characteristics of good behavioral objectives, as given by Mager (1962, p. 53).

1. A good behavioral objective identifies the behavior to be demonstrated by the learner (i.e., it specifically names and describes the skill).
2. A good behavioral objective states the conditions under which it will occur (i.e., it specifically tells how the learner will be tested).
3. A good behavioral objective indicates a standard of acceptable performance (i.e., it specifically tells what score is required to "pass" the test or it lists specific things that must be done).

Table 8.3 describes several typical objectives, with an analysis of the three desirable characteristics.

To read more examples of behavioral objectives written to meet Mager's specifications, we suggest rereading the objectives at the end of the chapters.

An instructor will quickly realize the practical value of behavioral objectives when evaluations begin. The instructor knows exactly what to test on, what test to use, and what score must be earned to achieve a passing grade.

Table 8.3. Behavioral Objectives

Behavioral Objective	Characteristics		
	Behavior to Be Demonstrated	Condition under which Behavior Will Occur	Standard of Acceptable Performance
1. From the 1-meter board, the student must perform a forward dive, pike position. To pass, the student must use a 3-step approach, a vertical hurdle, take-off at 10-20° angle, pike position without bending at knees, nearly vertical entry with legs straight and toes pointed.	Forward dive, pike position	Diving from the 1-meter board	Three-step approach, vertical hurdle, takeoff at 10-20° angle. No bend of knees in pike position. Nearly vertical entry with legs straight and toes pointed. NOTE: Instead, the standard could be: "Score at least 15 pts. (3 judges) in performing the dive." This is explicit enough for experienced judges, but not for novice judges.
2. Swim the sidestroke 50 yards, using the shallow arm-pull, scissors kick, and minimum glide of 2 seconds.	Swim sidestroke	Swim 50 yards	Shallow arm-pull, scissors kick, glide of 2 seconds. NOTE: Instead, the standard could be "Swim 50 feet in 8 strokes or less, using the shallow arm-pull and the scissors kick."
3. In a written examination, be able to define "massed" and "distributed" practice, according to the views of the authors of this text.	Defining "massed" and "distributed" practice	Written examination	*Massed practice:* When a certain amount of practice is given at a certain time. *Distributed practice:* Same amount of time is divided into several days' practice.
4. Demonstrate a favorable attitude toward swimming, as evidenced by voluntarily attending 5 recreational swim periods.	Favorable attitude toward swimming	Recreational swim period	Voluntary attendance at five sessions.
5. Indicate satisfactory swimming improvement by passing at least 8 tests at the end of the course which could not be passed at the beginning.	Satisfactory improvement	Taking tests at the end of the course	Passing 8 or more tests that could not be passed at the beginning of the course.

Again, students should know at the beginning of a course exactly what the objectives are. The job of the instructor is to help as many as possible achieve the desired standards. Much more motivation comes when the student knows exactly what he must do.

The Importance of the Mean Score and the Standard Deviation

All systems of evaluation are based on some comparison, either between test scores or between persons. This comparison can be subjective (based on judgment of the tester) or objective (based on mathematical figures). Objective evaluations generally are preferred. But, many instructors fear that they lack competence in simple statistical procedures.

To learn how to calculate the mean score and the standard deviation, you will need to consult a book with some emphasis on elementary statistics, such as Johnson's and Nelson's *Practical Measurements for Evaluation in Physical Education.* The calculations are not difficult, whatever your mathematical background. With the mean and standard deviation known, it is then possible to construct a logical and fair grading system, based either on achievement scores or the normal curve.

The Importance of Achievement Scales

How do we judge if a person is a good swimmer? Ordinarily we observe the swimmer doing a particular stroke over a distance, and judge proficiency on the basis of our knowledge and experience. A beginning instructor simply does not have the knowledge or experience to do this.

But, there are other ways to judge how skilled a swimmer is. By referring to a table of past scores for this test, we can quickly evaluate a current student. These tables of past scores (which actually list all the possible scores) are called scales or norms. A scale is composed of a number of scores, one of which tells how good one person is compared to others in the group. For example, if someone can swim twenty five yards of the sidestroke taking no more than four strokes, he or she scores higher than someone who takes ten strokes to cover the same distance. Or, someone who can swim 1,000 yards in twenty minutes is considered better than another person from the same group who can only swim 700 yards of the same stroke in twenty minutes.

Any instructor can construct crude scales with the following steps.

1. Have all students perform the same test following exactly the same procedure.
2. Record the results in some objective fashion (count, time with a watch, etc.).
3. Put the scores in one long list (best scores on top).
4. Note what the top, middle, and bottom scores are. If there are at least fifteen in the group, and they are judged to be normal in skill development, then the instructor can use these scores as a means of assigning letter grades *for this group only.*

Establishing scales according to correct statistical procedures is more time-consuming, but worthwhile because they can be used for any similar group, regardless of its number or variation in skill development. With scales, it is also possible to average certain scores (for example, distance swum underwater, and the time it takes to swim fifty yards of the back crawl) to arrive at one common number for grading purposes.

A scale for any test can be developed by a comparatively simple statistical procedure, if there are a sufficient number of scores. It is desirable to have at least a hundred scores from similar subjects, but scales can be made from as few as thirty test scores. (The greater the number of scores, the more assurance the instructor can have that the group is normal. The scores of several smaller classes can be combined into one large group for the purpose of constructing scales if the same test is administered the same way to each group.) There are different scales which can be used, such as T scores, z scores, 8 sigma, Hull, and others. We recommend the Hull Scale as the most useful because it provides for a great range of scores (from very high to very low) and yet rewards a very good test score with a high number. Study of any elementary statistics or physical education tests and measurements book will show you a simple way to construct achievement scales.

If Hull Scales are constructed for a number of tests, the points earned on different kinds of tests can be averaged as shown in Table 8.4.

The two important features of achievement scales, then, are that they permit you to evaluate current students on the basis of past students and allow you to average scores from different tests.

Table 8.4. Averaging Hull Scores (Hypothetical Data)

Hull Scale Points	Breaststroke Test (Yards per 5 minutes)	Crawl Stroke Test (Seconds per 50 yards)	Underwater Swim Test (feet)
55	200	28.3	
54	195	28.7	80
53	190	29.1	78
52	185	29.8	77
51	180	29.9	76
50	175	30.3	75
49	170	30.7	73
48	165	31.1	72
47	160	31.5	71
46	155	31.9	70

Calculation of average score for a hypothetical swimmer:

Performance	Hull Scale Points
180 yards breaststroke in 5 min.	51
50 yards of crawl stroke in 30.7 sec.	49
70 feet underwater	46
	146

146 ÷ 3 = 46.6 average

Assigning Letter Grades

The two methods most used for grading are the "standards" approach, and the "normal curve" approach. For the standards approach, the instructor arbitrarily decides that if all skills are passed, a grade of "A" will be earned; if 90 percent are passed, a grade of "B" will be earned, and so on. (Actually, to give a letter grade using ARC and YMCA standards is impossible, because in both of these organizations all test items must be passed before the certificate is earned. This, in effect, is the pass-or-fail grading system, which is not always appropriate for a school situation.)

This grading system has a major flaw. Several students will pass the same percentage of the tests, but some of these swimmers perform more proficiently than others. Also, some tests are considerably easier than others. A possible solution is to weight each test according to difficulty. For example, in a beginning swimmer class, one point is awarded for doing the tuck float for five seconds, five points for jumping off the high board, ten points for swimming twenty-five yards underwater. A class of college males may be awarded points by the following system:

5 points—75 ft. elem. back, 75 ft. side, 75 ft. breast, 75 ft. crawl, 75 ft. trudgen, 75 racing back

5 points—100 yd. elem. back, 100 yd. side, 100 yd. breast

15 points—30 ft. underwater

20 points—1-min. vertical tread without use of hands

30 points—450 yard swim, 5-minute tread

Such a system will offer a wider range of total points and motivate people to master the more difficult skills rather than a certain percentage of all skills required.

Instructors who use the standards approach predetermine what the standard shall be for a particular letter grade. If they weight the tests, they may say that 95 points of a possible 100 would be an A, 88-94 points, a B, 80-87 points a C, and 70-80 points a D. Anyone below 70 would fail. Of, if Hull Scales are used for all tests, an average of 80 or better would be an A, 60-79 a B, 40-59 a C, 20-39 would be a D, and below 20 would be a failure. An entire class might earn A or B grades or most members of a very poor class may be in the "D" bracket. Instructors who favor this approach point out that a person who earns a C grade in the current class is comparable to a C student in previous classes. This leads to consistency in grading.

The normal curve is more popular for assigning grades. (Instructors who favor the standards approach will indicate that they have already considered the curve. They say that experience with several similar groups has already shown them how good the A student is.) When using the normal curve method, the instructor assumes that the class is normal in ability (some are good students, some are poor, and the majority are average. Therefore, the grades should be about what a normal group would receive. Adequate statistical explanations are available in texts (see Johnson and Nelson, Chapter 3), which describe the way a normal group is distributed; generally, we know that the great majority are in the middle, and fewer students are found as we go above and below that middle of the group. The normal curve approach to grading says that if a certain part of the standard deviation is used, it is possible to assign letter grades. The most common standard deviation segment used is one, as shown in Chart 8.3.

Chart 8.4 shows how letter grades could be assigned.

Instructors must remember that in some test items, the smaller number is the better score (e.g.,

Chart 8.3. Grading by the Normal Curve

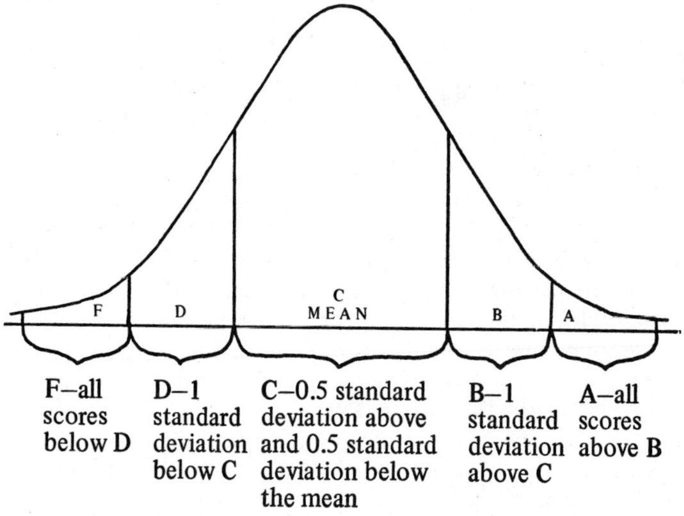

| F—all scores below D | D—1 standard deviation below C | C—0.5 standard deviation above and 0.5 standard deviation below the mean | B—1 standard deviation above C | A—all scores above B |

Chart 8.4. Example of Grading by the Normal Curve

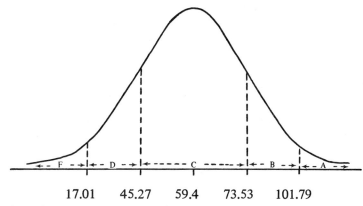

17.01   45.27   59.4   73.53   101.79

If mean = 59.4 and standard deviation = 28.26 (grade based on standard deviation units as shown in Chart 8.3) the grades would be:

A = 101.79 and up
B = 73.53 - 101.78
C = 45.27 - 73.52
D = 17.01 - 45.26

swimming a distance in two minutes is better than a time of three minutes). Therefore, before assigning grades, instructors must decide whether high scores are better or worse, and calculate accordingly.

Hull Scale scores can be easily combined with the normal curve approach to grading. When the averages for all students are found, a mean and a standard deviation for the group is calculated. It is then possible to calculate the A, B, C, D, and F grades according to the system described earlier.

Evaluation of Students at Private Pools and Country Clubs

The ARC program is quite common in private pools, which can lead to complications. These pools are usually the scene of private or semiprivate instruction, and while the usual ARC standards can be applied, sometimes considerable pressure is exerted by parents to have their children pass the course. While it is a temptation (for job security, if nothing else) to lower the standards to pass some students, this is not the aim of the ARC program. We strongly urge you to establish high performance norms and be firm in your demand that these standards be met. If you need help in deciding what the norms should be, talk with the local aquatic groups or veteran instructors.

CLASS ASSIGNMENTS

1. Talk to local ARC or YMCA instructors.
   a. What problems with evaluation do they have?
   b. What aids (e.g., skill sheets, stroke analysis sheets, achievement scales) are used?
   c. How is testing done—throughout the course, or at the end?

2. Talk to local school aquatic instructors.
   a. What problems with evaluation do they have?

b. What aids (e.g., skill sheets, stroke analysis sheets, achievement scales) are used?
c. How is testing done—throughout the course, or at the end?
d. How are grades determined?

BEHAVIORAL OBJECTIVES

Because all aquatic instructors must evaluate those in their classes, we expect our students to be able to respond correctly (based on material in this chapter) to questions calling for brief answers, as indicated below.

1. List the two basic questions to be considered before evaluation can be attempted, and explain why each is important.
2. Select one of these organizations: American National Red Cross, American YMCA, Canadian Red Cross. Then, list, by correct title, the publications of each group which give the skills and standards for all their aquatic courses.
3. Develop a worksheet for any aquatic class.
4. Create correctly worded behavioral objectives for a school swimming program.
5. Weight different aquatic skills according to the basic principle given in this text.
6. Determine letter grades according to the normal curve method.

REFERENCES

Johnson, Barry L., and Nelson, Jack K. *Practical Measurements for Evaluation in Physical Education.* Minneapolis: Burgess Publishing Company, 1979.
Kryspin, William J., and Feldhusen, John F. *Writing Behavioral Objectives.* Minneapolis: Burgess Publishing Company, 1973.

References

Each chapter of this text contains the primary references used for that section. The listing below is an attempt to provide further sources of aquatic information.

AQUATIC BIBLIOGRAPHY

Yates, Fern, Ed. *Swimming and Diving: A Bibliography.* Manassas, Va.: Council for National Cooperation in Aquatics, 1968.

AQUATIC ORGANIZATIONS

Aquatic Council of AAHPERD, 1900 Association Drive, Reston, Virginia 22109
Association of Canadian Underwater Councils, 333 River Road, Vanier City, Ontario K1L 8B9, Canada
Canadian Amateur Diving Association, 333 River Road, Vanier City, Ontario K1L 8B9, Canada
Canadian Amateur Swimming Association, 333 River Road, Vanier City, Ontario K1L 8B9, Canada
Canada Amateur Synchronized Swimming Association, 333 River Road, Vanier City, Ontario, K1L 8B9, Canada
Canadian Amateur Water Polo Association, 333 River Road, Vanier City, Ontario K1L 8B9, Canada
Council for National Cooperation in Aquatics, 9765 Bragg Lane, Manassas, Virginia 22110
National Aquatic Forum, c/o Ann Winter, Physical Education Department, University of Wisconsin, La Crosse, Wisconsin 54601
National Association of Underwater Instructors, Box 630, Colton, California 92324
National Association of Underwater Instructors Canada, 10 Monet Avenue, Etobicoke, Ontario M9C 3N7, Canada
National Swimming Pool Institute, 200 K Street, N.W., Washington, D.C. 20006
Professional Association of Diving Instructors, 2064 N. Busch Street, Santa Ana, California 92706
Royal Lifesaving Society Canada, 64 Charles Street E., Toronto, Ontario M4Y 1T1, Canada
United States Lifesaving Association, P.O. Box 366, Huntington Beach, California 92648

ORGANIZATIONS OFFERING AQUATICS PROGRAMS

American Alliance for Health, Physical Education, Recreation, and Dance (AAHPERD), 1900 Association Drive, Reston, Virginia 22109
American Camping Association, Bradford Woods, Martinsville, Indiana 46151
American National Red Cross, 17th and D Streets, N.W., Washington, D.C. 20006
Boy Scouts of America, North Brunswick, New Jersey 08902

Boy Scouts of Canada, 1345 Baseline Road, PO Box 5151 Station F, Ottawa, Ontario K2C 3G7, Canada

Boys Clubs of America, 711 First Avenue, New York, New York 10017

Camp Fire, Inc., 1740 Broadway, New York, New York 10019

Canadian Red Cross Society, 95 Wellesley Street E., Toronto, Ontario M4Y 1H6, Canada

Joseph P. Kennedy, Jr., Foundation, 1701 K Street, N.W., Suite 205, Washington, D.C. 20006

National Board of the Young Women's Christian Association, 600 Lexington Avenue, New York, New York 10022

National Council of YMCAs of Canada, 2160 Yonge Street, Toronto, Ontario M4S 2A9, Canada

National Council of YMCAs of the U.S.A., 291 Broadway, New York, New York 10007

National Industrial Recreation Association, 20 N. Wacker Drive, Chicago, Illinois 60606

National Jewish Welfare Board, 15 E. 26th Street, New York, New York 10010

National Recreation and Park Association, 1601 N. Kent Street, Arlington, Virginia 22209

National Safety Council, 444 N. Michigan Avenue, Chicago, Illinois 60611

President's Council on Physical Fitness and Sports, Suite 3030, Donahoe Building, 6th and D Streets, S.W., Washington, D.C. 20201

Cold Water Survival

Introduction

Scientists at the University of Victoria have been studying the effects on humans of immersion in cold ocean water under conditions similar to those experienced following boating accidents. The results are being used to find ways to increase survival time through various behavioral and technological means.

Even a small increase in survival time can mean the difference between being alive or dead when rescuers arrive.

Boaters (and others in danger of accidental immersion in cold water) should be aware of the factors that determine body cooling rate and eventual death from hypothermia. Such knowledge can improve chances of survival if an accident occurs. Remember, *drowning* is a problem that is easily solved by use of an approved personal flotation device (PFD). *Hypothermia* is a problem that is not easily solved, and deserves your careful attention.

The following questions attempt to focus attention on the major problems and recommendations about cold water survival.

1. What Is "Hypothermia" and How Does It Kill?

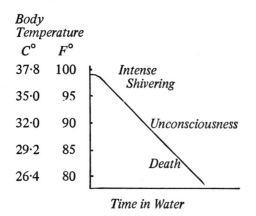

Body Temperature

C°	F°
37·8	100
35·0	95
32·0	90
29·2	85
26·4	80

Time in Water

Hypothermia means lowered, deep-body temperature. In cold water, the skin and peripheral (external) tissues become cooled very rapidly, but it takes 10–15 minutes before the temperature of the heart and brain begin to cool. Intense shivering occurs in a futile attempt to increase the body's heat production and counteract the large heat loss. Unconsciousness can occur when the deep-body temperature falls from the normal 37°C (99°F) to approximately 32°C (89.6°F). Heart failure is the usual cause of death when deep-body temperature cools to below 30°C (86°F).

Source: *Man in Cold Water,* pamphlet, no date. Used by permission of J. S. Hayward.

2. How Long Can I Survive in Cold Water?

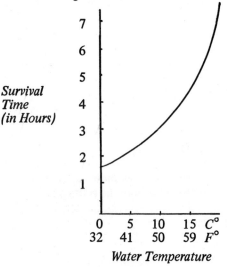

Survival
Time
(in Hours)

Water Temperature

The accompanying graph shows average predicted survival times of normal, adult humans in water of different temperatures. The figures are based on experimental cooling of average men and women who were holding-still in ocean water and wearing a standard lifejacket and light clothing. The graph shows, for example, that predicted survival time is about 2½-3 hours in water of 10°C (50°F). Predicted survival time is increased by extra body fat and decreased by small body size. Although women usually possess slightly more fat than men, they often cool faster because of their generally smaller body size. Due to even smaller body mass and relatively little fat, children cool much faster than adults.

3. Should I Swim to Keep Warm?

No! Although the body produces almost three times as much heat when swimming slowly and steadily (e.g. side stroke) in cold water compared to holding-still, this extra heat (and more) is lost to the cold water due to more blood circulation to the arms, legs and skin and increased water circulation through the clothing. Results show that the average person swimming in a lifejacket cools 35% faster than when holding-still.

4. How Far Can I Swim?

Shore *may* be close enough to reach by swimming despite a faster cooling rate with this activity. Tests conducted on people swimming in ocean water of 10°C (50°F), while wearing standard lifejackets and light clothing, showed that the average person could cover a distance of 0.85 mile before being incapacitated by hypothermia. It is not easy to judge distance, especially under emergency conditions in rough, cold water, but at water temperatures near 10°C (50°F), shore should be within one mile before making the decision to swim. The distance covered will obviously be affected by one's swimming ability, amount of insulation and water conditions.

5. What if I Have No Lifejacket or Other Flotation?

In this unfortunate situation, one is forced to adopt either of the following two "anti-drowning" techniques.

Treading Water

Continuous movement of arms and legs in various patterns keeps the head out of water. Test results showed an average cooling rate of subjects treading water that was 34% faster than while holding-still in a lifejacket.

Drownproofing

This involves restful floating with lungs full of air, interrupted every 10–15 seconds for raising the head out of the water to breathe. By this procedure, even nonswimmers can avoid drowning for many hours. Unfortunately, this behaviour resulted in a body cooling rate in cold water (10°C, 50°F) that was 82% faster than while holding-still in a lifejacket! This was mostly due to putting the head (high heat loss area) into the water along with the rest of the body. The University of Victoria research has shown drownproofing to be the fastest way to die from hypothermia of the behaviours studied to date.

6. What Body Regions Are the Most Critical for Heat Loss?

In addition to the head (which is normally out of the water), certain other body regions have high rates of heat loss while a subject is holding-still in cold water. Infrared pictures show that the sides of the chest (where there is little muscle or fat) are a major route for heat loss from the warm chest cavity. Also, the groin region loses more heat due to large blood and lymph vessels near the surface. If an effort is made to reduce body heat loss, these regions deserve special attention.

7. What Behaviour Will Increase Survival Time?

Based on the heat loss information in question 6, a technique was tested that attempted to reduce heat loss from the "critical areas": HELP (Heat Escape Lessening Posture).

HELP (Heat Escape Lessening Posture)

This technique involves holding the inner side of the arms tight against the side of the chest over the "hot region" shown in question 6. The thighs are pressed together and raised to close off the groin region. This body position was indeed a significant help, resulting in nearly a 50% increase in predicted survival time.

It should be noted that the picture shows a person wearing a traditional type of personal flotation device (PFD) that has all its buoyancy high on the body, close to the surface of the water. This type of device is especially suitable for the HELP. Where the buoyancy is more evenly distributed, as in a buoyancy vest or the UVic Thermofloat, the center of buoyancy is lower and the drawing up of the knees can lead to occasional instability in the water.

8. Do Different Types of "Lifejackets" Offer More or Less Thermal Protection?

Tests at the University of Victoria have shown that PFDs fall into three categories of thermal (heat) protection.

a) "Poor" Thermal Protection

All kapok lifejackets and loose-fitting, foam lifejackets of the vest type offered no significant protection from cold water.

b) "Fair" Thermal Protection

A few PFDs of two types offered significant thermal protection to the extent of a 50% to 75% increase in predicted survival time. The types were foam vests that possessed good adjustability for close fit to the chest and garment-type "flotation jackets" that use buoyant and insulative foam between the inner and outer layers of fabric.

c) "Good" Thermal Protection

Types of PFDs are now available that make a deliberate attempt to maximize thermal protection. These are based on improving the insulation potential of flotation jackets. One example, designed at the University of Victoria, is the "UVic Thermofloat" that has "convertible shorts" which help to trap water within insulative foam over the major heat loss regions of the body (like a "shorty" wet-suit). Recent findings showed that this jacket provides a predicted survival time more than 2½-times as long as a standard, kapok PFD.

9. Does It Help to Get Your Body Out of the Water?

The answer is almost invariably "yes". The body surrenders its heat to the water many times more quickly than to air of the same temperature, and it is often possible to stabilize body temperature once you are out of the water. Therefore, if possible, get on top of an over-turned boat or any wreckage that is available. This is particularly important for children due to their rapid cooling rate.

The "Sea-Seat" inflatable minicraft, designed by UVic scientists, takes advantage of the above information. The Sea-Seat can be inflated in 3–4 minutes of blowing into it, and enables an accident victim to get most of his body out of the water (all the body in the case of children). The Sea-Seat can be carried separately in a 9" x 12" plastic envelope or stored in a specially-designed pocket of the UVic Thermofloat. In recent tests, the combination of the Sea-Seat and the UVic Thermofloat produced predicted survival times that were equivalent to those of people wearing the most thermally-protective survival suits.

10. Does Alcohol Consumption Affect Survival Time?

A recent series of tests at the University of Victoria has shown that the cooling rate in cold water of legally-impaired subjects (blood alcohol near .08g/100ml) was not significantly different from their cooling rate when sober. The cold water seems to "overcome" the mild anesthesia of intoxication of this level. However, the consumption of alcohol while boating is still undesirable, because it makes you more likely to enter the water in the first place! (About ⅓ of boating fatalities involve significant alcohol impairment.)

11. Do People Ever Die of "Shock" When Falling into Cold Water?

Immersion in cold water (especially if sudden) causes immediate major changes in body function, and there are isolated instances of 'sudden death' being reported, but these are very uncommon. The cause of this 'sudden death' is not clear and a number of different reasons have been suggested. One is a form of heart attack resulting from the increase in heart-rate and changes in blood pressure which accompany immersion in cold water. However, this is unlikely to occur in someone with a healthy heart and circulatory system. Other possible causes of death are related to hyperventilation (over-breathing), which everyone experiences in response to the shock of cold water. It is possible that if one had plunged underwater or was in a rough sea that the hyperventilation could lead to uncontrolled aspiration (inhalation) of water and a form of drowning. Prolonged hyperventilation can lead to unconsciousness and subsequent drowning.

Because panic can magnify any of the above responses, it is important to remain calm and methodical if faced with a cold water emergency. If possible, enter the water gradually, allowing the body to adjust to the changing temperature. Consciously control your breathing as much as possible. The more clothing and insulation your body has, the less will be the initial shock on entry into cold water.

12. How Do You Rewarm Someone Who Has Been in Cold Water?

This is a difficult question because of the wide variety of circumstances regarding level of hypo-thermia and facilities available for rewarming. It is too complex a subject to give full, explanatory advice in a small pamphlet such as this. It is sufficient to indicate the spectrum of rewarming methods that have been used in different situations.

—body contact (warm person(s) huddle with the victim).
—exercise (for those with mild hypothermia).
—hot, wet towels and water-bottles.
—electric and chemical heating pads.
—heated blankets (electric or hot-water circulated).
—hot drinks (alcohol should be avoided).
—hot baths or showers
—heated, water-saturated air or oxygen (inhalation rewarming) using special "vaporizers", or the steam from a kettle directed (carefully) under a makeshift "hood" over the victim's head.
—peritoneal dialysis (warm solutions perfused through the abdominal cavity). This is obviously limited to application by a medical specialist.

In general, it is best to donate heat to the "core" of the body (head, neck and trunk) leaving arms and legs alone. Do not rub the surface of the body. If the person is severely hypothermic (probably unconscious), handle the body gently to avoid "jolts" that may adversely affect the heart's function. It is obvious that, if possible, the significantly-hypothermic victim should be transported to a site providing medical attention. More detailed, scientific information is available on request.

13. What if the Person Appears Dead from Hypothermia?

Recent examples have shown that persons who are *apparently* dead from hypothermia or drowning in cold water are often able to be resuscitated successfully even after quite a long period without breath-ing and blood circulation (10–40 minutes)! The main reason is that cold body tissues (e.g., brain) require less oxygen than when warm. Therefore, don't give up. Maintain artificial ventilation and circula-tion until medical assistance is available.

Summary

The danger of accidental hypothermia in cold water is a major reason to learn and practice safe boating techniques. In the unfortunate event of cold water immersion, your rate of progress into hypo-thermia depends on water temperature, who you are (body build), how you behave in the water, and what you were wearing when you went in. These factors have been reviewed in this pamphlet to help you be prepared for this important aspect of water safety.

Performance Analysis Sheets

Elementary Backstroke
Front Crawl Stroke
Sidestroke
Overarm Sidestroke
Breaststroke
Butterfly Stroke
Back Crawl Stroke
Single Trudgen Stroke
Double Trudgen Stroke
Trudgen Crawl Stroke
Inverted Breaststroke
Running Forward Dive in Layout Position
Running Forward Dive in Pike Position
Back Dive in Layout Position

The following pages contain performance analysis sheets for eleven strokes and three dives. For each skill, check items that apply to the performance of the skill. Note errors in the spaces provided.

ELEMENTARY BACKSTROKE

Directions: Check ✓ all items that apply to the performance of this skill. Note errors in the spaces provided.

Name _____   Name _____   _____
        (performer)   (analyst)

Illustration of Correct Technique   Analysis of Performance

Body Position

_____ The form *is* acceptable.
_____ The form is *not* acceptable because:
        _____ ears not in water
        _____ eyes not looking upward
        _____ arms not at sides
        _____ body not straight (_____ hips sag, _____ knees are bent, _____ toes not pointed, _____ arms not straight)
        _____ (other) _____

Legs

_____ The form *is* acceptable.
_____ The form for inverted whip kick is *not* acceptable because:
        _____ knees above surface during recovery
        _____ toes not pointed backward during recovery
        _____ thighs drop downward as legs extend
        _____ feet not turned outward during press
        _____ too little effort on backward press
        _____ (other) _____
_____ The form for inverted wedge kick is *not* acceptable because:
        _____ knees come above surface during recovery
        _____ knees not spread enough during recovery
        _____ thighs drop downward as legs extend
        _____ toes not pointed outward during kick
        _____ too little effort on backward press
        _____ legs not straight as they are squeezed
        _____ (other) _____

Arms

_____ The form *is* acceptable.
_____ The form is *not* acceptable because:
        _____ arms recovered too forcefully
        _____ arms recovered above the surface
        _____ arms not recovered close to body
        _____ arms not extended to bisect angle of shoulder and neck
        _____ pull and kick too forceful
        _____ stroke incomplete (_____ Legs do not press-squeeze until together, _____ arms end pull before hands are at thighs)
        _____ (other) _____

Coordination and Breathing

_____ The form *is* acceptable.
_____ The form is *not* acceptable because:
        _____ recovery of arms and legs too forceful
        _____ arms and legs not extended diagonally outward at same time
        _____ pull and kick not done at same time
        _____ glide poor (_____ no glide, _____ too brief)
        _____ breath not expelled as arms finish pull
        _____ breath not taken in immediately after exhalation
        _____ (other) _____

Method by Barbara S. Jones.

FRONT CRAWL STROKE

Directions: Check ✓ all items that apply to the performance of this skill. Note errors in the spaces provided.

Name _____   Name _____   Name _____
(performer)   (analyst)

Illustration of
Correct Technique

Analysis of Performance

Body Position

_____ The form *is* acceptable.

_____ The form is *not* acceptable because:
_____ face not looking ahead underwater
_____ head too deep in the water
_____ head held above the surface
_____ back overarched
_____ hips higher than the legs
_____ (other)

Legs

_____ The form *is* acceptable.

_____ The form is *not* acceptable because:
_____ too much bend at the knees
_____ not enough bend at the knees
_____ kick range too narrow (less than 12″–15″)
_____ too much splash
_____ toes not pointed with ankles extended
_____ (other)

Arms

_____ The form *is* acceptable.

_____ The form is *not* acceptable because:
_____ arm not bent during recovery
_____ arm not relaxed during recovery
_____ arm thrust rather than swung from shoulder
_____ elbow not higher than hand during recovery
_____ elbow enters water before hand enters
_____ hand enters water in front of opposite shoulder
_____ hand enters water in front of face and pushes forward before pulling back
_____ arm does not pull through under body
_____ elbow not bent when pull-push is executed
_____ pull-push of arms too short
_____ (other)

Coordination and Breathing

_____ The form *is* acceptable.

_____ The form is *not* acceptable because:
_____ arms and legs work independently
_____ arm action not rhythmic (swimmer gallops)
_____ head lifted for breathing rather than rolled to side
_____ breath taken in during late stage of arm recovery
_____ kick and arm stroke stopped while breath is taken
_____ Head turned from side to side
_____ (other)

Method by Barbara S. Jones.

SIDESTROKE

Directions: Check ✓ all items that apply to the performance of this skill. Note errors in the spaces provided.

Name _____ Name _____ _____
    (performer)   (analyst)

Illustration of
Correct Technique

Analysis of Performance

Body Position During Glide

_____ The form *is* acceptable.

_____ The form is *not* acceptable because:
_____ arms and legs not fully extended.
_____ legs not together
_____ body not stretched and straight
_____ body turned toward stomach-down position
_____ body turned toward back-down position
_____ head not turned toward the upper shoulder to facilitate breathing
_____ (other)

Legs

_____ The form *is* acceptable.

_____ The form is *not* acceptable because:
_____ legs separated vertically, resulting in a breast-stroke kick
_____ inverted scissors kick used
_____ legs do not bend enough at knees during recovery
_____ knees brought too far in front of stomach during recovery
_____ legs recovered too vigorously
_____ legs not straightened before the squeeze
_____ too little effort during squeeze
_____ ankles not extended to point toes during late part of squeeze
_____ legs pass each other at end of squeeze
_____ (other)

Arms

_____ The form *is* acceptable.

_____ The form is *not* acceptable because:
_____ pull of the leading (lower) arm too short
_____ pull of leading arm too deep
_____ leading arm not recovered with finger tips leading
_____ elbow of leading arm not brought to ribs before recovery of that arm
_____ trailing (upper) arm does not pull to thigh
_____ (other)

Coordination and Breathing

_____ The form *is* acceptable.

_____ The form is *not* acceptable because:
_____ both arms pull toward feet at same time
_____ leading arm begins pull immediately after recovery
_____ leading arm pulls at same time kick is delivered
_____ kick delivered before leading arm ready to recover
_____ exhalation is at a time other than during leg kick or during glide
_____ inhalation does not follow immediately after exhalation
_____ the duration of the glide is too brief
_____ (other)

Method by Barbara S. Jones.

OVERARM SIDESTROKE

Directions: Check √ all items that apply to the performance of this skill. Note errors in the spaces provided.

Name _____ Name _____
(performer)   (analyst)

Illustration of Correct Technique

Analysis of Performance

Body Position During Glide

_____ The form *is* acceptable.

_____ The form is *not* acceptable because:
_____ arms and legs not fully extended
_____ legs not together
_____ body not stretched and straight
_____ body turned toward stomach-down position
_____ body turned toward back-down position
_____ head not turned toward the upper shoulder to facilitate breathing
_____ (other) _____

Legs

_____ The form *is* acceptable.

_____ The form is *not* acceptable because:
_____ legs separated vertically, resulting in a breast-stroke kick
_____ inverted scissors kick used
_____ legs do not bend enough at knees during recovery
_____ knees brought too far in front of stomach during recovery
_____ legs recovered too vigorously
_____ legs not straightened before the squeeze
_____ too little effort expended during the squeeze
_____ ankles not extended to point toes during late part of squeeze
_____ legs pass each other at end of squeeze
_____ (other) _____

Arms

_____ The form *is* acceptable.

_____ The form is *not* acceptable because;
_____ pull of the leading (lower) arm too short
_____ pull of leading arm too deep
_____ leading arm not recovered with finger tips leading
_____ elbow of leading arm not brought to ribs before recovery of that arm
_____ trailing (upper) arm not recovered overwater
_____ trailing arm pounded into the water on recovery
_____ trailing arm reaches too far forward on recovery
_____ trailing arm does not pull through to thigh
_____ (other) _____

Coordination and Breathing

_____ The form *is* acceptable.

_____ The form is *not* acceptable because:
_____ both arms pull toward the feet at the same time
_____ leading arm begins to pull immediately after recovery
_____ leading arm pulls at the same time the kick is delivered
_____ kick delivered before the leading arm is ready to recover
_____ exhalation is at a time other than during leg kick or during glide
_____ inhalation does not follow immediately after exhalation
_____ duration of the glide too brief
_____ (other) _____

Method by Barbara S. Jones.

BREASTSTROKE

Directions: Check ✓ all items that apply to the performance of this skill. Note errors in the spaces provided.

Name _____ Name _____

_____ (performer)   _____ (analyst)

Illustration of
Correct Technique

Analysis of Performance

Body Position During Glide

_____ The form *is* acceptable.

_____ The form is *not* acceptable because:
  _____ body not straight and stretched
  _____ legs not extended and together
  _____ ears not between extended arms
  _____ (other) _____

Legs

_____ The form for whip kick *is* acceptable.

_____ The form for whip kick is *not* acceptable because:
  _____ knees outside the heels during recovery of legs
  _____ toes not pointed backward during recovery of legs
  _____ legs recovered too quickly and vigorously
  _____ legs not straightened before backward press
  _____ too little effort applied to backward press
  _____ toes of one foot turned inward during the press
  _____ (other) _____

_____ The form for wedge kick *is* acceptable.

_____ The form for wedge kick is *not* acceptable because:
  _____ heels inside the knees during recovery of legs
  _____ toes not pointed backward during recovery of legs
  _____ legs recovered too quickly and vigorously
  _____ legs not straightened before backward press
  _____ too little effort applied to backward press
  _____ toes of one foot turned inward during the press
  _____ (other) _____

Arms

_____ The form *is* acceptable.

_____ The form is *not* acceptable because:
  _____ arms pressed backward too far (_____ to ribs, _____ to thighs)
  _____ arms pulled too vigorously
  _____ hands not brought in front of the chest before extension forward
  _____ arm pull too much under body
  _____ elbows not bent for leverage
  _____ (other) _____

Coordination and Breathing

_____ The form *is* acceptable.

_____ The form is *not* acceptable because:
  _____ arm pull begins immediately at end of recovery of arms
  _____ leg recovery begins immediately at end of leg kick
  _____ leg kick and arm pull occur at the same time
  _____ one kick delivered to each pull of arms and one kick to each recovery of arms
  _____ duration of the glide is too brief
  _____ exhalation does not occur at end of glide
  _____ inhalation does not occur during early part of arm pull
  _____ (other) _____

Method by Barbara S. Jones.

BUTTERFLY STROKE

Directions: Check ✓ all items that apply to the performance of this skill. Note errors in the spaces provided.

Name _____

Name _____

(performer)

(analyst)

Illustration of
Correct Technique

Analysis of Performance

Body Position

_____ The form *is* acceptable.

_____ The form is *not* acceptable because:
_____ body inclines toward vertical
_____ legs too low
_____ head too high
_____ arms and legs not extended at the end of arm recovery
_____ (other)

Legs

_____ The form *is* acceptable.

_____ The form is *not* acceptable because:
_____ kick is a flutter kick
_____ legs bend too little at knees
_____ legs bend too much at knees
_____ feet come above water surface
_____ legs are not together
_____ leg kick lacks vigor
_____ ankles are not extended to point toes backward
_____ upward and downward movement of the hips too great
_____ (other)

Arms

_____ The form *is* acceptable.

_____ The form is *not* acceptable because:
_____ pull not started with the hands forward from shoulders
_____ arms press downward too far
_____ arms press downward too strongly
_____ arms do not bend during pull-push
_____ arm pull ends at shoulders rather than at thighs
_____ arms are not recovered over water
_____ arms thrust forward rather than swung from shoulders
_____ hands do not enter water before elbows enter
_____ head not lowered before arm entry
_____ (other)

Coordination and Breathing

_____ The form *is* acceptable.

_____ The form is *not* acceptable because:
_____ a leg kick and arm pull do not occur at the same time
_____ a leg kick and arm recovery do not occur at the same time
_____ spine is stiff; body does not undulate
_____ exhalation does not occur during glide or during early part of arm pull
_____ inhalation does not occur, as arms are pulled and pushed
_____ head raised too high for breathing
_____ (other)

Method by Barbara S. Jones.

BACK CRAWL STROKE

Directions: Check ✓ all items that apply to the performance of this skill. Note errors in the spaces provided.

Name _____ Name _____

(performer)   (analyst)

Illustration of
Correct Technique   Analysis of Performance

Body Position

_____ The form *is* acceptable.
_____ The form is *not* acceptable because:
    _____ body not straight
    _____ body position not horizontal
    _____ hips too low
    _____ head raised too high
    _____ head inclined backward
    _____ body lunges from side to side
    _____ (other)

Legs

_____ The form *is* acceptable.
_____ The form is *not* acceptable because:
    _____ toes not pointed
    _____ knees bend too much
    _____ feet come above the surface
    _____ feet too low in the water
    _____ kick too narrow
    _____ kick too wide
    _____ legs too stiff
    _____ trudgen kick used
    _____ (other)

Arms

_____ The form *is* acceptable.
_____ The form is *not* acceptable because:
    _____ arm pull is too deep
    _____ elbow leads the hand during pull
    _____ arm pull too jerky and vigorous, is not a steady press
    _____ arm does not pull through to thigh
    _____ an arm push does not follow arm pull
    _____ arm is thrust forward on recovery rather than swung from the shoulder
    _____ on recovery, elbow enters water before hand enters
    _____ on recovery, hand crosses the center line of body before entering water
    _____ (other)

Coordination and Breathing

_____ The form *is* acceptable.
_____ The form is *not* acceptable because:
    _____ too many kicks delivered to each arm stroke
    _____ too few kicks delivered to each arm stroke
    _____ legs and arms perform independently of each other
    _____ breathing not easy and rhythmic
    _____ (other)

Method by Barbara S. Jones.

SINGLE TRUDGEN STROKE

Directions: Check ✓ all items that apply to the performance of this skill. Note errors in the spaces provided.

Name _____ Name _____ Name _____
(performer) (analyst)

Illustration of Correct Technique

Analysis of Performance

Body Position During Glide

_____ The form *is* acceptable.
_____ The form is *not* acceptable because:
_____ arms and legs not fully extended
_____ legs not together
_____ body not stretched and straight
_____ body turned toward face-down position
_____ head not turned toward the upper shoulder to facilitate breathing
_____ head above the surface at all times
_____ (other)

Legs

_____ The form *is* acceptable.
_____ The form is *not* acceptable because:
_____ inverted scissors kick is used
_____ legs do not bend enough at knees during recovery
_____ knees brought too far in front of stomach during recovery
_____ legs recover too vigorously
_____ legs not straightened before the squeeze
_____ too little effort applied during squeeze
_____ ankles not extended to point toes during late part of squeeze
_____ legs pass each other at end of squeeze
_____ (other)

Arms

_____ The form *is* acceptable.
_____ The form is *not* acceptable because:
_____ pull-through of one arm shorter than pull-through of other
_____ recovery of one arm shorter than recovery of other
_____ arms not recovered over water
_____ on recovery, arms thrust forward rather than swung forward from shoulders
_____ hand does not enter water in front of shoulder of that arm
_____ (other)

Coordination and Breathing

_____ The form *is* acceptable.
_____ The form is *not* acceptable because:
_____ body does not roll onto the stomach after glide on the side
_____ kick delivered at the same time that arm on the breathing side recovered
_____ pull of leading arm begun immediately at end of recovery of that arm
_____ head lifted rather than turned to the side
_____ exhalation at a time other than during leg kick or during glide
_____ inhalation does not follow immediately after exhalation
_____ duration of the glide too brief
_____ (other)

Method by Barbara S. Jones.

DOUBLE TRUDGEN STROKE

Directions: Check √ all items that apply to the performance of this skill. Note errors in the spaces provided.

Name _____ Name _____ Name _____

(performer)   (analyst)

Illustration of
Correct Technique   Analysis of Performance

Body Position

____ The form *is* acceptable.
____ The form is *not* acceptable because:
____ body not straight and stretched
____ face above water at all times
____ body not in horizontal position
____ (other)

Kick

____ The form for narrow scissors kick *is* acceptable.
____ The form for narrow scissors kick is *not* acceptable because:
____ inverted scissors kick used
____ legs do not bend enough at knees during recovery
____ knees brought too far in front of stomach during recovery
____ legs recovered too vigorously
____ legs not straightened before the squeeze
____ ankles not extended to point toes during late part of squeeze
____ (other)

____ The form for breaststroke kick *is* acceptable.
____ The form for breaststroke kick is *not* acceptable because:
____ toes not pointed backward during recovery of the legs
____ legs recovered too vigorously
____ legs not straightened before backward press
____ too little effort applied to backward press
____ (other)

Arms

____ The form *is* acceptable.
____ The form is *not* acceptable because:
____ each arm begins pull immediately at end of recovery
____ pull-through of one arm is shorter than pull-through of other
____ recovery of one arm is shorter than recovery of other
____ arms are not recovered over water
____ on recovery, arms are thrust forward rather than swung forward from the shoulder
____ hand does not enter the water in front of shoulder of that arm
____ (other)

Coordination and Breathing

____ The form *is* acceptable.
____ The form is *not* acceptable because:
____ rate of stroking too rapid
____ duration of glide after each arm pull too brief
____ a kick does not accompany each arm pull
____ head lifted rather than turned sideward for breathing
____ hips not rolled enough to permit a scissors kick as the body is turned onto each side
____ (other)

Method by Barbara S. Jones.

TRUDGEN CRAWL STROKE

Directions: Check ✓ all items that apply to the performance of this skill. Note errors in the spaces provided.

Name _____ Name _____

_____ (performer) _____ (analyst)

Illustration of Correct Technique

Analysis of Performance

Body Position During Glide

_____ The form *is* acceptable.

_____ The form is *not* acceptable because:
_____ legs and arms not fully extended
_____ legs not together
_____ body not stretched and straight
_____ body turned toward face-down position
_____ head not turned toward upper shoulder to facilitate breathing
_____ (other)

Legs

_____ The form for trudgen kick *is* acceptable.

_____ The form for trudgen kick is *not* acceptable because:
_____ inverted scissors kick used
_____ legs do not bend enough at knees during scissors kick recovery
_____ knees brought too far in front of stomach during scissors kick recovery
_____ legs recovered too vigorously
_____ legs not straightened before scissors kick squeeze
_____ too little effort applied during squeeze
_____ ankles not extended to point toes during late part of scissors squeeze
_____ (other)

_____ The form for flutter kick *is* acceptable.

_____ The form for flutter kick is *not* acceptable because:
_____ toes not pointed backward
_____ knees bend too much
_____ width of the kick too narrow
_____ width of the kick too wide
_____ number of kicks too few
_____ number of kicks too many
_____ no flutter kick used
_____ (other)

Arms

_____ The form *is* acceptable.

_____ The form is *not* acceptable because:
_____ arms do not pull through to thighs
_____ pull-through of one arm is shorter than pull-through of other
_____ recovery of one arm is shorter than recovery of other
_____ arms are not recovered over water
_____ on recovery, arms thrust forward rather than swung forward from the shoulders
_____ hand does not enter the water in front of shoulder of that arm
_____ (other)

Coordination and Breathing

_____ The form *is* acceptable.

_____ The form is *not* acceptable because:
_____ one scissors kick not coordinated with pull of one arm
_____ flutter kicks not coordinated with pull of one arm
_____ face held above surface at all times
_____ head lifted rather than turned to one side for breathing
_____ duration of the glide in on-side position too brief
_____ (other)

Method by Barbara S. Jones.

INVERTED BREASTSTROKE

Directions: Check ✓ all items that apply to the performance of this skill. Note errors in the spaces provided.

Name _____   Name _____
(performer)   (analyst)

Illustration of
Correct Technique   Analysis of Performance

Body Position During Glide

_____ The form *is* acceptable.
_____ The form is *not* acceptable because:
  _____ ears not in the water
  _____ eyes not looking upward
  _____ body not straight (_____ hips sag _____ knees bent
       _____ toes not pointed)
  _____ after arm pull, arms not extended along sides
  _____ after leg kick, arms not extended forward
       beyond shoulders
  _____ (other) _____

Legs

_____ The form for whip kick *is* acceptable.
_____ The form for whip kick is *not* acceptable because:
  _____ knees come above surface during recovery
  _____ toes not pointed backward during recovery
  _____ thighs drop downward as legs extend
  _____ feet not turned outward during press
  _____ kick not vigorous enough
  _____ (other) _____

_____ The form for wedge kick *is* acceptable.
_____ The form for wedge kick is *not* acceptable because:
  _____ knees come above the surface during recovery
  _____ knees not spread enough during recovery
  _____ thighs drop downward as legs extend
  _____ toes not pointed outward during the leg press
  _____ kick not vigorous enough
  _____ legs not straight as they are squeezed together
  _____ (other) _____

Arms

_____ The form *is* acceptable.
_____ The form is *not* acceptable because:
  _____ arms recovered too forcefully
  _____ arms recovered above surface
  _____ arms not recovered close to body
  _____ elbows not lowered as arms recover
  _____ arms not fully extended after recovery
  _____ arms not fully extended after pull
  _____ arms not extended straight forward (in line of
       progress) from shoulders after recovery
  _____ (other) _____

Coordination and Breathing

_____ The form *is* acceptable.
_____ The form is *not* acceptable because:
  _____ kick occurs before hands recover to shoulders
  _____ arms begin the pull immediately at end of
       recovery
  _____ arms begin recovery immediately at end of arm
       pull
  _____ leg kick and arm pull occur at the same time
  _____ inhalation occurs during leg kick
  _____ inhalation occurs during arm pull
  _____ inhalation does not occur immediately after
       exhalation
  _____ (other) _____

Method by Barbara S. Jones.

RUNNING FORWARD DIVE IN LAYOUT POSITION

Directions: Check ✓ all items that apply to the performance of this skill. Note errors in the spaces provided.

Name _____ (performer)   Name _____ (analyst)

Illustration of Correct Technique	Analysis of Performance

Starting Position

_____ The form *is* acceptable.
_____ The form is *not* acceptable because:
_____ backward lean
_____ knees locked, body tense
_____ forward lean
_____ (other)

Approach

_____ The form *is* acceptable.
_____ The form is *not* acceptable because:
_____ arm swing not free
_____ forward lean
_____ steps too long
_____ head not erect
_____ run (walk) is too rapid
_____ (other)

Hurdle

_____ The form *is* acceptable.
_____ The form is *not* acceptable because:
_____ too long
_____ forward lean
_____ not high enough
_____ landing flat-footed
_____ knees bend on contact with board
_____ (other)

Takeoff

_____ The form *is* acceptable.
_____ The form is *not* acceptable because:
_____ too much lean forward
_____ arm and leg actions not synchronized
_____ actions of body and board not synchronized
_____ feet leave board too soon
_____ feet do not rise backward and upward
_____ arm circle is reversed
_____ (other)

Flight

_____ The form *is* acceptable.
_____ The form is *not* acceptable because:
_____ not enough height
_____ feet raised too much
_____ partial pike is assumed
_____ legs bend at knees
_____ feet not raised enough
_____ too much back arch
_____ arms do not flow into position sideward
_____ (other)

Entry

_____ The form *is* acceptable.
_____ The form is *not* acceptable because:
_____ too long
_____ too far out from the board
_____ body not straight
_____ too short
_____ ears not between arms
_____ legs flop over
_____ dive is shallow
_____ arms pull to sides
_____ (other)

Method by Barbara S. Jones.

RUNNING FORWARD DIVE IN PIKE POSITION

Directions: Check √ all items that apply to the performance of this skill. Note errors in the spaces provided.

Name _____   Name _____

(performer)   (analyst)

Illustration of Correct Technique	Analysis of Performance	Illustration of Correct Technique	Analysis of Performance

Starting Position

___ The form *is* acceptable.

___ The form is *not* acceptable because:
___ forward lean
___ backward lean
___ body tense
___ (other)_____

Approach

___ The form *is* acceptable.

___ The form is *not* acceptable because:
___ forward lean
___ arm swing not free
___ steps too long
___ head not erect
___ run (walk) is too rapid
___ (other)_____

Hurdle

___ The form *is* acceptable.

___ The form is *not* acceptable because:
___ too long
___ forward lean
___ not high enough
___ arm action not synchronized with leg action
___ landing flat-footed
___ knees bend on contact with board
___ (other)_____

Takeoff

___ The form *is* acceptable.

___ The form is *not* acceptable because:
___ forward lean; takeoff is outward
___ arm circle is reversed
___ arm and leg actions not synchronized
___ body and board actions not synchronized
___ feet leave board too soon
___ head is faced downward
___ (other)_____

Flight

___ The form *is* acceptable.

___ The form is *not* acceptable because:
___ not enough height
___ pike is partial
___ legs not straight
___ pike held too long
___ pike held too briefly
___ pike assumed too soon
___ feet brought up to hands
___ toes not pointed; ankles not extended
___ legs bend at knees
___ (other)_____

Entry

___ The form *is* acceptable.

___ The form is *not* acceptable because:
___ too short
___ too far out
___ ears not between arms
___ too long
___ body not straight
___ legs flop over
___ dive is shallow
___ arms pulled to sides
___ (other)_____

Method by Barbara S. Jones.

BACK DIVE IN LAYOUT POSITION

Directions: Check √ all items that apply to the performance of this skill. Note errors in the spaces provided.

Name _____   Name _____
　　　(performer)　　　　　　　(analyst)

Illustration of Correct Technique	Analysis of Performance

Starting Position

——— The form *is* acceptable.

——— The form is *not* acceptable because:
- ——— arms not used for balance during pivot
- ——— body bends forward at hips; body not erect
- ——— pivot on the one foot is not smooth
- ——— arm actions are too fast and uneven
- ——— (other)

Takeoff

——— The form *is* acceptable.

——— The form is *not* acceptable because:
- ——— leg and arm actions not synchronized
- ——— body and board actions not synchronized
- ——— feet lifted and returned to board before take-off
- ——— backward lean is too great
- ——— not enough height
- ——— spring is outward
- ——— (other)

Flight

——— The form *is* acceptable.

——— The form is *not* acceptable because:
- ——— body not stretched upward
- ——— backward lean
- ——— too much back arch
- ——— chest and hips not pressed upward
- ——— knees bend
- ——— body tends to twist
- ——— not enough height
- ——— head not tilted back
- ——— hips bend in pike
- ——— arms not level
- ——— (other)

Entry

——— The form *is* acceptable.

——— The form is *not* acceptable because:
- ——— too short
- ——— too far out from board
- ——— ears not between arms
- ——— too long
- ——— body not straight
- ——— legs flop over
- ——— dive is shallow
- ——— arms pull to sides
- ——— (other)

Method by Barbara S. Jones.

Index

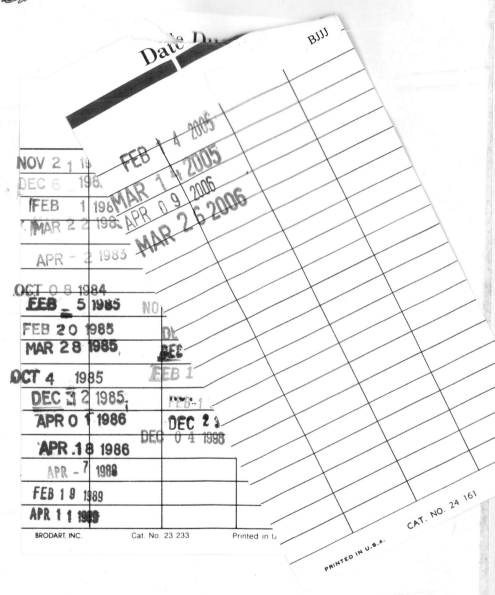